The Third Reich

The Third Reich

Fourth edition

David G. Williamson

Longman
is an imprint of

Harlow, England • London • New York • Boston • San Francisco • Toronto • Sydney • Singapore • Hong Kong
Tokyo • Seoul • Taipei • New Delhi • Cape Town • Madrid • Mexico City • Amsterdam • Munich • Paris • Milan

PEARSON EDUCATION LIMITED

Edinburgh Gate
Harlow CM20 2JE
United Kingdom
Tel: +44 (0)1279 623623
Fax: +44 (0)1279 431059
Website: www.pearsoned.co.uk

First edition published in 1982
Second edition published in 1995
Third edition published in 2002
Fourth edition published in 2011

© Pearson Education Limited 1982, 1995, 2002, 2011

The right of David G. Williamson to be identified as author
of this work has been asserted by him in accordance with
the Copyright, Designs and Patents Act 1988.

ISBN: 978-1-4082-2319-2

British Library Cataloguing in Publication Data
A CIP catalogue record for this book can be obtained from the British Library

Library of Congress Cataloging in Publication Data
Williamson, D. G.
   The Third Reich / D. G. Williamson. – 4th ed.
       p. cm.
   Includes bibliographical references and index.
   ISBN 978-1-4082-2319-2 (pbk.)
   1. Germany–History–1933–1945.   2. Germany–Politics and government–1933–1945.
3. Germany–Social conditions–1933–1945.   4. National socialism–History.   5 Hitler,
Adolf, 1889–1945.   6. Holocaust, Jewish (1939–1945)–Germany.   7. Germany–History–
1933–1945–Sources.   I. Title.
   DD256.5.W493 2011
   943.086–dc22

                                                                          2010045112

10   9   8   7   6   5   4   3   2   1
15   14   13   12   11

Set by 35 in 10/13.5pt Berkeley Book
Printed and bound in Malaysia, CTP-KHL

Introduction to the series

History is narrative constructed by historians from traces left by the past. Historical enquiry is often driven by contemporary issues and, in consequence, historical narratives are constantly reconsidered, reconstructed and reshaped. The fact that different historians have different perspectives on issues means that there is also often controversy and no universally agreed version of past events. *Seminar Studies in History* was designed to bridge the gap between current research and debate, and the broad, popular general surveys that often date rapidly.

The volumes in the series are written by historians who are not only familiar with the latest research and current debates concerning their topic, but who have themselves contributed to our understanding of the subject. The books are intended to provide the reader with a clear introduction to a major topic in history. They provide both a narrative of events and a critical analysis of contemporary interpretations. They include the kinds of tools generally omitted from specialist monographs: a chronology of events, a glossary of terms and brief biographies of 'who's who'. They also include bibliographical essays in order to guide students to the literature on various aspects of the subject. Students and teachers alike will find that the selection of documents will stimulate discussion and offer insight into the raw materials used by historians in their attempt to understand the past.

Clive Emsley and Gordon Martel
Series Editors

For A.B.R.W., 1901–1956, and D.R.L.W., 1912–1978

Contents

Publisher's acknowledgements

We are grateful to the following for permission to reproduce copyright material:

Photographs

We are grateful to the Bridgeman Art Library for permission to reproduce all the photographs that appear in the plate section. These images were supplied by the following collections: Peter Newark's Pictures and Peter Newark's Military Pictures.

Tables

Table on page 159 from *Design for Total War: Arms and Economics in the Third Reich [Studies in European History 17]*, De Gruyter Mouton (Berenice Anita Carroll 1968) p. 184.

Text

Extract on pages 147–9 from *Nazism, 1945: Vol. 1, The Rise to Power, 1919–1934, 2*, Exeter University Press (Nokes, J. Pridham, G. 1988) pp.14–16; Extract on pages 156–8 from *Nazism, 1919–1945, Vol. II State, Economy and Society, 1933–1939* 2ed (Nokes, J. Pridham, G. 2000) pp. 87–93; Extract on pages 166–7 from *A. Hitler, Mein Kampf (Introduction)*, Published by Pimlico. Reprinted by permission of The Random House Group Ltd (Watt, D. C. 1974); Extract on pages 168–9 from *A. Hitler, Mein Kampf*, Published by Pimlico. Reprinted by permission of The Random House Group Ltd (1974) pp. 295–6; Extract on page 169 from *A. Hitler, Mein Kampf*, Published by Pimlico. Reprinted by permission of The Random House Group Ltd pp. 558, 564–6, 598, 599; Extract on pages 170–2 from *From*

Documents on German Foreign Policy, 1918–1945, Series D, Vol. I (1937–41), HMSO (1950) pp. 29–38.

Chronology

1918

11 November   Armistice.

1919

January   German Workers' Party (DAP) is founded in Munich.

6 April   'Soviet' republic is set up in Munich.

28 June   Treaty of Versailles.

1920

24 February   DAP changes its name to the National Socialist German Workers' Party (NSDAP). Its 25 Point Programme is announced.

31 March   Hitler leaves the army.

1921

29 July   Hitler becomes Chairman of the NSDAP.

1923

11 January   Occupation of the Ruhr by French troops begins.

August   German currency is out of control: hyper-inflation.

8–9 November   The abortive Munich *Putsch*.

23 November   The Communist Party (KPD) and the NSDAP are banned.

1924

1 April   Hitler is given a five-year prison sentence.

9 April   Dawes Plan is announced.

20 December   Hitler is released from Landsberg Prison.

1925

27 February   Nazi Party is re-founded.

25 April   Hindenburg is elected President.

1926

14 February	Bamberg Conference: Hitler re-establishes control over the NSDAP.

1928

28 June	Grand Coalition is formed: NSDAP wins only 12 seats.

1929

9 July	Nazis and Nationalists (DNVP) jointly oppose the Young Plan.
24–29 October	US stock market crashes.

1930

30 March	Brüning becomes Reich Chancellor.
14 September	Reichstag elections: NSDAP gains 107 seats.

1931

February	Unemployment totals 5 million.
11 October	The Harzburg Front is formed.

1932

March–April	Presidential elections: Hindenburg is re-elected.
13 April	Prohibition of the SA and SS.
1 June	Papen becomes Chancellor.
14 June	Ban lifted on SA and SS.
20 July	Prussian government is suspended.
31 July	Reichstag elections: NSDAP becomes the largest party with 230 seats.
13 August	Hindenburg refuses to appoint Hitler Chancellor.
6 November	Reichstag elections: NSDAP loses 34 seats.
4 December	Schleicher becomes Chancellor.

1933

4 January	Papen–Hitler meeting.
30 January	Hitler is appointed Chancellor.
1 February	Dissolution of the Reichstag.
27 February	Reichstag fire.
28 February	The Decree for the Protection of People and State is promulgated.
5 March	Reichstag elections: NSDAP wins 288 seats.
23 March	Enabling Act is passed.
31 March	First Law for the Coordination of the Länder.
7 April	Law for the Restoration of a Professional Civil Service.
	Second Law for the Coordination of the Länder.

2 May	Trade unions are dissolved.
6 May	Plans for a German Labour Front are announced.
14 July	NSDAP is declared the only legal political party.
20 July	Concordat with the Catholic Church is ratified.
13 September	Reich Food Estate is set up.
29 September	Reich Entailed Farm Law.
12 November	Reichstag elections and referendum.
30 November	Gestapo set up.
1 December	Law to Ensure the Unity of Party and State is promulgated.

1934

20 April	Himmler is appointed 'Inspector of the Gestapo'.
17 June	Papen's Marburg speech.
30 June	'Night of the Long Knives' – Röhm is murdered.
20 July	SS is established, under Himmler, as an independent force from the SA.
2 August	Death of Hindenburg. Hitler becomes President as well as Chancellor. Schacht is made Economics Minister.
September	Schacht introduces the New Plan.

1935

13 January	Majority favour reunification with Germany in the Saar plebiscite.
16 July	Ministry of Churches is created under Hans Kerrl.
15 September	Nuremberg Laws.

1936

7 March	Military re-occupation of the Rhineland.
4 April	Göring is appointed Commissioner of Raw Materials.
17 June	Himmler is appointed Head of the German Police.
18 October	Decree on the Execution of the Four Year Plan.

1937

30 January	Reichstag prolongs Enabling Act for another period of four years.
14 March	Papal encyclical *Mit brennender Sorge* is published.
26 November	Schacht resigns as Economics Minister.

1938

25 January	Blomberg resigns.
4 February	Defeat of the Conservative elite is marked by the appointment of Ribbentrop to the Foreign Ministry; dismissal of Fritsch as Commander-in-Chief of the army and Hitler's assumption of command of the armed forces.

5 February	Last meeting of the Reich cabinet.
11 March	Annexation of Austria.
1–10 October	Occupation of the Sudetenland.
7–8 November	*Reichskristallnacht.*

1939

21 January	Schacht is dismissed from the Presidency of the *Reichsbank*.
15 March	Occupation of Bohemia.
25 March	Membership of Hitler Youth organisations becomes compulsory for all Germans between the ages of 10 and 18.
23 August	Nazi–Soviet Non-Aggression Treaty.
27 August	Food rationing is introduced.
1 September	Invasion of Poland.
27 September	Amalgamation of the Security Police and the office of Reichsführer SS to form the Reichssicherheitshauptamt (RSHA).

1940

9 April	Invasion of Denmark and Norway.
10 May	Offensive against the West begins.
10 June	Italy declares war on France and Britain.
22 June	Franco-German armistice.
17–23 June	USSR occupies the Baltic states.
June–September	Battle of Britain.
27 September	Tripartite Pact.
12 October	Invasion of Britain is cancelled.

1941

6 February	German troops are sent to North Africa under Rommel.
6 April	German invasion of Yugoslavia.
10 May	Hess's flight to Scotland.
29 May	Martin Bormann is appointed a minister.
22 June	Operation Barbarossa.
2 October–	
5 December	Battle for Moscow.
7 December	Pearl Harbor is attacked by the Japanese.
11 December	Germany and Italy declare war on USA.

1942

20 January	Wannsee Conference.
8 February	Speer becomes Armaments Minister.

26–27 March	First transports of Jewish emigrants from western Europe to Auschwitz.
28 March	RAF heavily damages Lübeck.
22 April	Central Planning Board is established to allocate raw materials and energy supplies.
August	More than 200,000 Jews are gassed in Chelmno, Treblinka and Belzec.
October	Axis troops are pushed back at El Alamein.

1943

14–24 January	Casablanca Conference: Britain and the USA insist on an unconditional surrender of the Axis powers.
27 January	Decree concerning the Registration of Men and Women for Reich Defence Tasks.
31 January	German Sixth Army surrenders at Stalingrad.
18 February	Goebbels' 'total war speech' in Berlin.
12 May	Axis armies surrender in Tunisia.
10 July	Western Allies land in Sicily.
12 July	Germans abandon the Kursk offensive.
24–30 July	Allied air attack on Hamburg kills 30,000 people.
26 July	Mussolini is replaced by General Badaglio.
20 August	Himmler replaces Frick as Interior Minister.
8 September	German troops occupy northern Italy.

1944

January	Gestapo breaks up the Kreisau Circle.
27 January	Soviet forces relieve Leningrad.
6 June	D-Day landings.
13 June	V-1 flying-bomb campaign begins.
20 July	The abortive bomb plot to kill Hitler.
30 August	Soviet forces enter Bucharest.
21 October	Aachen falls to American troops.

1945

30 January	Hitler's last radio speech.
25 April	American and Soviet troops meet on the Elbe.
30 April	Hitler's suicide. Dönitz becomes Chancellor.
7–8 May	Surrender of Germany.
23 May	Dissolution of Dönitz regime by the Allies.

Who's who

Amann, Max (1891–1957): Nazi politician and press baron. He joined the NSDAP in 1921 and looked after both the party's and Hitler's finances. A year later he took over the Eher publishing company, which included responsibility for the party newspaper, *Völkische Beobachter*. He was appointed President of the Reich Press Chamber in 1933.

Backe, Hermann (1896–1947): Before joining the NSDAP he had taught at the technical university at Hanover and had also been a farmer. He was a Nazi member of the Prussian *Landtag* in 1932, and became Reich Food Commissioner for the Four Year Plan in 1936. In 1942 he succeeded Darré as Food and Agricultural Minister. He committed suicide in prison in 1947.

Bästlein, Bernhard (1894–1944): German Communist, who was imprisoned in 1933. On his release in 1939 he helped build resistance cells in Hamburg and northern Germany. On 15 October 1942, the Gestapo began a wave of arrests and two days later they arrested Bästlein at work. In January 1944 he escaped from prison during an air raid, but was again arrested in September 1944 and executed shortly after.

Beck, General, Ludwig (1880–1944): Head of the General Staff of the *Wehrmacht* 1935–38. He resigned in August 1938 in protest against Hitler's plans to invade Czechoslovakia. He then remained in close contact with opposition forces in the *Wehrmacht*, and committed suicide when the 20 July 1944 bomb plot failed.

Bismarck, Prince Otto von (1815–98): Unifier of Germany in 1871 and first Chancellor of the Reich 1871–90.

Blomberg, General Werner von (1878–1946): Appointed Minister of Defence in January 1933. In 1935 he became War Minister, but was dismissed in January 1938 after he married Eva Grühn, a former prostitute. Hitler used his dismissal to abolish the War Ministry and replaced it with the OKW (High Command of the Armed Forces), which reported directly to him.

Bonhoeffer, Dietrich (1906–45): Protestant pastor, a member of the Confessing Church and later one of the leading members of the German resistance against Hitler. In 1942 he went to Stockholm to meet Bishop Bell of Chichester in an unsuccessful attempt to persuade the British government to support the German opposition. He was arrested in 1943 and hanged in Flossenburg concentration camp on 9 April 1945.

Bormann, Martin (1900–45): As Hitler's private secretary and head of the Party Chancellery, he was one of the most influential members of the Nazi Party. He joined the party in 1925 and became Hess's Chief of Staff and secretary in 1933. In 1941 after Hess's flight to Scotland, he became head of the Party Chancellery, and then in 1943 Hitler's secretary, a position he exploited to strengthen his own influence over the party. He committed suicide on 2 May 1945.

Bouhler, Phillip (1899–1945): Initially worked on the *Völkische Beobachter*; in 1934 he became Police President of Munich and then head of the *Führer* Chancellery. It was this office that was responsible for the euthanasia programme of 1939.

Brauchitsch, Field Marshal, Walther von (1881–1948): Served on the German General Staff during the First World War. He was appointed Commander-in-Chief of the German army in February 1938, but relieved of his command in December 1941 when Hitler himself became Commander-in-Chief. He opposed none of Hitler's military plans and was not a member of the military opposition.

Brüning, Heinrich (1885–1970): leader of the parliamentary group of the Centre Party and Chancellor of the Weimar Republic March 1930–May 1932. His rule by presidential decree and his deflationary economic politics, which alienated support from his government, did much to pave the way for the Papen–Hitler government. He emigrated to Britain and then the USA in 1934.

Chamberlain, Houston Stewart (1855–1927): Husband of the daughter of Richard Wagner and author of *The Foundations of the Nineteenth Century* published in 1899. He saw all European history since the Ancient Greeks in terms of racial struggle and argued that only the Aryans had the potential for a creative culture. His ideas were a considerable influence on Nazi racial ideology.

Chamberlain, Neville (1869–1940): British Conservative politician and Prime Minister of the United Kingdom from May 1937 to May 1940.

Daluege, Kurt (1897–1946): Joined the NSPAD in 1922 and became leader of the Berlin SS in 1928. After Heydrich's assassination he became Deputy Protector of Bohemia and Moravia.

Darré, Richard-Walther (1895–1953): Appointed Reich Farmers' Leader and Minister for Food and Agriculture in 1933. He passionately believed in preserving the peasantry as the 'bloodstock of the nation' and in encouraging settlements along the frontiers of the Reich, particularly in the east. Hitler became increasingly impatient with his theorising about 'blood and soil' and had him replaced as minister in 1941. He was tried at Nuremberg and sentenced to five years' imprisonment.

Delp, Alfred (1900–45): Jesuit and member of the Kreisau Circle. He was arrested just after the July bomb plot on 28 July 1944, tortured and hanged on 2 February 1945.

Dietrich, Otto (1897–1952): *SS-Obergruppenführer*. He was appointed Reich Press Chief for the NSDAP in 1931. From 1937 to 1945 he was State Secretary in the Propaganda Ministry.

Dönitz, Admiral Karl (1891–1980): Commander-in-Chief of the German navy (1943–45). He showed great loyalty to Hitler in the aftermath of the bomb plot in July 1944 and succeeded Hitler as Chancellor on 30 April 1945. He surrendered unconditionally to the Allies on 8 May, but by delaying capitulation enabled large numbers of German troops to escape the Russians. The British and Americans allowed his regime to continue until 23 May 1945.

Drexler, Anton (1884–1942): Founding member of the German Workers' Party. He helped Hitler compose the 25 Point Programme for the NSDAP. In July 1921 he was made honorary president of the NSDAP, while Hitler ran the party as chairman. He remained a member of the party until his death, but played no active role.

Eichmann, Adolf (1906–62): Joined the SD in 1934. In 1935 he was appointed head of the 'Office for Jewish Emigration', and in 1938–9 dealt with the expulsion of the Jews from Austria and Bohemia. In 1942, as a consequence of the decisions taken at the Wannsee Conference, he was given responsibility for carrying out the 'Final Solution', and in 1944 organised the deportation of the Hungarian Jews. In 1945 he fled to Argentina, but was kidnapped by the Israelis and executed in 1962.

Elser, Georg: Cabinet-maker, former Communist and committed Christian. He was sent to Sachsenhausen concentration camp and executed in 1945 after his attempt on Hitler's life. The Nazis were convinced that he was a British agent and hoped to stage a show trial after the war.

Fichte, Johann (1762–1814): Professor of Philosophy at Berlin. In his famous *Addresses to the German Nation* (1807–8), he gave intellectual leadership to the growing German hostility to Napoleon. He stressed the uniqueness of the German spirit, which in its depth, he claimed, was far superior to that of other nations.

Franco, General Francisco (1892–1975): Leader of the Spanish Nationalists and then ruler of Spain 1939–75.

Frank, Hans (1900–46): Trained as a lawyer and became head of the NSDAP's legal office in 1929. He was then appointed Minister of Justice in Bavaria, and in 1934 he became Reich Minister without Portfolio. He was Governor General of occupied Poland (1939–45), but was expelled from the party in 1942 for advocating a return to constitutional government. He was sentenced to death at Nuremberg.

Freislar, Roland (1893–1945): Nazi *Reichstag* deputy from 1932 and president of the Berlin *Volksgericht* (People's Court) 1942–5.

Frick, Wilhelm (1877–1946): Worked in the Munich police offices from 1904 until his election to the *Reichstag* in 1924 as a Nazi. In 1930 he became Minister of Interior in Thuringia, and in January 1933 was promoted to Reich Minister of the Interior. In 1943 he was replaced by Himmler and given the post of Protector of Bohemia and Moravia. He was hanged at Nuremberg in 1946.

Fritsch, General Werner Freiherr von (1880–1939): Commander-in-Chief of the *Wehrmacht* from 1934 until 1938. He was critical of the risks Hitler ran in his foreign policy and was forced to resign in January 1938 as a result of being falsely accused of homosexuality. He was killed in the Polish campaign in 1939.

Funk, Walther (1890–1960): editor of the conservative financial newspaper, *Die Börsenzeitung* (1922–32). When he joined the Nazi Party in 1931, he attempted to mediate between big business and the party. He became Government Press Chief in 1933, and then Economics Minister (1937–45). He was sentenced to life imprisonment at Nuremberg, although he was released in 1957.

Galen, Cardinal Archbishop, Graf Clemens von (1878–1946): Appointed Archbishop of Münster in 1933. While supporting Hitler's foreign policy, particularly the invasion of the USSR, he was a fierce critic of the anti-Christian strand in Nazi ideology. In 1941 he openly attacked the Nazi euthanasia programme, although he was unable to halt it completely. He was arrested in the aftermath of the July 1944 plot and sent to Sachsenhausen concentration camp. In 1945 he was appointed Cardinal.

Glaise-Horstenau, Edmund (1882–1946): From 11 to 13 March 1938 Vice-Chancellor of Austria under Seyss-Inquart. After the *Anschluss* he entered the *Wehrmacht* and was appointed Plenipotentiary General in the Independent State of Croatia on 14 April 1941.

Gobineau, Joseph Arthur de (1816–82): French diplomat and writer. In his *Essay on the Inequality of the Races of Man* (1853–55) he proclaimed the superiority of the white races. Together with H.S. Chamberlain (q.v.), his writings did much to influence Nazi racial ideology.

Goebbels, Paul Joseph (1897–1945): Joined the NSDAP in 1924 and became *Gauleiter* of Berlin in 1926 and Reich Director of Propaganda in 1929. He was given the key post of Minister of Enlightenment and Propaganda in 1933 and managed to build up a highly effective system for controlling the mass media and cultural life of the German state. In 1944 he was made Plenipotentiary for Total War. He committed suicide on 2 May 1945.

Goerdeler, Carl (1884–1945): Lord Mayor of Leipzig (1930–37) and Reich Price Commissioner (1934–35). He was critical of Hitler's rearmament policy and became a key figure in the conservative opposition to the regime. He was involved in the July 1944 conspiracy. In the wake of its failure he was arrested and executed.

Göring, Hermann (1893–1946): Joined the Nazi Party in 1922 and was briefly in charge of the SA the following year. He was elected to the *Reichstag* in 1928 and became its President (speaker) in 1932. On the take-over of power he was appointed first of all Prussian Minister of the Interior and then Prime Minister. He set up the Gestapo, but lost control of it to Himmler. He was also made Reich Aviation Minister and in 1935 became the Commander-in-Chief of the *Luftwaffe*. In 1936 Hitler put him in charge of the Four Year Plan, which made him a pivotal figure in the Third Reich. He was made Reich Marshal in 1940, but his failure to defeat the Royal Air Force that year caused his influence to decline. In April 1945 Hitler expelled him from the party and put him under house arrest for allegedly attempting to assume leadership of the Reich. He surrendered to the Americans and was tried at Nuremberg, but managed to commit suicide before being executed.

Greiser, Arthur (1897–1946): Joined the NSDAP in 1931 and succeeded Rauschning as President of the Danzig Senate in 1934. In 1939 he was appointed chief of the civil administration in Posen and in 1940 *Gauleiter* and Reich Governor of the Wartheland. He was sentenced to death in Poland in 1946.

Grynszpan, Herschl (born 1921): A German Jew, whose family originally came from Poland. He shot and fatally wounded the legation secretary in the German embassy in Paris in protest on hearing that 17,000 Polish Jews including his own family had been deported from Germany to Poland. This provided the Nazi regime with the excuse to unleash the *Reichskristallnacht*. He was handed over to the Germans by Vichy France and most probably died in prison in 1944/45.

Halder, General Franz (1884–1972): Replaced Beck as Chief of Staff of the *Wehrmacht* 1938–42, but as a result of disagreements with Hitler over the Russian campaign he was retired into the 'Führer Reserve' in 1942. He was arrested and imprisoned a day after the failed coup of 20 July 1944.

Hammerstein-Equord, Kurt Freiherr von (1878–1943): Because of his anti-Nazi views he was forced to resign as Commander-in-Chief of the *Reichswehr* in 1934, but he was recalled to military service in 10 September 1939. During the Second World War, he was involved in several plots to overthrow Hitler. He died of cancer in Berlin on 25 April 1943.

Harnack, Arvid (1901–42): Jurist, economist and university lecturer, who saw Germany as a bridge between Russia and the West. In 1933, Harnack obtained an appointment in the Reich Economic Ministry, and in 1936 secretly got in touch with the Soviet embassy. As a cover he joined the NSDAP in 1937. In 1939 he contacted the Schulze-Boysen group, which led to the formation of the *Rote Kapelle*. He was arrested and executed in 1942.

Hassell, Ulrich von (1881–1944): Career diplomat, who became German ambassador to Italy (1932–38). Hassell was one of the leading Conservative critics of the Nazi regime and was involved in the July 1944 plot, after which he was arrested and executed.

Henlein, Konrad (1898–1945): Leader of the Sudeten German Nazis. With backing from Hitler, he led the campaign against Czech rule. In 1939, after the annexation of the Sudetenland, he became Chief of the Civil Administration and *Gauleiter*. He was captured by the Americans in 1945 but committed suicide.

Hess, Rudolf (1894–1987): Worked as Hitler's secretary from 1920, became Deputy Leader of the party in 1932 and then Minister without Portfolio in 1933. He played a key role in the complexities of party–state relations. In 1941 he flew to Scotland apparently to negotiate peace with the British government, but was interned until 1945. At Nuremberg he was sentenced to life imprisonment.

Heydrich, Reinhard (1904–42): Joined the NSDAP and SS in 1931 and became Himmler's deputy in 1933. In January 1939 he was appointed head of the Reich Central Office for Jewish Emigration and, in September, of the Reich Security Head Office. He organised the deportation of the Jews to occupied Poland and briefed the *Einsatzgruppen* in 1941 before their entry into the USSR. He replaced Neurath as Reich Protector of Bohemia and Moravia in 1941, but was assassinated by the Czech underground in 1942.

Himmler, Heinrich (1900–45): Briefly after the First World War he was a poultry farmer in Bavaria. He took part in the Munich *Putsch* and in 1929 was made head of the SS. He was made Chief of the Police in Bavaria in 1933, and by December was able to establish his control over the political police in the other non-Prussian states. In 1934 he became the head of the Prussian police and the Gestapo and by 1936 had consolidated his grip on the whole police apparatus in Germany. In 1939 he was made Commissar for the Consolidation of German Nationhood (RKVDV), which gave him a powerful say in Nazi racial and extermination policy in the occupied areas. In 1943 he became Minister of the Interior, but his premature attempt to end the war in April 1945 led to Hitler ordering his arrest. He was captured by British troops in May, but committed suicide before his trial.

Hindenburg, Paul von Beneckendorff und von (1847–1934): Hindenburg came out of retirement in 1914 to defeat the Russians at Tannenberg. He was made a Field Marshal and in 1916 Chief of the General Staff. Together with General Ludendorff, he controlled German military and civil policy from July 1917 to November 1918. He was elected President in 1925 and re-elected in 1932. During the crisis years of 1930–33 he allowed the governments of Brüning, Papen and Schleicher to rule by presidential decree. Without his consent in January 1933 Hitler would not have been appointed Chancellor.

Hitler, Adolf (1889–1945): Born in Braunau am Inn, Upper Austria. In *Mein Kampf* he painted an exaggerated picture of a poverty-stricken childhood, but his father, Alois, an Austrian customs official, drew a reasonable salary and provided adequately for his family. Alois was strict, humourless and often violent, while his mother compensated by an over-protectiveness. Inevitably, beneath the surface, as Kershaw has written, 'the later Hitler was

. . . being formed', but psycho-historians have been unable to come up with anything more than speculation about the impact of these years on his character (Kershaw, I, 1998: 13). Hitler left school without any qualifications in 1905 and, convinced of his artistic talents, tried unsuccessfully to gain a place at the Academy of Fine Arts in Vienna. He refused to resign himself to the humdrum task of earning a living and up to 1914 lived the life of an increasingly penniless drifter in Vienna and Munich. In Vienna he absorbed the gist of the current Social Darwinistic, *völkisch* and racist thinking. He also followed the tactics of the Austrian Social Democrats, the pan-German Nationalists and the Christian Social Party, noting particularly how the latter drew support from 'those sections of the population whose existence was threatened' (*Mein Kampf*, 1974: 91). In August 1914 Hitler joined a Bavarian regiment and fought for the next four years with considerable personal bravery and won the Iron Cross (First Class). He was wounded in a British gas attack in 1918, but returned in late November to his regiment in Munich. In the summer of 1919 he was employed to counter the effects of Bolshevik propaganda among the troops. He also joined the German Workers' Party, which was subsequently renamed the NSDAP, and became its chairman in July 1921. After the failure of the Munich *Putsch* in November 1923 he was imprisoned at Landsberg where he wrote *Mein Kampf*. When he came out of prison, he rebuilt the NSDAP and planned to gain power legally. The Depression made the NSDAP the largest party in the *Reichstag*, but Hitler never secured a majority of seats and was ultimately only brought to power to head a Nazi–Nationalist coalition because Papen convinced Hindenburg that Hitler could be controlled by the conservative–nationalist elites. The Enabling Act of March 1933 gave his administration virtually unlimited powers and on Hindenburg's death in August 1934 Hitler himself, thanks to the elimination of Röhm, gained the support of the army for combining the post of Chancellor and President and named himself '*Führer* of the German Reich'. Up to 1937 he concentrated largely on solving the unemployment problem, laying the foundations for rearmament in depth and dismantling the Versailles system. From 1938 onwards his foreign, domestic and racial policies became increasingly radical. He annexed Austria, Bohemia and Moravia and invaded Poland, which caused war with Britain and France. In June 1941 he made the cardinal error of attacking the USSR while leaving Britain undefeated in the west. His assumption of responsibilities for military operations in December 1941 ensured that the military disasters in Russia severely damaged the *Führer* myth that did much to underpin the *Volksgemeinschaft*. Hitler survived the July bomb plot in 1944, but committed suicide on 30 April 1945.

Hossbach, Friedrich (1894–1980): German staff officer who in 1937 was the military adjutant to the *Führer* of the Third Reich. He was the author of the 'Hossbach Memorandum', which recorded the meeting between Hitler and key ministers and service personnel on 5 November 1937.

Hugenberg, Alfred (1865–1951): Businessman and press magnate during the Weimar Republic. He was a member of the DNVP from 1919 to 1933 and his newspapers backed Hitler (1930–33). He was Minister of Economics and Food in Hitler's government up to June 1933.

Jacob, Franz (1906–44): Former Communist member of the Hamburg *Landtag*. He was arrested in August 1933 and only released in 1940. On his release he worked in the Hamburg shipyards and formed a Communist resistance group with Bernhard Bästlein and Robert Abshagen. He escaped arrest in Hamburg by fleeing to Berlin in 1942. He had contacts with the Kreisau Circle and with von Stauffenberg, but was arrested on 4 July and executed in September.

Jodl, General Alfred (1890–1946): Chief of the Operations Staff of the Armed Forces High Command (*Oberkommando der Wehrmacht*, or OKW) during the Second World War, and Hitler's closest military adviser. At Nuremberg he was tried, and sentenced to death.

Kahr, Gustav Ritter von (1862–1934): Conservative and monarchist Prime Minister of Bavaria 1920–21. In September 1923 he was appointed state commissioner of Bavaria with dictatorial powers. Initially he supported Hitler's plans for a *Putsch* but he withdrew support. In 1924 he was forced to resign from his post when Hitler's trial revealed his administration's involvement in the initial planning for the *Putsch*. He was murdered on 30 June 1934 by the SS.

Keitel, Wilhelm (1882–1946): Appointed Chief of Staff to the War Minister Werner von Blomberg in 1935. He was head of the OKW 1938–1945. He was tried and found guilty of war crimes at Nuremberg in 1946.

Kerrl, Hans (1887–1941): June 1934 appointed Reich Minister without Portfolio. A year later he became Reich Minister for Church Affairs.

Krosigk, Graf Schwerin von (1887–1977): Served in the short-lived Flensburg government of Dönitz. He had been appointed German Finance Minister in 1932 and held the post until 1945.

Krupp, Gustav von Bohlen und Halbach (1907–67): German arms manufacturer and leader of the Reich Estate of German Industry. He was tried as a war criminal at Nuremberg.

Lammers, Hans Heinrich (1879–1962): A career civil servant who joined the Nazi Party in 1932. He was appointed in 1933 a State Secretary and chief of the Reich Chancellery and then Minister without Portfolio in 1937. In this position, he became the centre of communications and chief legal adviser for all government departments. From 30 November 1939 he was a member of the Council of Ministers for the Defence of the Reich.

Leber, Julius (1891–1945): SPD journalist and Reichstag Deputy. He was arrested and incarcerated in concentration camps 1933–37. He then joined the resistance and later had close connections with the Kreisau Circle. He was arrested in July 1944 and executed three months later.

Leuschner, Wilhelm (1888–1944): Trade unionist and Minister of the Interior in Hesse. He was imprisoned by the Nazis in May 1933. On his release he was involved in resistance groups centring around Beck and Stauffenberg. He was arrested and executed after the failure of the July 1944 plot.

Ley, Robert (1890–1945): Worked for IG Farben and then joined the NSDAP in 1924. He was elected to the *Reichstag* in 1930 and was appointed leader of the German Labour Front in 1933. He committed suicide in 1945.

Lichtenberg, Father Bernhard (1875–1943): Bitter opponent of the Nazis, and one of the few priests to champion the Jews during the Third Reich. Heydrich called him 'that gutter priest from Berlin'. Lichtenberg was arrested in 1941 and died in 1942 while being transferred to Dachau concentration camp.

Lubbe, Marinus van der (1909–34): Dutch Communist accused of, and executed for, setting fire to the German *Reichstag* building on 27 February 1933. He was posthumously pardoned in 2008.

Ludecke, Kurt (1890–1960): German nationalist, and socialite who joined the Nazi Party in the early 1920s and used his social connections to raise money for the NSDAP.

Ludendorff, General Erich von (1865–1937): Chief of Staff and Quarter Master General of the German army. He became Hindenburg's right-hand man in 1917–18. He resigned in 1918 and took part in the Munich *Putsch* of 1923. He sat as a Nazi deputy in the *Reichstag* (1924–28), but thereafter became estranged from Hitler.

Mendelssohn, Felix (1809–47): German-Jewish composer and conductor who was the grandson of the philosopher Moses Mendelssohn. His work includes oratorios, symphonies, piano, violin and chamber music.

Mierendorff, Carlo (1897–1943): An active member of the SPD since 1920, he was appointed chief press officer for the Ministry of the Interior, Hessen, and was elected to the *Reichstag*, 1930–33. He was a member of the Kreisau Circle and died in an air raid in 1943.

Milch, Edward (1892–1972): The key figure in creating the Luftwaffe. In 1940 he was given the rank of Field Marshal and was placed in charge of the production of military aircraft in Germany. In 1947 he was tried at Nuremberg and sentenced to life imprisonment. In June 1954 he was released. He was the son of a Jewish pharmacist, but Göring defended him from the Gestapo by producing an affidavit that claimed that his real father was a Gentile.

Moltke, Helmuth Count von (1907–45): The great-grandnephew of Helmuth von Moltke the Elder, the victorious commander in the Austro-Prussian and Franco-Prussian Wars. He was a lawyer by profession and the owner of the Kreisau Estate in Prussian Silesia. In January 1944, he was arrested by the Gestapo and a year later was tried in the People's Court by Roland Freisler. He was executed in January 1945.

Müller, Ludwig, Bishop (1883–1945): As the leading figure in the association of German Christians and a supporter of Nazism, he was appointed the

Reich Bishop of the German National Church (Reichskirche). He committed suicide at the end of the Second World War.

Mussolini, Benito (1883–1945): Originally a socialist, but was expelled from the party when he supported Italy's entry into the war in 1915. He created the Italian Fascist Party in 1919 and successfully exploited the post-war economic and political crisis to gain power in 1922. By 1929 he had consolidated his position and established a one-party government. Mussolini was determined to turn the Mediterranean into an Italian lake. However, his fatal mistake was to enter the war as an ally of Hitler in 1940. Hitler was a great admirer of Mussolini and in many ways regarded him as a political role model.

Neurath, Constantin Freiherr von (1873–1956): German Foreign Minister (1932–38) and then Reich Protector of Bohemia and Moravia (1939–41), when he was 'retired' and replaced by Heydrich.

Niemöller, Martin (1892–1984): He was initially a conservative nationalist, but became hostile to Nazi Church policy. He helped found the Pastors' Emergency League and became the leader of the Confessing Church. He was sent to Sachsenhausen and Dachau concentration camps for seven years. After 1945 he became active in the peace movement.

Oberfohren, Ernst (1881–1933): Leader of the DNVP in the *Reichstag*. Although he voted for the Enabling Bill, he became increasingly sceptical of the Nazis and was accused of sending the *Manchester Guardian* a critical account of the *Reichstag* fire. He was found shot dead in Kiel on 8 May 1933.

Olbricht, General Friedrich (1888–1944): Chief of the General Army Office and of the Armed Forces Replacement Office in Berlin. He played a key role in developing Operation *Valkyrie*, the 20 July plot in 1944. When it failed he was court-martialled by the army and shot.

Oster, Gerneral Hans (1887–1945): Deputy head of the *Abwehr*, which dealt with espionage and counter-espionage, under Wilhelm Canaris, and one of the earliest and most determined opponents of Adolf Hitler and Nazism. He was a leading figure in the German resistance from 1938 to 1943. It was Oster who supplied English-made bombs to Tresckow's group for their various attempts to assassinate Hitler in 1943. Oster was arrested a day after the failed 20 July 1944 plot and executed in April 1945.

Papen, Franz von (1879–1969): Soldier and diplomat. He was elected to the Prussian *Landtag* in 1920 for the Centre Party and was Chancellor from June to December 1932. He laid the foundations for the restoration of authoritarian rule by abolishing the Prussian government. In January 1933 he agreed to serve in Hitler's government as Vice-Chancellor. In June 1934 he was highly critical of Hitler's handling of Röhm and the SA, and narrowly missed being murdered after the 'Night of the Long Knives'. He was sent first as ambassador to Vienna and then to Turkey (1938–44). He was sentenced to eight years' imprisonment in 1947 by a German court, but was freed in 1949.

Pétain, Marshal Henri Philippe (1856–1951): Hero of the battle of Verdun in 1916. He was appointed French Prime Minister in 1940 to negotiate peace with the Germans. In unoccupied France he headed an authoritarian government based at Vichy.

Pol Pot (1928–98): Communist leader of Cambodia, 1975–79. His attempts to 'ethnically cleanse' the country resulted in the death of an estimated 1.7 to 2.5 million people.

Popitz, Johannes (1884–1945): Appointed Prussian Finance Minister in 1933. He was a conservative and monarchist, who offered his resignation after *Kristallnacht*, which was not accepted. He was a member of the *Mittwochsgesellschaft* (Wednesday Society), a centre for conservative opposition to the National Socialist regime. In the summer of 1943, Popitz conducted secret talks with Heinrich Himmler, whose support he sought to win for a *coup d'état*, and whom he tried to convince to take part in attempts to negotiate with the Western powers for an acceptable peace deal. He was arrested in Berlin on 21 July 1944, and hanged in February 1945.

Raeder, Admiral E. (1876–1960): Commander-in Chief of the German navy, 1939–43 when he resigned in favour of Karl Dönitz.

Rauschning, Hermann (1887–1982): An ultra conservative who became a Nazi in 1932. From 1933 to 1934 he was President of the Danzig Senate. In 1934 he renounced his Nazi Party membership and fled to the United States where he bitterly attacked Nazism. In 1939 he wrote his most famous book, *Germany's Revolution of Destruction*.

Reinhardt, Fritz (1895–1969): State Secretary in the German Finance Ministry. In 1937 he was appointed SA *Obergruppenführer*.

Ribbentrop, Joachim von (1893–1946): Joined the NSDAP in 1932 and acted as Hitler's foreign affairs adviser in 1933. In 1936 he became ambassador to Britain and in 1938 Foreign Minister. His main success was the Nazi–Soviet non-aggression treaty of August 1939. He was condemned to death at Nuremberg and executed in 1946.

Röhm, Ernst (1887–1934): Participant in the Munich *Putsch*. After a few years in Bolivia he was appointed head of the SA in 1930. He became a bitter critic of Hitler's opportunism after 1933 and pressed for a 'second revolution'. His radicalism threatened to alienate the conservative elite from Hitler and he was subsequently murdered in the 'Night of the Long Knives' in 1934.

Rosenberg, Alfred (1893–1946): A Baltic German who fled to Bavaria during the Russian Revolution. He was involved in the Munich *Putsch* and temporarily became leader of the Nazi Party when Hitler was in prison. He developed his racial theories in his book the *Myth of the Twentieth Century*, which was published in 1930. He was made responsible for ideological training within the NSDAP. In 1941 he became Minister for the Occupied Eastern Territories. He was sentenced to death at Nuremberg.

Rust, Bernhard (1883–1945): Joined the NSDAP in 1922 and was appointed *Gauleiter* of Hanover and Braunschweig in 1925. In 1933 he became Prussian Minister of Science and then in 1934 Reich Minister of Education. He committed suicide in 1945.

Saefkow, Anton (1903–44): Leading Communist functionary. He was arrested by the Nazis in 1933 and imprisoned until 1939. After the invasion of the USSR, he managed to form the biggest KPD resistance group in Germany, the so-called 'Operative Leadership of the KPD'. In April 1944, the Social Democrat Adolf Reichwein established contact with Saefkow to include the KPD group in the 20 July 1944 plot. On its failure he was arrested and sentenced to death.

Sauckel, Fritz (1894–1946): Joined the Nazi Party in 1923 and was appointed *Gauleiter* in Thuringia in 1927. In March 1942 he was appointed Plenipotentiary-General for Labour Mobilisation and given orders by Hitler to recruit the necessary workers from the eastern occupied territories. He was sentenced to death at Nuremberg.

Schacht, Hjalmar (1877–1970): Appointed Reich Currency Commissioner and then president of the *Reichsbank* in 1923. In 1932 he advocated Hitler's appointment as Chancellor. Under Hitler he was reappointed to the *Reichsbank* and played a key role in devising the *Mefo* bills to finance rearmament. He was made Economics Minister in 1934 and Plenipotentiary-General for the War Economy in 1935. In 1936, however, serious disagreements with Hitler about the pace and financing of rearmament led to the introduction of the Four Year Plan under Göring and a decline in Schacht's influence. He was dismissed from the Economics Ministry in 1937 and the *Reichsbank* in 1939, but he remained a Minister without Portfolio until 1943. He was cleared of war crimes by the Nuremberg Tribunal.

Schirach, Baldur von (1907–74): Nazi Youth leader 1931–40 and then *Gauleiter* and Governor of Vienna. He was sentenced to 20 years' imprisonment at Nuremberg.

Schleicher, General Kurt von (1882–1934): Head of the Ministerial Bureau within the Defence Ministry, he played a key role in advising Hindenburg during the period 1930–32. He was appointed Chancellor in December 1932, only to be replaced by Hitler on 30 January 1933. He was murdered during the 'Night of the Long Knives'.

Schmitt, Kurt (1886–1950): Chairman of the Allianz AG insurance company 1921–33, and then Reich Economic Minister 1933–34.

Scholl, Sophia Magdalena (1921–43): German student, active within the White Rose group. She was convicted of high treason after having been found distributing anti-war leaflets at the University of Munich with her brother Hans (1918–43).

Scholtz-Klinik, Gertrud (1902–99): Joined the NSDAP in 1930 and was leader of the Nazi women's organisation in Baden. In 1934 she was appointed Reich's Women's Leader and then head of *Frauenwerk*, the women's section of the DAF. In 1948 she was arrested and sentenced to 18 months' imprisonment by the French.

Schroeder, Kurt von (1899–1966): Rhineland banker who was an early financial contributor to the NSDAP. He arranged the crucial meeting between Hitler and Papen in January 1933 with the purpose of bringing down the Schleicher government.

Schulze-Boysen, Heinz (1909–42): Left-wing commentator and journalist. He joined the *Luftwaffe* in 1933. In 1936 he made contact with Arvid Harnack and his circle, and also with the Communists, which resulted in the creation of what the Gestapo called the Red Orchestra (*Rote Kapelle*). From 1940 to 1942, the group was in wireless contact with Soviet agents, but in July 1942 it was broken up by the Gestapo and Schulze-Boysen was arrested and executed in December 1942.

Schuschnigg, Kurt von (1897–1977): Chancellor of Austria (1934–38). Imprisoned by the Nazis after the *Anschluss*. In 1945 he moved to the USA.

Seldte, Franz (1882–1947): Co-founder of the *Stahlhelm*. He joined the Nazi Party in 1933 and was appointed Reich Labour Minister, a post he held until 1945.

Seyss-Inquart, Arthur (1892–1946): Regarded as a moderate Nazi in the 1930s and appointed to the Austrian State Council by Schuschnigg, who hoped thereby to appease the Nazis, but in February 1938 Hitler insisted that he should become Interior Minister. After the *Anschluss* he became Governor of Austria and then, later, Reich Commissioner of the German-occupied Netherlands. He was executed at Nuremberg in 1946.

Speer, Albert (1905–81): Architect who joined the Nazi Party in 1931. He stage-managed the great rallies at Nuremberg and designed the new Reich Chancellery and Party Headquarters in Munich. In January 1942 he was appointed Armaments Minister and did much to increase and rationalise production. He was sentenced to 20 years' imprisonment at Nuremberg.

Stalin, Josef (1879–1953): Born Djugashvili in Georgia. By 1929 he was in control of the Bolshevik Party and was able to launch successive Five Year Plans which enabled the USSR to survive the German invasion in 1941. In May 1941 he became Chairman of the Council of Ministers. The Soviet victory was celebrated in the USSR as his supreme achievement.

Stauffenberg, Claus Schenk Graf von (1907–44): After being wounded in Africa he returned to staff duties in Berlin in 1943. He took a leading role in organising the abortive plot of 20 July 1944 and was executed within hours after it became clear that Hitler was still alive.

Stennes, Walther (1895–1989): Served with distinction in the First World War and in its aftermath joined the *Freikorps*. In 1927 he became a Nazi and was appointed leader of the SA in east Germany in 1928, but was dismissed when he criticised Hitler for having forsaken the revolutionary path. In 1933 he fled to China, and only returned to Germany in 1949.

Strasser, Gregor (1892–1934): Leader of the north German Nazis during the 1920s and the main representative of the 'socialist', anti-capitalist wing of the Nazi Party. He resigned from the party when Hitler vetoed his acceptance of Schleicher's offer of the Vice-Chancellorship in December 1932. He was murdered in the 'Night of the Long Knives' in June 1934.

Streicher, Julius (1885–1946): Bavarian teacher who founded *die Deutsche Soziale Partei* in 1919. He joined the Nazi Party in 1921 and founded *Der Stürmer*, a rabidly anti-Semitic journal, which led the campaign for repressive measures against the Jews. He was hanged in 1946.

Stuckart, Wilhelm (1902–53): A lawyer by profession, he joined the Nazi Party in 1922. From March 1936 he was a State Secretary in the Reich Ministry of Interior, leading the 'Constitution and Legislation' department. He represented Frick at the Wannsee Conference.

Thierack, Otto (1889–1946): A lawyer who joined the Nazi Party in 1932 and was appointed Minister for Justice in Saxony in 1933. He was President of the People's Court 1936–42, and Minister of Justice 1942–45, He committed suicide in 1946.

Todt, Fritz (1891–1942): He studied civil engineering and joined the Nazis in 1922. In 1931 he was appointed an SS colonel. He was made Inspector General of German Roads in 1933, which made him responsible for the construction of the motorways and military fortifications along the frontiers. In 1940 he was appointed Armaments Minister, but was killed in an air crash in January 1942.

Tresckow, Major-General Henning von (1901–44): Attempted to assassinate Hitler in March 1943 and played an important role in drawing up plans for Operation *Valkyrie*. He committed suicide on the Eastern Front when the plot failed.

Wagener, Adolf (1890–1944): Joined the NSDAP in 1923, and was appointed *Gauleiter* of Munich–Upper Bavaria in 1929. In 1933 he was made the Bavarian Minister of the Interior and then in 1936 the Bavarian Minister of Education. In 1939 he became Defence Commissioner for the Munich and Nuremberg districts.

Wagener, Otto (1888–1971): Reich Commissar for the Economy from April to June 1933. He was replaced by Wilhelm Kepler after complaints from the Reich Association of German Industry. He became a major-general in the Second World War.

Weizsäcker, Ernst Freiherr von (1882–1951): German diplomat, who became Chief State Secretary in the Foreign Office. From 1943 to 1945 he was ambassador to the Vatican.

Willikens, Werner (1893–1961): Joined the NSDAP in 1925 and later became a member of the SS. In 1933 he became State Secretary in the Prussian Ministry of Agriculture, and two years later joined the Reich Ministry for Food and Agriculture. In 1940 he produced a plan to settle peasants from Baden and Württemberg in the newly annexed area of Poland.

Witzleben, Field Marshal Erwin von (1881–1944): Commander-in-Chief of German forces in western Europe 1941–42 and then a key conspirator in the 20 July 1944 plot.

Glossary

Alte Kämpfer The veterans of the Nazi Party, literally the 'old fighters'. These were the men who had joined it mostly before 1923 and had taken part in the Munich *Putsch* of November of that year, as compared to the 'March violets', who flocked to the party for opportunist reasons after March 1933. The *Alte Kämpfer* wanted radical measures taken against the Jews and the *Mittelstand* to be protected from big business. In 1933–34 Hitler sacrificed their interests to rearmament and economic recovery.

Anschluss The incorporation of Austria into Germany, which had been the aim of many Germans and Austrians since 1918. It was, however, prohibited by Article 80 of the Treaty of Versailles. Italy was particularly hostile to the prospect of an *Anschluss*, but after the rupture with Britain and France caused by his conquest of Abyssinia, Mussolini abandoned his opposition and accepted the *fait accompli* of the *Anschluss* on 13 March 1938.

Aryan Originally a Hindu word meaning a member of the highest class, Gobineau used the term to describe the Caucasian races. It was much used by the Nazis to denote gentile Germans as opposed, for the most part, to Jews.

asocials People such as tramps and the homeless who did not conform to the normal rules of society.

Atlantic Charter A statement of fundamental democratic principles for the post-war world issued jointly by Churchill and Roosevelt in 1941.

atomised Literally reduced to individual atoms. In the political context the term means a society reduced to a total of isolated individuals lacking support from independent political parties or clubs.

Blitzkrieg Literally, a lightning war, which would, in Hitler's words, 'defeat the enemy as quick as lightning'. These tactics had been first practised by the *Reichswehr* in the 1920s in western Russia, where the Soviet government had allowed it to organise manoeuvres which could not be monitored by Anglo-French officials. Later, economic historians came to see the *Blitzkrieg* as a means for waging war without making massive demands on the German population. In fact, while Hitler clearly welcomed quick victories, Germany was being prepared for a long war of 10–15 years.

Bolsheviks Originally the majority faction of the Marxist Russian Social Democratic Labour Party which split from the Mensheviks in 1903. They ultimately became the Communist Party of the Soviet Union and came to power in Russia as a consequence of the October Revolution of 1917.

Bonapartism Political system employed by Napoleon III of France (1851–70). He created a dictatorship which was supported by the wealthy elites and the lower middle classes. He attempted to strengthen it through a vigorous assertion of French national interests.

cadre party Political group or party which formed a core unit for later mass expansion.

Centre Party The Catholic Centre Party was created in December 1870 to represent the interests of Catholic Germans in the new Reich, and rapidly became involved in a bitter struggle (*Kulturkampf*) with Bismarck and the Prussian state, but by 1895 the government began to see the party as a counter-force to the SPD. Between 1907 and 1918 there was never a government majority without the backing of the Centre Party. During the Weimar Republic the Centre Party, or prominent members of it, participated in every government up to 1932.

collateral Pledge made by a borrower of specific property to a lender, to secure repayment of a loan. The collateral serves as protection for a lender against a borrower's default.

collective farms The Soviet collective farm system consisted of a mixture of state-run farms (*Sovkoz*) and farms run by the peasants themselves along cooperative lines (*Kolkhozy*).

Comintern The Communist international movement set up in 1919 to organise worldwide revolution.

Committee for National Liberation Formed in Algiers in June 1943. It was committed to an Allied victory and the defeat of Vichy France.

Confessing Church (Bekennende Kirche) This was set up in reaction to the Reich Church (*Reichskirche*) by the Pastors' Emergency League in October 1934. It rejected outright the totalitarian claims of the Nazi state over the Church.

corporate body A body such as a company which has its own legal identity.

corporatist Used to describe attempts to defuse class hatred by giving both the state, capital and labour a role in running industry.

Dawes Plan The report on the German economy issued in 1924 by a committee chaired by the American Charles Dawes. It provided for a loan to Germany and a reorganisation of reparation payment.

deficit financing When the expenditure of a government is greater than its tax revenues, a deficit in the government budget is created. In a depression an increase in government expenditure can help revive the economy.

Deutsche Arbeitsfront (**DAF**) The German Labour Front. This was created and put under the control of Robert Ley on 6 May 1933, both to replace the trade unions and to weaken the more radical NSBO, which was subordinated to it. Both workers and employers were members of the DAF, but it had no part in determining wages or relations with the employers. Nevertheless, under the leadership of Robert Ley, it did become influential in social policy and developed the 'Beauty of Labour' and the 'Strength through Joy' schemes.

Deutsches Jungvolk The junior section of the Hitler Youth, for boys between the ages of 10 and 14.

fascism Between 1919 and 1945 there were many varieties of fascism, the essence of which was: a nationalist ideology and an authoritarian state with a charismatic leadership ready to use force to achieve national aims.

foreign exchange Foreign-currency holdings in the Reich.

Freikorps Companies of right-wing volunteers, which sprang up spontaneously during the winter of 1918/19.

Führer Leader. This title was adopted by Hitler to emphasise his absolute leadership of the Nazi Party. At the Bamberg Conference of 1926 he was successful in asserting the primacy of the *Führer* over the party. After Hindenburg's death in August 1934, Hitler was able to nominate himself *Führer* and Reich Chancellor.

Führerprinzip Literally, the 'principle of *Führer*-leadership', based on Hitler's charismatic, absolute leadership. Hitler's power as *Führer* was supposed to be based on his 'exceptional' qualities of leadership. All power was concentrated in his hands and theoretically no major decision could be made without his consent, although in practice party and government officials tried to 'work towards the *Führer*' and anticipate his consent.

Gau (**pl.** *Gaue*) A regional territorial division of the NSDAP. In the reorganisation of the party of 1925–29, Germany was divided into *Gaue*, each under a *Gauleiter*. In 1928 the boundaries of the *Gaue* were reorganised to correspond to the 35 parliamentary electoral districts. *Gau* is originally an old Germanic term meaning a subdivision of a tribe.

Gauleiter (**pl.** *Gauleiter*) A regional party leader in charge of a *Gau*. In April 1933 the senior *Gauleiter* in each state, with the exception of Bavaria and Prussia, was appointed Reich Governor. The *Gauleiter* controlled the local and district party organisations, and as such were able to influence local government in the early days of the take-over of power.

Generalgouvernement Government-General. The area of Poland which was not annexed by the Reich but was directly controlled by a German civil administration in Cracow.

German idealism Philosophical movement originating in Germany in the late eighteenth and early nineteenth centuries. It developed from the work of

Immanuel Kant, and became closely linked with romanticism and the revolutionary politics of the Enlightenment.

Gestapo (*Geheime Staatspolizei*) The Secret State Police. During the Weimar Republic, Department 1a of the Berlin Police *Praesidium* ran the Prussian political police. In April 1933 Göring, as acting Prussian Interior Minister, set up a new Secret State Police Office (*Gestapa*). In November 1933 he created the Gestapo and appointed Himmler its Inspector in April 1934. Its task was to maintain discipline in the factories and to keep political and ideological opponents of the regime under surveillance.

Gleichschaltung Literally, coordination or streamlining. The process of putting everything under Nazi control not only involved the abolition of all the non-National Socialist political parties, the elimination of the *Reichstag* as an independent assembly and the taking over of state and local governments, and, right down to local level, clubs and societies, ranging from singing associations to horticultural societies, were all placed firmly under Nazi control.

Halbstarken Literally translated as half strong. The term was used in the 1950s to describe an adolescent subculture whose members were mostly male and working class and aggressive and provocative in public in the Federal Republic of Germany. The *Halbstarken* can be compared to the 'Teddy Boys' in Britain.

intentionalists Historians who stress the importance of the *individual* and personal *intention* in history. Thus intentionalists, such as Andreas Hillgruber, Klaus Hildebrand and Lucy Davidowicz, stress the aims and intentions of Hitler and emphasise his key role in the formulation of policies, particularly foreign policy and the campaign against the Jews ending in the Holocaust.

Jungmädel-Bund The junior section of the League of German Girls, for girls aged between 10 and 14.

Kapp Putsch Conspiracy by right-wing nationalists and the *Freikorps* led by Wolfgang Kapp to overthrow the Weimar Republic.

Kashubians West Slavic ethnic group in Pomerelia, north-central Poland. Their language or dialect is Kashubian.

Knauer case Herr Knauer, the father of a severely handicapped child appealed to Hitler for permission to have the child killed. The appeal reached Hitler through his private Chancellery, and was approved.

Kommunistische Partei Deutschlands (KPD) The German Communist Party was founded in 1919 and in November 1932 won 100 seats in the *Reichstag*. After the *Reichstag* fire, 4,000 Communist officials, party members and members of the *Reichstag* were arrested and, by the end of 1933, approximately half its total membership was in prison or concentration camps. The Communist opposition was initially run by the Central Committee of the KPD, based in Paris.

Land (*pl. Länder*) The Reich had 25 federal states. The largest was Prussia, which covered two-thirds of Germany and contained three-quarters of the population. The Reich reconstruction law of January 1934 merged the Prussian ministries with the relevant Reich departments. In the other states cabinets remained in existence as agents of the central government. The *Landtage* were abolished.

Landtag Each German state had an elected *Landtag* or assembly. In July 1932 Papen dissolved the Prussian government and put Prussia under the control of a Reich Commissioner. On 31 March 1933 the state assemblies were reconstituted to reflect the Nazi/Nationalist majority in the *Reichstag*, and in January 1934 they were finally abolished.

Lebensraum Literally living space. Convinced that Germany was over-populated, Hitler argued from the end of 1922 onwards that the destruction of Soviet Russia would enable Germany to gain sufficient land for settlement there rather than overseas. These ideas were then elaborated in *Mein Kampf* and became a central component of Hitler's foreign policy.

Locarno Treaties Signed in December 1925, the most important of which was the treaty guaranteeing the inviolability of the Franco-German and Belgo-German frontiers and the demilitarisation of the Rhineland.

Luftwaffe The German Air Force. Under the Treaty of Versailles Germany was forbidden to possess an air force, but in 1933 Hermann Göring was appointed Reich Aviation Minister with the brief to build up in secret a strong air force.

Manichaean interpretation Manichaeism, a Persian religion, believed in the struggle between a good, spiritual world of light and an evil, material world of darkness.

Maquis French resistance movement.

Marxist Referring to Marxism Philosophical system constructed by Karl Marx (1818–83). Its essence was that the economic system of a country determined its political and social structures. Marx was convinced that capitalism would be overthrown by the workers.

Masurians Ethnic group along the former East Prussian–Polish borders. They are descended from Masovians who migrated to Prussia mainly during the sixteenth century and were largely Protestant.

Mein Kampf Literally meaning *My Struggle*, this was Hitler's major political work. It comprises two volumes. The first was dictated to Emil Maurice and Hess in Landsberg Prison in 1924 and published in July 1925. The second volume appeared in December 1926. Once Hitler came to power it rapidly became obligatory reading. In April 1936 the Reich Ministry of the Interior recommended that every bridal couple should be presented with a copy.

Ministerpräsident The head of a state government in the German states. Invariably these officials, even when they were Nazis, resented the power and the claims of the newly appointed Reich Governors, who were usually the senior local *Gauleiter*. Party–state relations at this level were therefore in a state of permanent conflict.

Mittelstand Literally, this term means members of the 'middle estate'. Essentially, it embraced the lower middle classes: farmers, small business-men, self-employed artisans and white-collar workers.

Nationalsozialistische Betreiebszellen-Organization (NSBO) National Socialist Factory Cell Organisation.

Nationalsozialistische Deutsche Arbeiterpartei (NSDAP) National Socialist German Workers' Party. In February 1920 the German Workers' Party changed its name to the NSDAP to stress that it was both a nationalist and socialist party. In July 1921 Hitler was elected chairman. The party was banned after the Munich *Putsch*, but was re-founded in February 1925. On 14 July 1933 it was declared the only legal political party in Germany.

'Night of the Long Knives' The name given to the murders beginning in the night of 29–30 June 1934, which were carried out on Hitler's orders. In Wiessee, near Munich, Röhm and six other SA leaders were seized and shot. Throughout the Reich Hitler settled old scores. Schleicher and Gregor Strasser were also eliminated. At least 85 people were killed; only 50 of these were SA men.

new orthodoxy The evolution of what was originally a revisionist historical interpretation into an almost universally held interpretation.

Oberpräsidenten Senior administrative officials in the Prussian provinces.

public corporation A corporation created to perform a governmental function or to operate under government control.

Putsch A revolt or attempted take-over of power, such as the Kapp *Putsch* in 1920, when Nationalists supported by army officers attempted to seize power; the Munich *Putsch* in November 1923, when a coalition of Nazis and Nationalists made an abortive attempt to seize power; and the failed *Putsch* in Vienna by the Austrian Nazis in July 1934.

RKFDV (Reichskommissar/Reichskommissariat für die Festigung des Deutschen Volkstums) Himmler was appointed Reich Commissioner of the office of the Commissariat for the Strengthening of the German Race in October 1939. His task was (a) to remove all people of 'alien race' from the annexed territories in eastern Europe, and (b) to strengthen the Germanic element there by transferring ethnic Germans from the occupied territories.

Regierungspräsident Literally, District President, who is in charge of a sub-division of a *Land* province – a *Regierungsbezirk*. These officials survived the Nazi take-over of power and were relied upon by the Ministry of the Interior in Berlin as a counter-balance to the *Gauleiter* and Reich Governors.

Reichsbank The German central bank, which was responsible for currency issue. Hitler re-appointed Schacht to its Presidency in March 1933 where he developed the means for financing rearmament through the *Mefo* bills.

Reichskirche The German National Church was an attempt to unite the various churches into which German Protestantism was divided, and was set up on 27 May 1933. The government refused to accept von Bodelschwingh as the new Reich Bishop and engineered the election of Ludwig Müller, a convinced Nazi. As this led to bitter dissension and the formation of the Confessing Church, Hitler withdrew his support for Müller.

Reichskristallnacht Literally 'Night of Broken Glass': the wave of anti-Semitic violence of 9 November 1938.

Reichsrat The upper house of the German parliament in which the federal states were represented. This was abolished by the 'Law on the Reform of the Reich' in January 1934 which transferred the sovereign rights of the *Länder* to the Reich.

Reichstag The lower house of the German parliament which, since 1919, had been voted by universal male and female suffrage on an electoral system of proportional representation. It lost much of its power under the Enabling Act of March 1933. In the elections of 12 November 1933 and 10 April 1938 voters were presented with a single list of candidates called the *Führer*'s list. These elections were also combined with referenda on the decision to leave the League of Nations (1933) and the *Anschluss* with Austria (1938).

Reichswehr The German army. A term in use up to 1935 and then replaced by *Wehrmacht* (q.v.).

Resistenz Medical term meaning immunity or resistance to a disease. Hence the failure of Nazi ideology to penetrate certain sections of the German population can also be characterized by the term *Resistenz*.

SA (Sturmabteilung) Nazi storm- or assault-troops, also known as the 'Brownshirts'. The SA was founded in 1921 to protect party meetings from being disrupted by the Communists and other hostile groups. It was dissolved after the Munich *Putsch* and re-founded in 1926 under a former *Freikorps* leader, Pfeffer von Salomon. In January 1931 Ernst Röhm took over its leadership. During the period September 1930–January 1933 Hitler had to restrain an increasingly impatient SA from attempting to seize power. After the *Reichstag* fire, the SA played a key role in neutralising opponents of the Nazi take-over, but by July 1933 the SA's demand for a 'second revolution' was threatening to alienate the conservative elites on whose support Hitler still relied. With the elimination of Röhm on 30 June 1934 it effectively lost its power to the SS.

SS (Schutzstaffel) Literally, protection squad. It was founded in 1925 to protect the leading Nazis. It began to play a key role, first of all within the Nazi Party, when it was taken over by Himmler in 1929, and then, after

1933, within the Nazi regime. Its initial role was to eliminate the enemies of the new *Volksgemeinschaft*. When Himmler successfully established control over the whole police and security systems within the Reich in 1936, its influence was greatly strengthened. Through control of the police and then the occupied territories, the SS also played a dominant role in formulating the racial policy of the Third Reich.

SD (Sicherheitsdienst) Security service of the SS. It was created in 1932 and in July 1934 became the sole political intelligence agency of the Reich. In September 1939 the SD, Gestapo and Reich Criminal Police Department were amalgamated into one agency – the Reich Security Head Office (RHSA).

Silesians Inhabitants of Silesia, who speak a distinctive Slav dialect.

Sinti and **Roma** Minority ethnic groups generally known as 'Gypsies'.

Sorbs A distinct racial group living in south-eastern Germany in an area originally called Lusatia. In 2000 there were still some 80,000 Sorb speakers.

SPD (Sozialistische Partei Deutschlands) The German Social Democratic Party unwittingly helped pave the way for Hitler's eventual success by resigning from the Great Coalition in March 1930. Nevertheless, it 'tolerated' Brüning's government (September 1930–May 1932), and in March 1933 it was the only party to vote against the Enabling Act. It was banned on 22 June, but continued to operate underground. Leaflets were smuggled into Germany from its headquarters in Prague.

structuralists The name given to the school of historians, the most eminent members of which are Hans Mommsen, Broszat and Wehler, which applies a structural analysis to modern German history, particularly the Third Reich. They play down the role of Hitler and instead place more emphasis on the German elites and the polycratic nature of the regime.

Totenkopfverbände Literally meaning 'Death's-Head Units', were the SS units responsible for administering the concentration camps in the Third Reich. The first unit was formed to guard Dachau in June 1933, which became the training centre for the *Totenkopfverbände*.

völkisch This term can be literally translated as 'folkish', but in reality there is no English translation. It was an ideology based on the creation and preservation of a traditional Germanic, national and, above all, racial community. It was xenophobic and became increasingly anti-Semitic as the Jews were perceived to be in the forefront of the powerful forces destroying old Germany. It formed an important component of the Nazi Party, which in *Mein Kampf* Hitler called a *völkisch* party.

Volksgemeinschaft Literally, 'People's Community'. This was to be brought about by unifying the population primarily on the basis of nationalism. Hitler believed that fusing nationalism with some elements of socialism would end class conflict and enable him to create a new national community based on race.

Volkssturm A conscript home guard created in September 1944. The Nazi Party was made responsible for its organisation, although Himmler was to decide how it should be deployed. All males between 16 and 60 were liable for service. Most of the *Volkssturm* units served locally, although initially some were posted to the front.

Waffen-SS Armed or militarised SS. In the aftermath of the 'Night of the Long Knives' Hitler gave permission for the creation of three SS regiments. These formed the nucleus of the *Waffen-SS* – a term introduced in 1940.

'Water Poles' Poles in Silesia who speak a dialect composed of Czech, Slovak and German.

Wehrmacht In 1919 the German army was reduced to 100,000 men. Hitler rebuilt and expanded the armed forces, and in March 1935 he reintroduced conscription. The *Reichswehr* changed its name to *Wehrmacht*, a term which also included the navy and air force. From February 1938 onwards Hitler took over the ultimate command of the *Wehrmacht*. In December 1941 he appointed himself Commander-in-Chief of the army and assumed responsibility for military operations.

Westwall Defence system stretching more than 630 km (390 miles) with more than 18,000 bunkers, tunnels and tank traps. It went from Kleve on the border with the Netherlands, to the Swiss border.

Young Plan Plan produced by a committee chaired by the American Owen D. Young for the payment of German reparations over a period of 58 years.

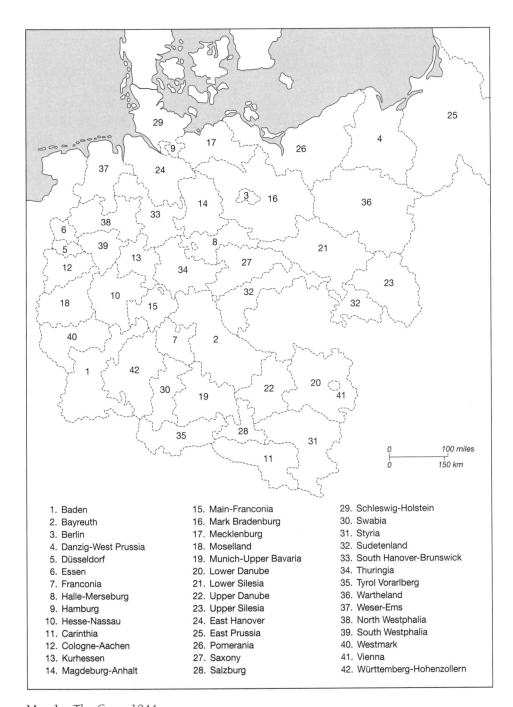

1. Baden	15. Main-Franconia	29. Schleswig-Holstein
2. Bayreuth	16. Mark Bradenburg	30. Swabia
3. Berlin	17. Mecklenburg	31. Styria
4. Danzig-West Prussia	18. Moselland	32. Sudetenland
5. Düsseldorf	19. Munich-Upper Bavaria	33. South Hanover-Brunswick
6. Essen	20. Lower Danube	34. Thuringia
7. Franconia	21. Lower Silesia	35. Tyrol Vorarlberg
8. Halle-Merseburg	22. Upper Danube	36. Wartheland
9. Hamburg	23. Upper Silesia	37. Weser-Ems
10. Hesse-Nassau	24. East Hanover	38. North Westphalia
11. Carinthia	25. East Prussia	39. South Westphalia
12. Cologne-Aachen	26. Pomerania	40. Westmark
13. Kurhessen	27. Saxony	41. Vienna
14. Magdeburg-Anhalt	28. Salzburg	42. Württemberg-Hohenzollern

Map 1   The Gaue, 1944

From M. Freeman, *Atlas of Nazi Germany*, Longman, London, 1995, p. 67

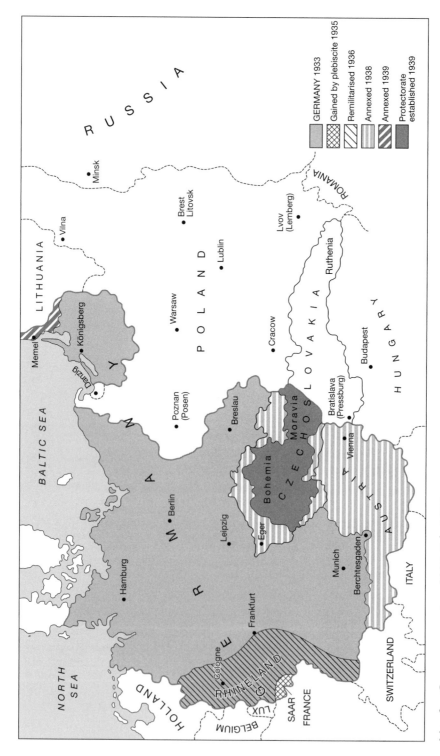

Map 2   German expansion, 1935–July 1939

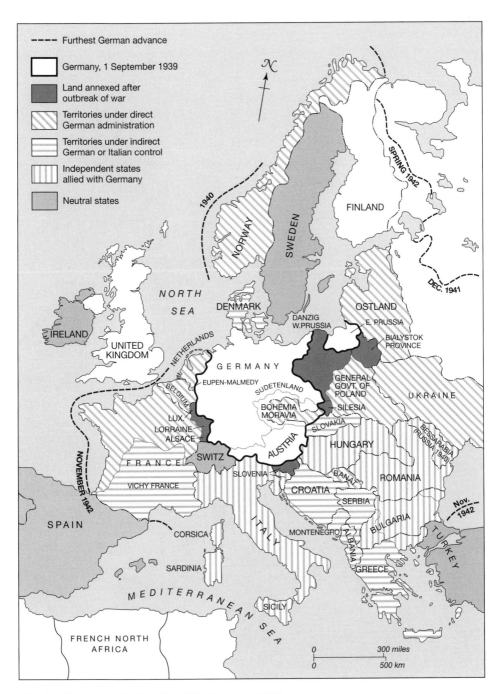

Map 3   Europe at the height of Nazi power, 1942

Map 4   The situation in Germany, 8 May 1945

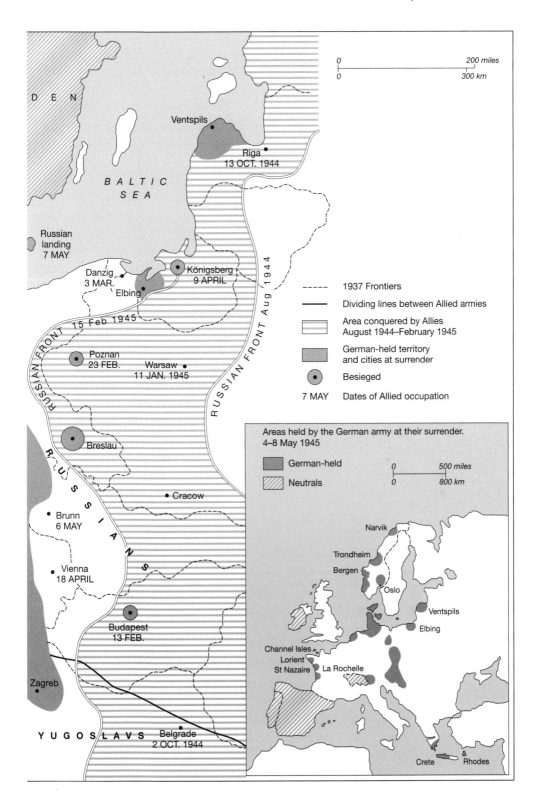

DEN

Ventspils

BALTIC
SEA

Riga
13 OCT. 1944

Russian
landing
7 MAY

Danzig   Königsberg
3 MAR.   9 APRIL
Elbing

RUSSIAN FRONT 15 Feb 1945

RUSSIAN FRONT Aug 1944

Poznan
23 FEB.   Warsaw
11 JAN. 1945

RUSSIANS

Breslau

Cracow

Brunn
6 MAY

Vienna
18 APRIL

Budapest
13 FEB.

Zagreb

YUGOSLAVS   Belgrade
2 OCT. 1944

- - - -   1937 Frontiers

———   Dividing lines between Allied armies

Area conquered by Allies
August 1944–February 1945

German-held territory
and cities at surrender

Besieged

7 MAY   Dates of Allied occupation

Areas held by the German army at their surrender.
4–8 May 1945

German-held

Neutrals

0   500 miles
0   800 km

Narvik

Trondheim

Bergen

Oslo

Ventspils

Elbing

Channel Isles
Lorient
St Nazaire   La Rochelle

Crete   Rhodes

0   200 miles
0   300 km

Part One

INTRODUCTION

1

The historical debate

The Third Reich has had a truly global impact. Not only did its destruction act as a catalyst for the Cold War, and the subsequent partition of Germany for 45 years, but it also accelerated de-colonisation and the creation of the Israeli state. Attempts to define the nature of National Socialism (hereafter Nazism) began as soon as it became a major political force in the 1930s and have continued unabated ever since, which has resulted in an academic literature 'beyond the scope even of specialists' (Hildebrand, 1991: 101).

In assessing the nature of Nazism, contemporaries raised questions which are still relevant today: was it a version of **fascism** or totalitarianism (see below), which had more in common with Stalin's Russia than Mussolini's Italy, or was it a unique revolutionary phenomenon? On the Left, Nazism was defined in broadly **Marxist** terms. Orthodox Marxist thinkers perceived it to be a mass movement manipulated by big business and finance in a last-ditch attempt to defend capitalism from socialism. Georgi Dimitrov, the General Secretary of the **Comintern**, defined fascism, in which he included Nazism, in 1935 as 'the open terrorist dictatorship of the most reactionary, most chauvinist and most imperialist elements of finance capital' (in Kershaw, 1993: 10). In this context Hitler was nothing more than a puppet of big business and finance. Other more independent Marxist thinkers took their arguments from Marx's seminal essay on Napoleon's coup of 2 December 1851, *The Eighteenth Brumaire of Louis Bonaparte*, and compared fascism to **Bonapartism** in the France of Napoleon III. On the one hand this had made life safe for capitalism as it destroyed working-class political power, but it also had its own dynamism and ended up by controlling the capitalist class, too, even though it created an environment basically favourable to capitalism [**Doc. 1, p. 146**].

A different approach was taken by the broadly nationalist school of historians within Germany in 1933, who interpreted Hitler's rise to power as a national revolution, which was both anti-liberal and anti-Marxist. Johannes

fascism Between 1919 and 1945 there were many varieties of fascism, the essence of which was: a nationalist ideology and an authoritarian state with a charismatic leadership ready to use force to achieve national aims.

Marxist Referring to **Marxism** Philosophical system constructed by Karl Marx (1818–83). Its essence was that the economic system of a country determined its political and social structures. Marx was convinced that capitalism would be overthrown by the workers.

Comintern The Communist international movement set up in 1919 to organise worldwide revolution.

Bonapartism Political system employed by Napoleon III of France (1851–70). He created a dictatorship which was supported by the wealthy elites and the lower middle classes. He attempted to strengthen it through a vigorous assertion of French national interests.

Haller, for instance, argued that it was one of the most powerful ideas of the time that 'national and social were not opposites' (in Michalka, 1984: 361). This assessment met with some understanding in Britain, where, as late as 1935, Churchill still believed that Hitler might one day be regarded by history as one of those 'great figures whose lives have enriched the story of mankind' (Hildebrand, 1974: 602), while Lloyd George saw him as a liberator of the German people. [**Doc. 14, p. 156**] By far the most penetrating of the early non-Marxist studies of Nazism was written by Hermann Rauschning, the former Nazi President of the Danzig Senate, who in his classic study *Germany's Revolution of Destruction* argued that Nazism was a 'revolutionary power whose creed was action for action's sake and whose tactics were the destruction and undermining of all that is in the existing order' (Rauschning, 1939: 13) [**Doc. 2, p. 146**].

In the war years and early post-war period, both Western and Soviet historians and propagandists, like Rohan Butler (1941), Sir Robert Vansittart (1941) and Edmond Vermeil (1945), in their search for the origins of Nazism, attempted to identify lines of continuity in German history, which allegedly stretched 'from Luther to Hitler'. In response to this blanket condemnation of their nation's past, German historians such as Friedrich Meinecke and Gerhard Ritter argued that Nazism could only be understood within the context of the general European crisis triggered by the First World War.

The outbreak of the Cold War in Europe had a considerable impact on the historical debate on Nazism. Both East and West Germany sought to interpret their common Nazi past differently. For East German historians, Georgi Dimitrov's definition of fascism remained valid and an essential rallying cry against the capitalist West. For West Germans, and increasingly the West as a whole, Nazism was seen as a variant of totalitarianism. According to Carl Friedrich, the German *émigré* political scientist in the USA, it had in common with Russian Communism 'a total ideology, a single mass party, a terroristic secret police, a monopoly of mass communications, a monopoly of weapons, and a centrally directed planned economy' (Friedrich and Brzezinski, 1956: 294).

This 'totalitarian' definition of Nazism was the dominant theme in western research on Nazism until the 1960s, when an increasing number of specialised studies began to show that the concept of totalitarianism did not do justice to an understanding of the structure of the Third Reich and the role of Hitler. A dramatic change in historical thinking was signalled by the Fischer controversy of the early 1960s. In his *Griff nach der Weltmacht*, Fischer returned to the thesis of continuity in German history by arguing that the expansionist territorial aims of the German elites in the First World War were broadly similar to Hitler's. His book had a profound influence on German historians and helped to direct historical research back to the vital question of continuities in the role of elites and social structure between Wilhelmine Germany and the Nazi period. In that sense Fischer could be called the father of the new structuralist school of historians which dominated modern German history for the next 30 years.

This methodology was further developed by Hans-Ulrich Wehler in his study of the German Empire (1871–1918), where he deliberately avoided close studies of personalities and analysed the empire 'as a totality' with its interconnections between politics, the economy and society. Primarily, Wehler was motivated by the desire 'to investigate why Hitler's National Socialist regime came to power some dozen years after the end of the monarchy' (Wehler, 1985: 7). He established a '**new orthodoxy**', which argued that Germany's failure to develop into a parliamentary democracy during the *Kaiserreich* set Germany on the special path, or *Sonderweg*, that ultimately led to the Third Reich. Applying similar analytical methods to the Third Reich, **structuralists**, like Martin Broszat and Hans Mommsen, have challenged the orthodox view of a virtually all-powerful Hitler and stressed that the study of political leaders and 'great men' needs to be complemented by a structural analysis of contemporary society (Broszat, 1981; Mommsen, 1979). They argue that historians should concentrate more on explaining how Nazi society worked and on showing that Hitler himself was often a prisoner of forces and structures which he might have unleashed or created but could not always control. Inevitably this emphasis on structural determinants, which played down political and diplomatic history as well as the role of the individual in history, met with fierce opposition from the more traditional historians, or **intentionalists**, such as Andreas Hillgruber and Klaus Hildebrand, who see Hitler and his aims as central to the study of the Third Reich. This debate between the intentionalists and structuralists, as will be seen in the chapters that follow, still pervades every aspect of modern research on the Third Reich and Nazism.

CAN THE THIRD REICH BE 'HISTORICISED'?

One of the dilemmas confronting historians of the Third Reich is that the appalling atrocities carried out by the Nazis make historical objectivity, or historicisation, difficult to achieve. When the orders for dealing with the Russians were issued to the German army in 1941 (see pages 103–4), Major-General von Tresckow observed with horror to his fellow officer, Rudolf von Gersdorff, that guilt would fall on the Germans for a hundred years 'and not just on Hitler alone, but on you and me, your wife and mine, your children and my children, the woman crossing the road now, and the

new orthodoxy The evolution of what was originally a revisionist historical interpretation into an almost universally held interpretation.

structuralists The name given to the school of historians, the most eminent members of which are Hans Mommsen, Broszat and Wehler, which applies a structural analysis to modern German history, particularly the Third Reich. They play down the role of Hitler and instead place more emphasis on the German elites and the polycratic nature of the regime.

intentionalists Historians who stress the importance of the *individual* and personal *intention* in history. Thus intentionalists, such as Andreas Hillgruber, Klaus Hildebrand and Lucy Davidowicz, stress the aims and intentions of Hitler and emphasise his key role in the formulation of policies, particularly foreign policy and the campaign against the Jews ending in the Holocaust.

boy playing with a ball over there' (Burleigh, 2000: 707). Despite the fact that there *was* a courageous German opposition to Hitler, many Germans, even today, would still agree with Tresckow's comment. The long shadows of the genocidal war in Russia and the Holocaust have made it very difficult for historians to 'normalise' or treat the Third Reich like any other period of German history. Dan Diner, one of the most trenchant critics of historicisation, has, for instance, argued that 'Auschwitz is a no-man's-land of understanding, a black box of explanation, a vacuum of extra historiographic interpretation' (Kershaw, 1993: 214). Attempts to put the Third Reich into perspective led to the *Historikerstreit*, or historians' dispute, which erupted into a major public controversy in West Germany in 1985. Ernst Nolte, for instance, put forward the thesis that the Holocaust should be seen within the context of the atrocities committed by Stalin and **Pol Pot** (Nolte, 1985). Other historians, who can also broadly be described as 'right wing', such as Michael Stürmer, resent the intense concentration on the Third Reich and argue that it has effectively made earlier German history inaccessible to post-1945 generations, but to historians on the Left this emphasis has been welcome, as it has forced the Germans to learn the lessons of the immediate past. Jürgen Habermas, for instance, uncompromisingly insisted that 'a commitment to universal constitutional principles rooted in conviction has only been feasible in the cultural nation of the Germans after – and through – Auschwitz' (in Kershaw, 1993: 199).

The perception that the fall of Nazism in 1945 had effectively brought to an end the history of united Germany changed with the fall of the Berlin Wall and the reunification of Germany in 1990. Ultimately, then, Hitler had not permanently destroyed the German nation and state, and, as Saul Friedländer, the Israeli historian, observed, reunification had 'given back natural continuity to German history' (Kershaw, 1993: 2000). The Third Reich could now be seen as an episode in German history rather than its climax or indeed termination. A consequence of this is that particularly the younger generation of German historians, such as Michael Prinz and Rainer Zitelmann (Prinz and Zitelmann, 1991) have become increasingly interested in the modernising impact of the Nazi regime and its economic and social influence on the post-war West Germany. Other historians such as Richard Overy (Overy, 2004) have shed fresh light on the Nazi dictatorship by carrying out comparative analyses of both 'Stalinism' and 'Hitlerism', while Adam Tooze has explored the links between ideology and the German war economy (Tooze, 2007) and Mark Mazower (Mazower, 2008) has looked afresh at German-occupied Europe. The challenge for historians is to historicise the Third Reich and to put it into the context of German and indeed world history without making an apologia for its horrors.

Part Two

ANALYSIS

2

The origins and rise of National Socialism

THE IDEOLOGICAL ROOTS

National Socialism was, as Karl Dietrich Bracher has pointed out, 'a conglomerate of ideas and precepts, hopes and emotions, welded together by a radical political movement in a time of crisis' (Bracher, 1973: 38). A key component was the belief in German racial superiority, the origins of which can be traced back to the potent merging of nationalism and romanticism during the Napoleonic Wars at the beginning of the nineteenth century. The philosopher Johann Fichte, in his *Addresses to the German Nation* in 1807, for instance, helped lay the foundations for a new Romantic German Nationalism, which invested the German race with heroic qualities and almost mystical racial purity. Fichte's ideas, from which could be distilled 'a deadly cocktail of ethnic, cultural and linguistic nationalism' (Berger, 1997: 480), in the second half of the nineteenth century became the basis of the new **völkisch** or Germanic racial ideology, which was implacably opposed to liberalism, socialism and democracy. Fichte's philosophy, as absorbed and transmuted by the *völkisch* movement, influenced emotionally a whole generation of university professors, grammar-school teachers, army officers, bankers and businessmen. It made them, initially at least, responsive to the *völkisch* strand of thought within Nazism. Hitler recognised this when he wrote in **Mein Kampf** that '[a]ll sorts of people with a yawning gulf between everything essential in their opinions are running around today under the blanket term "folkish"' (Hitler, 1974: 344).

Further important strands in Nazi thought were social Darwinism and the new pseudo-scientific studies of race. Social Darwinism, the crude application of Darwin's theories of evolution and natural selection to human society, became increasingly popular in northern Europe and America in the late nineteenth century. Social Darwinists interpreted international relations in terms of struggle and the survival of the fittest, and were increasingly receptive to the theories of racial inequality put forward by the French aristocrat

völkisch This term can be literally translated as 'folkish', but in reality there is no English translation. It was an ideology based on the creation and preservation of a traditional Germanic, national and, above all, racial community. It was xenophobic and became increasingly anti-Semitic as the Jews were perceived to be in the forefront of the powerful forces destroying old Germany. It formed an important component of the Nazi Party, which in *Mein Kampf* Hitler called a *völkisch* party.

Mein Kampf Literally meaning *My Struggle*, this was Hitler's major political work. It comprises two volumes. The first was dictated to Emil Maurice and Hess in Landsberg Prison in 1924 and published in July 1925. The second volume appeared in December 1926. Once Hitler came to power it rapidly became obligatory reading. In April 1936 the Reich Ministry of the Interior recommended that every bridal couple should be presented with a copy.

Count Joseph Gobineau, and the naturalised German Houston Stewart Chamberlain, the son of a British admiral. Gobineau, in his *Essay on the Inequality of the Races of Man*, written in 1853–55, proclaimed the racial supremacy of the white, or '**Aryan**', races and the crucial importance of racial 'purity' for the life of a nation. It was not, however, until 1894 that his ideas were seriously disseminated in Germany when a Gobineau society was set up. Chamberlain, in his best-selling *The Foundations of the Nineteenth Century* (1899), interpreted history as a racial struggle in which the purity of the 'Aryan' races had at all costs to be defended. Racial purity was seen to be the key to the future survival and greatness of Germany. Shortly before his death in 1927 he was celebrated by the Nazi Party as the 'prophetic seer of National Socialism' (Bracher, 1973: 30), and his ideas formed the basis of *The Myth of the Twentieth Century*, written in 1930 by Alfred Rosenberg, the philosopher of National Socialism.

Aryan Originally a Hindu word meaning a member of the highest class, Gobineau used the term to describe the Caucasian races. It was much used by the Nazis to denote gentile Germans as opposed, for the most part, to Jews.

THE BISMARCKIAN REICH: AN INCUBATOR OF NATIONAL SOCIALISM?

To Wehler and the other historians of the 'new orthodoxy' (see page 5), a knowledge of the German Empire between 1871 and 1918 remains 'absolutely indispensable' for an understanding of events from 1919 to 1945 (Wehler, 1985: 246). His argument is essentially that the constitution that Bismarck drew up for the new German Reich in 1871 failed to provide a satisfactory framework in which the German people could come to terms with the problems of a modern, pluralist, industrial society, as he attempted at all costs to preserve the political power of the Prussian aristocracy. When Bismarck resigned in 1890, his 'neo-Bonapartist system', which depended on a pliant Kaiser, a successful foreign policy and the constant manipulation of the parties in the *Reichstag* to form temporary majorities, was already beginning to become unworkable. Successive chancellors up to 1914 tried to build up anti-democratic blocs in the *Reichstag* and to unite the country behind grandiose plans for naval expansion and an assertive foreign policy. By 1912, when the *Reichstag* elections produced a marked swing to the Left, it was clear that this policy had failed, and increasingly in military, aristocratic and heavy industrial circles there was, as in 1930–33, talk of a pre-emptive **Putsch** against the *Reichstag*. The polarisation between Right and Left consequently made the evolution of a broadly accepted political consensus impossible to achieve and by 1914 German domestic politics were in a state of deadlock from which, as Volker Berghahn argues, the only escape was forwards into war (Berghahn, 1973).

Reichstag The lower house of the German parliament which, since 1919, had been voted by universal male and female suffrage on an electoral system of proportional representation. It lost much of its power under the Enabling Act of March 1933. In the elections of 12 November 1933 and 10 April 1938 voters were presented with a single list of candidates called the *Führer*'s list. These elections were also combined with referenda on the decision to leave the League of Nations (1933) and the *Anschluss* with Austria (1938).

There is, however, no simple straight line running from the Bismarckian Reich up to 1933. There were 'complex tendencies at work' (Blackbourn, 1997: 496) in Germany in 1914, which pointed towards both the development of a democracy and a more authoritarian solution. On the one hand, there was the backward-looking *völkisch* ideology, the paranoid tendency to see politics in terms of friends and bitter enemies, the role of pressure groups, the anti-democratic sentiments of the elites and the longing for a strong man who could unite the country. On the other hand, for all its imperfections, Wilhelmine Germany was very much a state where the rule of law was a reality, as was freedom of speech and the press. There were even signs that some consensus was beginning to emerge in the *Reichstag*. In 1913, for instance, the **German Social Democratic Party (SPD)** voted for a government bill taxing the great landed estates. Wilhelmine Germany might have been the seedbed of Nazism, but, if it were not for the disastrous impact of the First World War, these seeds would not have germinated.

The outbreak of war in August 1914 temporarily created a euphoric mood of national unity, but, as the prospects of a quick victory receded, the divisions in German society re-emerged in intensified form. The conservative Right, the Prussian officer corps and many of the industrialists continued their implacable opposition to political reform, hoping that victory would consolidate the Bismarckian state. In 1917, when the government appeared to be unable to control the *Reichstag*, the German High Command forced the Kaiser to appoint an unknown and inexperienced civil servant as a puppet chancellor.

The urgent need to mass produce armaments and the ever tightening impact of the British blockade also created widespread distress. By 1917 one-third of Germany's small artisan workshops had been closed down. Food shortages, inflation, inadequate wages and worsening living conditions created intense bitterness against war profiteers and the black market. In their desperate search for scapegoats, the Jews became vulnerable targets and were accused of profiting from the war while Germans laid down their lives at the front. Bitter divisions also opened up between the farmers and the government, which attempted to control food prices and stamp out the profitable black market in the interests of the urban workers. All these were themes which Hitler and other right-wing politicians were able to exploit in the early 1920s.

Putsch A revolt or attempted take-over of power, such as the Kapp *Putsch* in 1920, when Nationalists supported by army officers attempted to seize power; the Munich *Putsch* in November 1923, when a coalition of Nazis and Nationalists made an abortive attempt to seize power; and the failed *Putsch* in Vienna by the Austrian Nazis in July 1934.

SPD (Sozialistische Partei Deutschlands) The German Social Democratic Party unwittingly helped pave the way for Hitler's eventual success by resigning from the Great Coalition in March 1930. Nevertheless, it 'tolerated' Brüning's government (September 1930–May 1932), and in March 1933 it was the only party to vote against the Enabling Act. It was banned on 22 June, but continued to operate underground. Leaflets were smuggled into Germany from its headquarters in Prague.

THE GERMAN REVOLUTION, 1918–19: A TURNING POINT THAT DID NOT TURN?

To avoid certain military defeat on the western front the German High Command in late September 1918 urged the creation of a parliamentary government in the hope that this would facilitate an appeal to the Americans for a generous armistice. The formation of the new government under Prince Max von Baden was essentially a revolution from above, but it came too late to give the new regime any real authority. Both the monarchy and the new cabinet were swept away in the wave of strikes and demonstrations against the war that erupted in early November. Soldiers' and Workers' Councils sprang up all over Germany, and the new government, under the leader of the SPD Friedrich Ebert, could initially only survive by basing its power on these councils. Consequently, there was briefly an opportunity to purge the *ancien régime*. Had this occurred it seems unlikely that Hitler would have been able to gain power in 1933. Ebert, however, refused to create a republican people's militia and his unwillingness to purge the bureaucracy and judiciary allowed the enemies of the regime to stay in power and ultimately to act as 'stirrup holders for Hitler' in 1933 (Wehler, 1985: 231). In retrospect, it is easy to see that Ebert overestimated the strength of the Communists, yet at the time the success of the **Bolsheviks** in Russia made him determined to avoid a Russian-style revolution with all its bloody excesses breaking out in Germany.

Ebert's enemies on the Right also exaggerated the Communist danger. The Communist uprising in Berlin in January 1919 and the proclamation of the 'Soviet Republic' of Bavaria in April were inevitably judged against the background of the Russian Revolution. Even though they were quickly crushed, they struck terror into the minds of the **Mittelstand** and property-owning classes and fuelled their fears of socialism and 'Jewish' Bolshevism.

ADOLF HITLER AND THE FORMATION OF THE NSDAP, 1919–24

One of the most dramatic events in contemporary history has been Hitler's metamorphosis from 'the nobody of Vienna into the leader of Greater Germany' (Stern, 1975: 12). When Hitler was temporarily blinded in a British gas attack near Comines in 1918, he was an obscure corporal in the Sixth Bavarian Division (for earlier biographical details see 'Who's who'). He experienced the first two months of the German revolution in hospital, but in late November returned to his regiment in Munich where he witnessed the dramatic events surrounding the establishment of the Munich 'Soviet Republic' in April 1919. Far from joining one of the **Freikorps** to fight Communism, his priority was to escape demobilisation by remaining in the army as long as possible. Ironically, as the Munich Soldiers' Council supported the revolution in Munich, Hitler, who was elected representative of his

Bolsheviks Originally the majority faction of the Marxist Russian Social Democratic Labour Party which split from the Mensheviks in 1903. They ultimately became the Communist Party of the Soviet Union and came to power in Russia as a consequence of the October Revolution of 1917.

Mittelstand Literally, this term means members of the 'middle estate'. Essentially, it embraced the lower middle classes: farmers, small businessmen, self-employed artisans and white-collar workers.

Freikorps Companies of right-wing volunteers, which sprang up spontaneously during the winter of 1918/19.

company, gained his first political experience in the service of the revolution, and may even have considered joining the SPD, but after the collapse of the 'Soviet Republic' on 3 May his basic counter-revolutionary sympathies came to the notice of the military authorities, and he was employed as a *V-Mann*, or informant, to counter the effects of Bolshevik propaganda among the troops. In this role he joined the German Workers' Party (DAP), which was one of the numerous *völkisch*, radical parties which had sprung up throughout Germany in the aftermath of the November revolution. Hitler left the army in April 1920 and worked full time for the party, which in February had changed its name to the German National Socialist Workers' Party (***Nationalsozialistische Deutsche Arbeiterpartei* (NSDAP)**). Within two years he had not only wrested control from the party's original founders, but had begun to create an organisational structure which subordinated it to his leadership. Within Bavaria the NSDAP rapidly became the most dynamic force on the Right, especially when its impact was sharpened by the formation of the paramilitary **SA (*Sturmabteilung*)** in August 1921, which by November 1923 had 55,000 members.

How much of this success was due to what Gordon Craig calls his 'political genius' (Craig, 1978: 544) and how much to luck and circumstances? There is no doubt that the early history of the Weimar Republic could hardly have been more favourable for the development of political extremism. The Republic inherited the unsolved social and political conflicts of the Second Reich, all of which were exacerbated by the consequences of the lost war: the high inflation rate, internal unrest and the stiff terms of the Versailles Treaty. The programme of the NSDAP, the 25 Points [**Doc. 3, p. 147**], which was drawn up by Hitler and Anton Drexler in January 1920, was in itself a jumble of *völkisch* and nationalist ideas, which most of the other far Right groups shared. Hitler's strength lay not in the originality of his ideas but in the way in which he expressed them and captured the incandescent anger, fear and deep resentment of the middle classes about what was happening to them and their country [**Doc. 4, p. 150**]. National Socialism could certainly have existed without Hitler, but it was he who turned it into a major force, first in Bavaria and later in the Reich as a whole, through his ceaseless propaganda and mobilisation of the masses. By the end of 1922 Hitler was increasingly being compared to Mussolini by his followers. However, unlike Mussolini's fascists, the Nazis were not yet a national party with representation in parliament. In Italy the Fascist Party dominated the extreme Right, whereas in Germany the Nazi Party was still a part of the mosaic of right-wing political and paramilitary groups, which could do nothing without the support of the **Reichswehr**.

In 1923 the Ruhr crisis presented Hitler with an opportunity to play a greater role in national politics. Initially, the French occupation of the Ruhr

Nationalsozialistische Deutsche Arbeiterpartei **(NSDAP)** National Socialist German Workers' Party. In February 1920 the German Workers' Party changed its name to the NSDAP to stress that it was both a nationalist and socialist party. In July 1921 Hitler was elected chairman. The party was banned after the Munich *Putsch*, but was re-founded in February 1925. On 14 July 1933 it was declared the only legal political party in Germany.

SA (*Sturmabteilung*) Nazi storm- or assault-troops, also known as the 'Brownshirts'. The SA was founded in 1921 to protect party meetings from being disrupted by the Communists and other hostile groups. It was dissolved after the Munich *Putsch* and re-founded in 1926 under a former *Freikorps* leader, Pfeffer von Salomon. In January 1931 Ernst Röhm took over its leadership. During the period September 1930–January 1933 Hitler had to restrain an increasingly impatient SA from attempting to seize power. After the *Reichstag* fire, the SA played a key role in neutralising opponents of the Nazi take-over, but by July 1933 the SA's demand for a 'second revolution' was threatening to alienate the conservative elites on whose support Hitler still relied. With the elimination of Röhm on 30 June 1934 it effectively lost its power to the SS.

Reichswehr The German army. A term in use up to 1935 and then replaced by *Wehrmacht* (q.v.).

united the Reich behind the government and its campaign of passive resistance, but by the autumn hyper-inflation, the separatist movements in the Rhineland and the threat of Communist uprisings in Hamburg and Saxony all combined to force the government to seek a compromise with the French. The NSDAP gained support in proportion to the degree of national distress, and it was a measure of Hitler's new standing in right-wing Bavarian circles that in September 1923 he became the political leader of the *Kampfbund*, an association of militant groups on the far Right formed to coordinate tactics against the Republic. The SA was integrated into the military wing of the *Bund*, and Hitler's task was to mobilise public opinion to support a *Putsch* in Munich as a preliminary to taking Berlin by force. General von Ludendorff acted as the figurehead of the conspiracy.

To have any chance of success the *Kampfbund* needed the backing of Kahr, the Bavarian State Commissioner, and the heads of the Bavarian police and the local *Reichswehr* units, but after hearing that the *Reichswehr* would not nationally oppose the elected government in Berlin, these officials began to have second thoughts. This left Hitler in an exposed situation. His followers expected action, and if he delayed for too long the favourable moment would pass. Backed by Ludendorff, he now decided upon a *Putsch*: he would march on Berlin, install himself as head of the new Reich government, while Ludendorff would take over control of the army.

He now attempted to coerce Kahr and his colleagues into supporting these plans by seizing them at a public meeting in the *Bürgerbräukeller* on the evening of 8 November. He was momentarily successful in winning their immediate support, but by the following morning this had evaporated. The planned march to the city centre was broken up by the police and a few days later Hitler was arrested. In February 1924 he was given the minimum sentence of five years' imprisonment with a virtual promise that he would be released early on probation. The publicity the *Putsch* received and the subsequent trial turned Hitler into a national figure.

THE RENAISSANCE OF THE NAZI PARTY, 1925–30

Dawes Plan The report on the German economy issued in 1924 by a committee chaired by the American Charles Dawes. It provided for a loan to Germany and a reorganisation of reparation payment.

When Hitler came out of prison in December 1924 he faced a daunting task to re-establish his position. The Greater German National Community, the successor party to the NSDAP, which had been banned after the *Putsch*, was on the verge of dissolution. The political and economic environment was also unfavourable to the revival of the extreme Right since, with the stabilisation of the currency and the acceptance of the **Dawes Plan**, the Weimar Republic seemed well on the way to recovery.

Once the ban on the Nazi Party in Bavaria had been lifted in January 1925, Hitler was able to reassert his control. Convinced now that he was no longer a 'drummer' but a man of destiny called to save Germany, he systematically defeated all attempts to debate policy or share decision-making and promoted an image of himself as a 'myth person' or 'demi-god' who stood far above the mundane arguments and bitter disagreements that frequently occurred within the party. In that sense the **Führer** cult helped integrate the disparate groups with conflicting interests, which made the Nazi Party, into a coherent whole. In northern Germany there was some criticism of the new cult. Gregor Strasser and Joseph Goebbels attempted to commit the party to an updated version of the 1920 programme, but at a carefully staged conference at Bamberg in February 1926 Hitler defeated the attempt and reinforced the **Führerprinzip** to the point of 'his self-deification' (Orlow, I, 1971: 70).

Over the next four years the party was rebuilt and its essential nature was determined until its dissolution in 1945. Hitler was not interested in organisational matters and would only personally intervene if a real crisis occurred. Day-to-day control of the NSDAP increasingly became institutionalised through party bureaucrats in Munich, such as Rudolf Hess, who protected Hitler's image without threatening his power. Laying the foundations for the party's mushroom growth during the Depression was essentially the work of Gregor Strasser, who became the Organisational Leader of the Nazi Party in January 1928. Germany was divided into 35 **Gaue** or regions, each supervised by a **Gauleiter**, below which were the local branches staffed by a cadre of dedicated activists varying in number from district to district. The political party was organised vertically from the party offices in Munich, and each level was subordinated to the one above it. Reflecting the party's new electoral priorities, the *Gaue* were progressively adjusted to overlap with the *Reichstag* constituencies. This apparently neat vertical pattern was, however, marred by the increasing tendency of the organisations affiliated to the party – the SA, the Hitler Youth, the Nazi Teachers' Association, and so on – to see themselves as responsible to the *Führer* alone rather than being mere cogs in the party system.

Hitler was unwilling formally to revise the 1920 programme [**Doc 3, p. 147**], but he never hesitated to jettison its economic radicalism to win over new supporters. On the other hand, Mein Kampf, most of which was written in prison, provides the essential key to understanding his first principles, even though it is not a precise blueprint for the future. Page after page bears witness to Hitler's **Manichean interpretation** of the world as an arena where the supposedly creative forces of the Aryan races clash with the allegedly cunning and evil agents of world Jewry, who operated from their base in Bolshevik Russia [**Doc. 30, p. 168**]. His linking of Jewry with Bolshevism had an 'explosive political effect' (Nolte, 1969: 419). In his eyes

Führer Leader. This title was adopted by Hitler to emphasise his absolute leadership of the Nazi Party. At the Bamberg Conference of 1926 he was successful in asserting the primacy of the *Führer* over the party. After Hindenburg's death in August 1934, Hitler was able to nominate himself *Führer* and Reich Chancellor.

Führerprinzip Literally, the 'principle of *Führer*-leadership', based on Hitler's charismatic, absolute leadership. Hitler's power as *Führer* was supposed to be based on his 'exceptional' qualities of leadership. All power was concentrated in his hands and theoretically no major decision could be made without his consent, although in practice party and government officials tried to 'work towards the *Führer*' and anticipate his consent.

Gau (pl. *Gaue*) A regional territorial division of the NSDAP. In the reorganisation of the party of 1925–29, Germany was divided into *Gaue*, each under a *Gauleiter*. In 1928 the boundaries of the *Gaue* were reorganised to correspond to the 35 parliamentary electoral districts. *Gau* is originally an old Germanic term meaning a subdivision of a tribe.

Gauleiter (pl. Gauleiter)
A regional party leader in charge of a *Gau*. In April 1933 the senior *Gauleiter* in each state, with the exception of Bavaria and Prussia, was appointed Reich Governor. The *Gauleiter* controlled the local and district party organisations, and as such were able to influence local government in the early days of the take-over of power.

Manichean interpretation Manichaeism, a Persian religion, believed in the struggle between a good, spiritual world of light and an evil, material world of darkness.

Lebensraum Literally living space. Convinced that Germany was overpopulated, Hitler argued from the end of 1922 onwards that the destruction of Soviet Russia would enable Germany to gain sufficient land for settlement there rather than overseas. These ideas were then elaborated in *Mein Kampf* and became a central component of Hitler's foreign policy.

Nationalsozialistische Betreiebszellen-Organization (NSBO) National Socialist Factory Cell Organisation.

Young Plan Plan produced by a committee chaired by the American Owen D. Young for the payment of German reparations over a period of 58 years.

it justified his crusade to find in western Russia the **Lebensraum**, which he argued Germany so urgently needed. Hitler defined the state in ethnic terms and his whole programme for regenerating Germany depended ultimately on creating a racially pure state, which would be strengthened by the colonisation of western Russia. As a politician, he was flexible and opportune, but he never abandoned his core ideas.

A key lesson Hitler drew from the failure of the Munich *Putsch* was the importance of gaining power through the ballot box. While still in prison he told one of his associates, Kurt Ludecke: 'Instead of working to achieve power by armed conspiracy, we shall have to hold our noses and enter the *Reichstag* against Catholic and Marxist deputies' (Noakes and Pridham, I, 1998: 37).

Up to 1927 Hitler's priority, following the example of Italian fascism, was to gain political control of the cities, but this campaign was not helped by his refusal to sanction the creation of surrogate Nazi trade unions until 1929, when belatedly the National Socialist Factory Cell Organisation (**Nationalsozialistische Betreiebszellen-Organization (NSBO)**) was set up. The NSDAP's natural constituency remained the *Mittelstand*, impoverished by the war, inflation, government cuts and the unprofitability of agriculture. Throughout the 1920s the *Mittelstand* had increasingly voted for small or local special-interest parties and by 1928 these parties were able to win 14 per cent of the vote. Part of the success of the Nazi Party after 1930 was that it was able to attract these votes. A major step was taken in this direction in the winter of 1927–28, when, with the onset of the agricultural depression, Hitler dropped the Urban Plan in favour of more intensive campaigning in the countryside. Despite his frequent avowals that he would never alter the 1920 programme, he toned down the emphasis on land confiscation in Point 17 [**Doc. 3, p. 147**]. Although this switch in priorities came too late to benefit the Nazi Party much in the elections in May 1928, its potential was shown by the fact that in some rural areas in north-west Germany the Nazis gained over 10 per cent of the vote.

In the Autumn of 1929 Alfred Hugenberg, the hard-line leader of the German nationalists invited Hitler to join his referendum campaign against the **Young Plan**. This gave him access to the funds of the nationalists and much-needed publicity in the papers owned by Hugenberg. The association with the nationalists also made the Nazis potentially more attractive to the conservative and nationalist middle-class voters. In the subsequent campaign, which failed by a large margin to reject the Young Plan, the Nazi Party gave the impression of being the most dynamic party on the Right.

It was the economic crisis of 1930–33 that turned the Nazi Party into a mass party of protest. The repercussions of the Wall Street Crash were soon felt in Germany, whose economy since 1924 had been dangerously dependent on short-term American loans. By January 1930 there were already over 3 million unemployed, a number which doubled by 1932. The peasantry sank ever more deeply into debt, and the profits of both large and small businesses declined alarmingly. The fear of bankruptcy and unemployment affected all sections of society.

The Nazis were well placed to exploit this misery, but they would have remained on the fringes of power if it had not been for the break-up of the Grand Coalition in March 1930, which was caused by the resignation of the SPD over the contentious issue of increasing employees' national insurance contributions at a time when wages were falling. This triggered the long political crisis that ended in Hitler's appointment as Chancellor three years later. When the Grand Coalition collapsed, President Hindenburg seized the chance to appoint Heinrich Brüning, the right-wing leader of the parliamentary group of the **Centre Party**. Hindenburg and his advisers, particularly General Schleicher, the head of the Ministerial Bureau in the Defence Ministry, had been waiting to replace the Social Democratic Chancellor Müller with a more authoritarian and 'anti-Marxist' figure. The character of the new government was seen when its finance bill was defeated on 18 July. Instead of attempting to negotiate a compromise, Brüning tried to bulldoze the bill through by resorting to the use of emergency powers contained in Article 48 of the Weimar constitution. When the *Reichstag* rejected this as unconstitutional, it was dissolved and a general election was held on 14 September. This was a decision of 'breathtaking irresponsibility' (Kershaw, I, 1998: 324) which allowed the Nazi Party to become a major political force.

In the subsequent electoral campaign the Nazis' main theme was that only Hitler could unite a Germany that under parliamentary democracy had become deeply divided and split into competing interest groups. This message was propagated with great energy throughout Germany. In some regions, such as Upper and Middle Franconia, whole areas were saturated with canvassers and electoral meetings. Hitler himself gave 20 major speeches in the big cities, while overall some 34,000 meetings were planned throughout the Reich. The results on 14 September were 'a political earthquake' (Kershaw, I, 1998: 333). The Nazis increased their seats from the 12 they won in 1928 to 107, which made them the second largest party in the *Reichstag*.

Centre Party The Catholic Centre Party was created in December 1870 to represent the interests of Catholic Germans in the new Reich, and rapidly became involved in a bitter struggle (*Kulturkampf*) with Bismarck and the Prussian state, but by 1895 the government began to see the party as a counter-force to the SPD. Between 1907 and 1918 there was never a government majority without the backing of the Centre Party. During the Weimar Republic the Centre Party, or prominent members of it, participated in every government up to 1932.

NAZI VOTERS, 1930–32

In 1930 18.3 per cent of the electorate (6.5 million) voted for the Nazis; in July 1932 this increased to 37.3 per cent (13.7 million). Where did these votes come from? Historians agree that many of the 3 million young voters who came on to the electoral roll between May 1928 and July 1932 and the sharp increase in the numbers of over 21-year-olds who actually bothered to vote in 1930 and 1932 contributed to the Nazi successes. Exactly how many of these voted for the Nazis is impossible to determine, but obviously mass unemployment and Hitler's pledges to create work made the Nazis attractive to unemployed first-time voters. The Nazi vote was also significantly boosted by voters switching from the smaller middle-class interest parties, such as the Economics Party or the Bavarian Peasants' League. The NSDAP had built up a network of middle-class organisations which were able to target farmers, small traders, clerical workers, students and women, as well as the medical, teaching and legal professions. It managed both to champion the specific interests of these groups while also integrating them into one national party.

It is clear from the statistics that the NSDAP did best in the mainly Protestant and rural districts of northern Germany, but less well in the Catholic areas and the big cities. This does not mean, however, that the party did not attract votes from all sections of society. Jürgen Falter has shown that some 40 per cent of Nazi voters and 60 per cent of the SA were workers (Falter, 1984). As the SPD became increasingly associated with Brüning's deflationary policy (see below), the Nazis offered an attractive alternative of work-creation projects and a classless party which promised a new national community.

THE ROAD TO POWER, SEPTEMBER 1930–JANUARY 1933

Although the NSDAP had become a major force on 14 September, its ultimate triumph was not a foregone conclusion. Initially Brüning's position seemed secure, as he was kept in power by Hindenburg and his deflationary policies were 'tolerated' by the SPD, if only to keep Hitler from the Chancellorship. Provided the Hindenburg–Brüning–SPD axis remained intact, there was no obvious way forward for Hitler. As one commentator, Helmuth Gerlach, observed in 1930, it was quite possible that 'if the sun [shone] once more on the German economy, Hitler's voters [would] melt away like snow' (Burleigh, 2000: 133).

Up to late summer 1932 the NSDAP continued to expand at an impressive rate, but the problem remained of how it was to maximise this support to seize power. Hitler hoped to win power constitutionally through the ballot box and then, semi-legally, implement the Third Reich [**Doc. 5, p. 150**]. His first chance to test this out came in the presidential elections of spring 1932, when Hindenburg's seven-year term came to an end. In the second ballot against Hindenburg Hitler gained 36.6 per cent of the vote, as opposed to Hindenburg's 52.9 per cent. There then followed on 24 April a series of state and city elections covering some four-fifths of Germany. In these the Nazis gained results which ranged from 28.4 per cent in Württemberg to 40.9 per cent in Anhalt. Impressive as these successes were, they did not give Hitler the decisive majorities he needed. His ambiguous constitutional tactics subjected the Nazi Party to increasing strains. As the party expanded, friction increased between the party's political organisation and the SA, which resented the sudden proliferation of party bureaucracy and the stress on electoral success. There were consequently a series of minor but potentially explosive SA strikes and mutinies, which might have led to the disintegration of the Nazi Party, but in May 1932 it suddenly looked as if Hitler's tactics might after all succeed.

The conservative elites saw Brüning's appointment as a prelude to the replacement of the Weimar Republic by a more authoritarian regime. To achieve this, however, they needed to secure popular backing which they increasingly realised only the Nazi Party could provide. By the spring of 1932 Brüning had lost the confidence of Hindenburg and Schleicher. Both his economic and foreign policies appeared to have failed, his government was also considering scrapping grain subsidies to the great East Elbian landowners, and General Groener, the Reich Minister of the Interior, had alienated Hitler by banning the SA. It was this last action which persuaded Hindenburg, on Schleicher's advice, on 29 May to replace Brüning with Franz von Papen, who, it was hoped, would be able to win Nazi support for an authoritarian regime backed by the *Reichswehr*. Hitler responded to Schleicher's overtures with caution. He was determined not to enter a coalition in a subordinate position and only initially agreed to support Papen provided that the SA ban was lifted and a general election was held.

The election took place on 31 July and resulted in the Nazi Party gaining 230 seats, but it stopped tantalisingly short of an overall majority. Hitler suffered a major political setback when Hindenburg, instead of asking him to form a government, merely offered him the Vice-Chancellorship in Papen's cabinet. Papen, who had already suspended the Prussian government in July, had ambitious plans for dissolving the *Reichstag* and delaying elections until he had drafted a new constitution. Through a restricted franchise and a non-elected first chamber he intended drastically to reduce the powers of the legislature, but the timing of his plans went wrong when he was forced to dissolve the *Reichstag* prematurely after a massive vote of no confidence in his government on 12 September.

The elections of 6 November were another setback for the Nazis. As a result of growing disillusionment with Hitler, who appeared to be unable to win power, and electoral fatigue, the Nazis actually lost 2 million voters and their number of seats fell to 196. Hitler's refusal to serve under Papen led to the latter's resignation and the appointment of Schleicher on 3 December as Chancellor. Schleicher hoped both to win the backing of the SPD and the trade unions through a package of economic reforms and work-creation projects, and to divide the NSDAP by offering Gregor Strasser the posts of Vice-Chancellor and Minister President of Prussia. This plunged the Nazi Party into its most serious crisis since 1925. When Hitler vetoed the deal, Strasser resigned from the party in protest, although he did not join the cabinet. Hitler had to move rapidly to take over the political organisation which Strasser had built up in the party, and was able to prevent a split by appealing to the loyalty of the *Reichstag* deputies, *Gauleiter* and Regional Inspectors to their *Führer*.

The problem of gaining power, however, remained. The party was arguably well on its way to 'the rubbish pile of history' (Orlow, I, 1971: 308) when it was rescued, in January 1933, by the Cologne banker Baron Kurt von Schroeder, and Papen. Schroeder, on his own initiative, arranged a meeting on 4 January between Hitler and Papen. Initially Hitler appeared to be ready to accept office in a Papen cabinet, provided that he controlled the Defence and Interior Ministries. Over the next two weeks Hitler's bargaining powers were strengthened both by Nazi electoral success in the state election of Lippe, where the party won 39.5 per cent of the vote, and by the mounting difficulties facing the government. Schleicher had failed to reconcile the SPD or the unions and had also alienated the great East Elbian landowners by refusing to increase tariff duties on imported food. When he was refused permission by Hindenburg to dissolve the *Reichstag* and postpone new elections, he resigned on 28 January. Hitler was now able successfully to demand the Chancellorship and that the NSDAP should be given the Ministries of the Interior in both the Reich and Prussia. Papen optimistically hoped that by appointing reliable conservative figures to the other nine cabinet appointments, he would be able to contain Hitler. On the evening of 28 January this arrangement was accepted by Hindenburg and the new Hitler cabinet was sworn in on 30 January.

Hitler's appointment as Chancellor was not inevitable. Support for the Nazi Party was after all 'a mile wide, but beyond a hard-core of fanatics, only an inch deep' (Burleigh, 2000: 143), and was already unravelling by the autumn of 1932. On the other hand, there were compelling reasons for his appointment. The Weimar Republic was already fatally weakened by 1932, but unlike most of the states of central and eastern Europe and Spain and Portugal, the traditional elites were not strong enough to set up an authoritarian regime themselves. They had no option but an alliance with Nazism. The very fact that the NSDAP had suffered an electoral reverse in November 1932 was welcome to them as it indicated that the party might be more easily manipulated.

3

The legal revolution and the consolidation of power, 1933–34

In 1930 Hitler had publicly declared that 'the constitution only maps out the area of battle, not the goal' (Bracher, 1973: 245). Having been appointed Chancellor on 30 January 1933 by President Hindenburg, acting under the terms of Article 48 of the Weimar constitution, his most immediate aim was to secure complete power, but it was important for him to preserve a camouflage of legality as his repeated emphasis on legal revolution and national unity both won over and fatally confused many who might otherwise have worked against him [**Docs 5 and 6, pp. 150 and 151**]. In view of the overwhelming non-Nazi majority in the cabinet, Papen's rash boast that within two months 'we will have pushed Hitler so far into a corner that he'll squeak' (Bracher, 1973: 248) seems understandable, but Hitler enjoyed several advantages: two Nazi ministers, Göring and Frick, were responsible respectively for the Ministries of the Interior in Prussia and the Reich; Papen's deposition of the Prussian government in July 1932 (see page 19) had seriously weakened opposition among the other German states to further centralisation; and Hitler was able to exploit the state of emergency that had existed since 1930. He invoked Article 48, which theoretically invested emergency powers in the President, to issue a string of emergency decrees. Hitler was also the only politician on the Right to head a mass party. Although the Nazi Party was incapable of achieving power by itself, it was a powerful force held together by loyalty to Hitler and by the prospect of power and the rewards that go with power.

THE DISSOLUTION OF THE *REICHSTAG* AND THE ELECTION OF 5 MARCH 1933

Hitler aimed first to eliminate the remaining powers of the *Reichstag*. He rejected the chance of a pact with the Centre Party, which would have gained him a working majority and secured cabinet agreement for a fresh election. The Nazis then proceeded to launch a dynamic electoral campaign initiated by a broadcast to the German people on 1 February 1933 in which Hitler cleverly played on the nation's longing for unity and recovery. He hid his brutal anti-Semitism and his grandiose plans for expansion into eastern Europe and instead concentrated on the 'appalling inheritance which we are taking over', stressing the total failure of the 'November parties' and the imminent danger of a Communist *Putsch*. He appealed to the conservative millions of Germany by pledging that the new government would 'take under its firm protection Christianity as the basis of our morality and the family as the nucleus of our nation and state'. Hitler's economic plans were vague, but he did promise 'two big Four Year Plans' to save the farmer and to launch 'a massive and comprehensive attack on unemployment' (Noakes and Pridham, I, 1998: 132).

Even during the election campaign in February Hitler started to lay the foundations of the Nazi dictatorship by presidential decree. On 4 February the government acquired the power to forbid political meetings and to ban newspapers. Two days later the Reich's grip on Prussia was strengthened by the dissolution of the Prussian *Landtag*. Göring now emerged as a key figure in the Nazi take-over of power and began a systematic purge of the Prussian civil service and police. On 17 February the Prussian police, which effectively meant the police in three-fifths of Germany, were ordered actively to support the Nazi Party machine and an extra 50,000 men, predominantly from the SA, were enrolled as auxiliary police.

An important element in the Nazi campaign was the constant reference to the Communist threat. In fact the Communists, still following instructions from Moscow, were disappointingly docile, and the Nazis were driven to fabricate proof of an impending Red *Putsch* by raiding the Communist Party headquarters in Berlin. It was, however, the *Reichstag* fire that gave Hitler his best chance to exploit the alleged Red threat. Although the fire was so opportune that contemporaries assumed the Nazis started it, the Dutch Communist Marinus van der Lubbe was in fact the arsonist. But it is academic to worry about who actually started the fire for, as Fest has aptly remarked, 'by instantly taking advantage of the fire the Nazis made the deed their own' (Fest, 1977: 588). On the initiative of Wilhelm Frick, the Reich Minister of the Interior, the draconian 'Decree for the Protection of People and State' was drafted and promulgated on 28 February 1933, empowering the central government not only to arrest individuals at will, censor the post and search private houses, but also to take over the state governments should they refuse to enact 'measures for the restoration of public security'. The decree gave Hitler sufficient power to entrench himself and ensured that his government's fate did not, in the final analysis, depend on the forthcoming

Landtag Each German state had an elected *Landtag* or assembly. In July 1932 Papen dissolved the Prussian government and put Prussia under the control of a Reich Commissioner. On 31 March 1933 the state assemblies were reconstituted to reflect the Nazi/Nationalist majority in the *Reichstag*, and in January 1934 they were finally abolished.

election. It has therefore been described with some justification as 'a kind of *coup d'état*' (Noakes and Pridham, I, 1998: 142).

Hitler also began to forge the *de facto* coalition with the generals, big business and industry, upon which his second government was initially to be based. On 3 February, at a dinner organised by Kurt von Hammerstein, the Commander-in-Chief of the *Reichswehr*, Hitler outlined in full his plans for rearmament and consequently won the grudging recognition that 'at any rate no chancellor has ever expressed himself so warmly in favour of defence' (Wheeler-Bennett, 1961: 291). Hitler's anti-socialism and determination to destroy the trade unions was increasingly appreciated by big business. When he met a group of leading industrialists a little over two weeks later, he was able to win not only their goodwill but also considerable sums for his campaign funds by stressing the anti-democratic and anti-socialist nature of his campaign.

When Germany went to the polls on 5 March 1933, Hitler did not secure the decisive majority he was hoping for. The Nazis won 43.9 per cent of the votes and could only claim a majority on the strength of their alliance with the Nationalist Party, which was supported by a mere 8 per cent of the electorate. In many Catholic and working-class areas the Nazi Party suffered a decisive defeat and it failed to gain an overall majority in Bavaria, Baden, Württemberg, Hesse and Saxony.

THE 'REVOLUTION FROM BELOW' AND THE ENABLING ACT

Nevertheless, the momentum of the Nazi drive for power was not checked. On the contrary, the election results released a new burst of revolutionary and terrorist activities which won the Nazis the physical control of Germany. While the sheer force of this 'revolution from below' undoubtedly strengthened Hitler's hand and enabled him to neutralise opposition and to force the remaining non-Nazi **Länder** governments into resignation (see below), it would be a simplification to argue that Hitler manipulated this explosion at will. To a degree that is hard to determine, Hitler had initially to go with the tide of Nazi violence, but he was also concerned that excessive popular violence would alienate both his coalition partners and the Reich President. He appealed on 10 March to both the SA and the SS to end the gratuitous violence against individuals and particularly the 'obstruction or disturbance of business life'. This message of moderation was then apparently contradicted the same day by Göring in a speech in Essen which condoned the settling of accounts with 'traitors' (Noakes and Pridham, I, 1998: 150–51)

Land (pl. Länder) The Reich had 25 federal states. The largest was Prussia, which covered two-thirds of Germany and contained three-quarters of the population. The Reich reconstruction law of January 1934 merged the Prussian ministries with the relevant Reich departments. In the other states, cabinets remained in existence as agents of the central government. The *Landtage* were abolished.

SS (*Schutzstaffel*) Literally, protection squad. It was founded in 1925 to protect the leading Nazis. It began to play a key role, first of all within the Nazi Party, when it was taken over by Himmler in 1929, and then, after 1933, within the Nazi regime. Its initial role was to eliminate the enemies of the new *Volksgemeinschaft*. When Himmler successfully established control over the whole police and security systems within the Reich in 1936, its influence was greatly strengthened. Through control of the police and then the occupied territories, the SS also played a dominant role in formulating the racial policy of the Third Reich.

and Hitler had to renew his appeal two days later, which this time appears to have had more effect. All over the Reich, however, Nazis continued to seize administrative positions in local government, and there was a growing danger that the German administrative machine would disintegrate in the hands of incompetent Nazi activists. Consequently, on 7 April, the hastily drafted Law for the Restoration of the Professional Civil Service confirmed the continued existence of the traditional state bureaucracy even though it was purged of Jews and socialists (see page 38).

In the meantime, on 21 March, in a contrived but impressive ceremony at Potsdam, Hitler celebrated the opening of the new *Reichstag* in the presence of the Crown Prince and the military establishment of the *ancien régime*, and skilfully reawakened memories of the unity of August 1914. Two days later the *Reichstag* met to consider the Enabling Bill, the aim of which was to legalise the transfer of full legislative and executive powers to the cabinet for a period of four years. As it entailed a major change in the constitution, the government had to secure a two-thirds majority. Hitler simplified his task by locking up the 81 Communist deputies and winning over the splintered liberal parties, but he still needed the votes of the Centre Party if the bill was to have a secure passage. Against Brüning's advice, the Centre Party decided to support the government, believing mistakenly that it would in time be able to influence Hitler [**Doc. 7, p. 151**].

The debate on the Enabling Bill in the Kroll Opera House took place in the atmosphere of a *coup d'état*. The square outside was packed with enthusiastic supporters of the Nazis while inside the building SA and SS men lined the walls and corridors. Although Hitler went out of his way to stress that the *Reichstag* and **Reichsrat**, the Presidency, the Christian Churches and the *Länder* would not be permanently impaired by the bill, he also made it absolutely clear that if the *Reichstag* did not give him the necessary majority he was 'prepared to go ahead in face of the refusal and the hostilities which will result from that refusal' (Bullock, 1962: 269). This combination of terror and specious pledges won Hitler the required two-thirds majority, and the Enabling Bill passed through both houses and duly became law – only the SPD dared vote against it.

The Enabling Law was of immense propaganda value. Although its constitutional validity is debatable, as it was passed by a *Reichsrat* which, 'after the dismemberment of the state governments by coups, unquestionably was not properly constituted' (Bracher, 1973: 250), it maintained the façade of the legal revolution and removed any doubts the civil service or the judiciary had as to the legality of the Nazi take-over. It was this pseudo-legality that inhibited and confused all but the most clear-sighted opponents of the Nazi regime.

Reichsrat The upper house of the German parliament in which the federal states were represented. This was abolished by the 'Law on the Reform of the Reich' in January 1934 which transferred the sovereign rights of the *Länder* to the Reich.

THE PROCESS OF *GLEICHSCHALTUNG*

Hitler rapidly completed the process of coordinating or bringing the *Länder* into line with the new National Socialist regime (***Gleichschaltung***), which had started before the Enabling Bill was passed. Nazi governments had already gained power in Thuringia, Brunswick, Oldenburg, Anhalt and Mecklenburg, while Prussia had been under the control of a Reich Commissioner since July 1932. After 5 March pressure had also been brought to bear on the other *Länder* governments, both centrally from the Reich Minister of the Interior and locally from the Nazi regional leadership. Through this mixture of 'revolutionary pressure from below and action from above' (Broszat, 1981: 99) National Socialist Reich Commissioners were first able to take over the police forces in the city states of Hamburg, Bremen, Lübeck and the *Länder* of Schaumberg-Lippe, Hesse, Baden, Württemberg, Saxony and Bavaria. Then, on 31 March, the *Länder* Diets were reconstituted to reflect the ratio of the parties in the *Reichstag* and, a week later, Reich Governors, who in most cases were the local *Gauleiter*, were appointed with full powers to dismiss recalcitrant ministers and to insist on carrying out the policies set out by the Reich Chancellor. *Gauleiter* were also made ***Oberpräsidenten*** of the Prussian provinces. In January 1934, despite Hitler's promises to the contrary, the Diets were finally abolished and all the state governments were firmly subordinated to the Reich government (see page 37).

Hitler's potentially most formidable opponents were the trade unions. In 1920 they had defeated the **Kapp *Putsch*** by calling a general strike, but by 1933 their members, like most other Germans, were shell-shocked by the slump and the dole queue, and in no psychological position to oppose the apparently inevitable Nazi revolution. The leaders of the socialist unions, which were by far the largest and most powerful in Germany, hoped to salvage at least the essentials of their organisation by assuring Hitler that they would not meddle in politics and would limit themselves merely to protecting the economic and social welfare of their members. On 13 April they even provisionally agreed to the creation of a Nazi *Reichskommissar* for the unions, but any compromise with Hitler was of course impossible. Goebbels outmanoeuvred the union leadership by appealing over its head to the workers. He declared 1 May as a national holiday in honour of labour and invited the workers to participate in the processions and ceremonies which were to mark it. Then, on 2 May, the SA and SS occupied trade-union offices throughout Germany, and both unionised and non-unionised workers were enrolled in the new German Labour Front (***Deutsche Arbeitsfront* (DAF)**). Hitler carefully ensured that it would not become dominated by the activists in the NSBO, the National Socialist Factory Cell Organisation, by handing

Gleichschaltung Literally, coordination or streamlining. The process of putting everything under Nazi control not only involved the abolition of all the non-National Socialist political parties, the elimination of the *Reichstag* as an independent assembly and the taking over of state and local governments, and, right down to local level, clubs and societies, ranging from singing associations to horticultural societies, were all placed firmly under Nazi control.

Oberpräsidenten Senior administrative officials in the Prussian provinces.

Kapp *Putsch* Conspiracy by right-wing nationalists and the *Freikorps* led by Wolfgang Kapp to overthrow the Weimar Republic.

***Deutsche Arbeitsfront* (DAF)** The German Labour Front. This was created and put under the control of Robert Ley on 6 May 1933, both to replace the trade unions and to weaken the more radical NSBO, which was subordinated to it. Both workers and employers were members of the DAF, but it had no part in determining wages or relations with the employers. Nevertheless, under the leadership of Robert Ley, it did become influential in social policy and developed the 'Beauty of Labour' and the 'Strength through Joy' schemes.

over responsibility for fixing wages at plant level and for preserving 'industrial peace' to specially created Trustees of Labour, who were directly responsible to the Ministry of Labour. The NSBO was purged of its more radical members and firmly subordinated to the DAF. The carefully neutered Labour Front could now become the symbol of the 'National Community', to which the employers would also belong (see below).

Hitler also moved to coordinate all the various extra-parliamentary associations and private armies that had proliferated on both the Right and the Left before 1933. The left-wing organisations were speedily dissolved, but their right-wing counterparts were integrated into existing Nazi affiliates. The Christian Farmers' Union Association, for example, was merged into the party's Political Agrarian Apparatus, while the *Stahlhelm*, the right-wing ex-soldiers' league, was incorporated into the SA. The Law against the New Formation of Parties of 14 July confirmed the dissolution of the political parties and made the Nazi Party the only legal party in Germany. Except for the SPD and the Communists (***Kommunistische Partei Deutschlands* (KPD)**), the parties had voluntarily dissolved themselves. The mysterious death of Ernst Oberfohren, the head of the Nationalist Party's *Reichstag* delegation, who had dared to criticise Hitler's policies and to question whether his party's coalition with the Nazis should continue, was in the final instance a reminder of what could befall political dissenters of any political colour!

Nazi control of education, the media and the cultural life of the Reich was established with little difficulty. By the spring of 1933 Goebbels, as Minister of Propaganda, controlled broadcasting and, adroitly, through a system of internal press conferences and directives, imposed uniform news coverage and interpretation on the papers (see page 56). In September 1933 all 'intellectual workers' were forced to join the Reich Chamber of Culture, which enabled a rigorous check to be kept on their activities. In May the Ministry of the Interior compelled the German states to introduce new syllabuses into the schools and universities. All teachers' and university lecturers' associations were affiliated to the National Socialist Teachers' Organisation. At the universities, gangs of Nazi students terrorised left-wing or independent-minded lecturers and forced them to resign.

Businessmen and industrialists were more effective in defending their essential interests. The populist or radical wing of the Nazi Party, led by Gottfried Feder and Otto Wagener, the Party Commissioner for Economic Matters, campaigned vigorously for the immediate realisation of the original Nazi programme, involving the destruction of the department stores and industrial cartels and the subsequent enhancement of small-scale business. As Hitler needed an effective modern industry to stabilise the economy and to rearm Germany, at the end of June 1933, after 'a chaotic interim period' (Schoenbaum, 1967: 129) in which the initiative in economic policies had

Kommunistische Partei Deutschlands (KPD) The German Communist Party was founded in 1919 and in November 1932 won 100 seats in the *Reichstag*. After the *Reichstag* fire, 4,000 Communist officials, party members and members of the *Reichstag* were arrested and, by the end of 1933, approximately half its total membership was in prison or concentration camps. The Communist opposition was initially run by the Central Committee of the KPD, based in Paris.

threatened to pass to the party radicals, economic reality forced Hitler to stop party attacks on big business. He appointed Kurt Schmitt, the managing director of Germany's largest insurance company, to replace Hugenberg as Economics Minister. Industry and business did not, however, entirely escape coordination. In June the employers' associations were formed into the Reich Estate of German Industry, and seven months later the whole of German business was regrouped along functional and territorial lines under the umbrella of the Reich Economic Chamber; but, unlike other victims of coordination, businessmen and industrialists were effectively able to manage their own affairs and keep the more radical members of the Nazi Party out of key positions. Gustav Krupp von Bohlen und Halbach, for instance, became the Reich Estate's 'Leader'. As there was no danger of the DAF becoming the genuine representative of Labour, Krupp had little difficulty in recommending its membership to the employers. On 1 June 1933 he also suggested that German industry should pay a special 'Adolf Hitler donation' to express its gratitude for the elimination of the trade unions and in anticipation of the coming rearmament boom. Krupp's thinking behind this proposal was that industry, by making voluntary donations, would be able to head off any attempts by the party to demand more money. Big business was, as Norbert Frei has observed, putting up 'a clear marker of its independence' (Frei, 1993: 55).

THE CHURCHES

Like big business, the Catholic Church was ready to negotiate an agreement with Hitler which would in essentials preserve its independence. The Concordat signed between the Vatican and the German government on 14 July 1933 appeared to give the Catholic Church substantial advantages which it had not secured from the Weimar Republic, and to more than compensate for the dissolution of the Centre Party. Not only was it guaranteed religious freedom, the right to administer itself and appoint its clergy, but privileges which previously had existed in only a few Catholic areas were now extended to the whole of the Reich. In any *Land*, for instance, parents could now demand Catholic confessional schools, provided there were sufficient numbers to warrant the request. Hitler was ready to make these apparently generous concessions both because he hoped to end the Church's intervention in politics and saw the Concordat as a temporary measure that would not ultimately stop the coordination of the Catholic Church in Germany. It was significant, for instance, that Article 31 sought to make a distinction between Catholic organisations, which were purely ecclesiastical, and 'those that serve other purposes, such as social or professional interests' with a view to the latter's eventual dissolution. The Concordat was ratified in September 1933, but attempts to implement Article 31 led to growing friction between the Nazis and the Roman Catholic Church (see page 57).

It was, however, from the 28 regional Protestant Churches that Hitler unexpectedly met opposition. He hoped to group these into one united Reich Church under an elected Reich bishop, which would be more easy to control politically, but these attempts drew him into a 'minefield of inter-mingled religion and politics' (Kershaw, I, 1998: 489). The first attempt to get his nominee, Bishop Otto Müller, an ardent Nazi and former military chaplain, elected failed. Only after his successful rival was forced to resign and a state Commissioner for the Evangelical Churches in Prussia had been appointed to draw up a constitution for the Reich Church, did Müller succeed in a second attempt. His election in July 1933 was immediately challenged by a strong dissident group, the Pastors' Emergency League, led by Martin Niemöller, the pastor of the Berlin parish of Dahlem. Müller at first attempted to intimidate the opposition. In the autumn a major crisis caused by the arrest of the two Protestant bishops of Bavaria and Württemberg blew up, which not only threatened to embarrass Hitler, but led to the Pastors' Emergency League setting up a breakaway church – the **Confessing Church** – in October 1934. Hitler withdrew his support from Müller and, in July 1935, created a new Ministry of Church Affairs. This, however, also failed to coordinate the German Protestants, who remained divided into three main groups: the German Christians under an increasingly marginalised Bishop Müller, the Confessing Church and the mainstream Church establishment, which tried to tread the tightrope between cooperating with the regime and preserving a degree of independence.

Confessing Church (Bekennende Kirche)
This was set up in reaction to the Reich Church (*Reichskirche*) by the Pastors' Emergency League in October 1934. It rejected outright the totalitarian claims of the Nazi state over the Church.

THE DEFEAT OF THE SECOND REVOLUTION

It is a cliché that revolutions devour their children. Both Robespierre in France and Lenin in the USSR were compelled to liquidate over-zealous revolutionaries whose opposition threatened their policies. Hitler was not spared this process. The ambiguities and apparent compromises of the 'legal revolution' of 1933, which left the military and big business elites still intact, were increasingly criticised by the SA and the populist wing of the party. The Nazi activists had hoped that the seizure of power would entail both real economic benefits and the immediate availability of prestigious new posts, but the party was never to enjoy a monopoly position in the state comparable to that possessed by the Communist Party in Russia. By July 1933 it was becoming only too clear that Hitler could not afford to give free rein to its more radical policies. Although there was considerable resentment in the party at the delay in implementing a real Nazi revolution involving the destruction of large-scale capitalism, and the replacement of the *Reichswehr* and the traditional bureaucracy by new, party-dominated structures, only Ernst Röhm possessed a sufficiently strong power base to become an effective critic of, or, in the final resort, a challenge to, Hitler. As the Chief of Staff of the SA, he controlled a unique and potentially revolutionary instrument which was a combination of an embryonic people's army and a revolutionary pressure group that had played a key role in destroying opposition to the Nazi seizure of power.

Once Hitler had declared an end to the 'legal revolution' in July 1933 [**Doc. 9, p. 153**], the SA increasingly became an 'embarrassing legacy of the years of struggle' (Bullock, 1962: 286), and was in the process of becoming a mere political auxiliary army whose task was to raise money and to run propaganda activities. Röhm, of course, was unwilling to accept this role and continued to expand the SA until, by the end of 1933, it was a potential force of some 2.5 million men. He saw the SA and SS, which was still attached to the SA, as the guarantors of a second and much more radical revolution. Röhm's thinking on the social, political and economic aspects of the Second Revolution was vague and incoherent. He had considerable sympathy with the more socialist aspects of the Nazi programme, but one can only say with certainty that, for him, the Second Revolution would hinge on turning the SA into a 'huge militia base for a thoroughly rearmed Germany organised along more or less national-bolshevik lines' (Orlow, II, 1973: 57). It was this growing insistence on creating a new people's army, which in the end would surely absorb the *Reichswehr*, and his assertion of the primacy of the SA over the political wing of the party that threatened Hitler.

Ultimately Röhm's elimination was inevitable. Although Hitler's whole system of government both encouraged and resulted in rivalry between the various Nazi leaders and their departments, Röhm was in a different category from the other Nazi barons, as he had the means to challenge Hitler and was not dependent upon him. An SA revolution would have inevitably damaged the prospects of the other party leaders, who were already ensconced in powerful positions and for the most part dependent on the skills of the traditional bureaucracy. Consequently, by the spring of 1934, at the latest, they were ready to push Hitler into a show-down with the SA. Yet it is quite possible that Hitler would have put off a confrontation with Röhm, if in the summer of 1934 the growing rivalry between the SA and the army and, more importantly, the imminent question of the succession to the Presidency which was posed by Hindenburg's ill-health and great age, had not become acute.

The continued existence of the *Reichswehr* was essential if Hitler was to embark upon a major rearmament programme and reintroduce conscription [**Doc. 10, p. 153**]. It can thus be argued that this fact alone made a Hitler–Röhm clash inevitable. In all crucial military decisions Hitler favoured the *Reichswehr*. In a series of policy statements in 1933 he confirmed that the SA would be put under the command of the *Reichswehr* and be relegated to supervising the military education of youth groups. In January 1934 Hitler made a more fundamental decision when he consented to the drawing up of plans for the eventual reintroduction of traditional military conscription, thereby finally destroying Röhm's hopes of a people's army. However, only in retrospect can these decisions be seen as a victory for the *Reichswehr*, because right up to June 1934 there was no guarantee that Röhm would not use the SA to force Hitler to initiate a second revolution.

By the spring of 1934 the imminent prospect of Hindenburg's death confronted Hitler with the dual necessity of both preventing a second revolution and nipping in the bud what could amount to a potential counter-revolution. In both operations the army's support was the key to success. The 'legal revolution' had left the army and the conservative elites in industry and the civil service still unbroken. There was the possibility that after Hindenburg's death they might unite in the demand for a monarchist restoration, which was arguably the last remaining chance of checking or even toppling Hitler. The national-conservative elites were having second thoughts about having brought Hitler to power and were hoping that a crisis over the SA might enable them to establish an authoritarian government under their own control. Edgar Jung, a right-wing intellectual and speech-writer for Papen, openly conceded that 'We are partly responsible that this fellow has come to power [and] we must get rid of him again' (Kershaw, I, 1998: 508). The Nazi regime was also becoming increasingly unpopular in the country as a whole. Millions were still unemployed [**Doc. 15, p. 156**], the peasants were becoming disillusioned with the excessive bureaucracy and red tape of the Reich Food Estate (see page 46), and many businessmen were critical of the currency and credit restrictions (see page 48) and the continual shortages of raw materials. A report from the SPD executive in exile, based in Prague, commented that many former Nazi voters in the business world 'say with dismay that they had not imagined things would turn out as they have' (Frei, 1993: 4). The embarrassing results of the elections in March and April 1934 for the newly established Councils of Trust (*Vertrauensrate*) in the factories (see page 64) also showed the deep mistrust many workers had for the regime. NSBO candidates were so decisively defeated that in many factories the results were not announced.

However, provided that Hitler could control the SA, the *Reichswehr* at least would hesitate to support a restoration, as both Blomberg, the Defence

Minister, and Fritsch, the new Commander-in-Chief of the army, as well as a significant number of junior officers, were impressed by Hitler's determination to rearm Germany. It is debatable whether Hitler actually concluded a secret pact with the generals, whereby in exchange for the elimination of Röhm they would back him as Hindenburg's successor, but it is obvious that both parties had strong reasons for cooperating, and there is indisputable evidence that the *Reichswehr* supplied weapons and lorries to the SS units which liquidated Röhm at the end of June.

From March 1934 onwards Hitler 'moved erratically and with spells of doubt and indecision towards a show-down with the SA' (Craig, 1978: 588). His occasionally flagging resolution was bolstered by Göring, Himmler and Hess, who were impatient to remove once and for all the dangerous potential of the SA. The months of May and June were a period of growing tension, even though on 6 June Röhm agreed to relieve it by sending his men on leave during July, a concession which clearly shows that he had no immediate plans for a *Putsch*. Eleven days later, however, Hitler received a sharp reminder from Papen, who informed him in a sensational speech, drafted by Edgar Jung and delivered at Marburg University, that the longer he delayed in solving the Röhm problem the more likely he was to face growing conservative opposition to his regime. Papen specifically warned against a second revolution and criticised the excessive *Führer* cult [**Doc. 11, p. 154**].

Goebbels attempted to prevent its circulation, but copies of the speech were leaked and made a huge impact on the public. 'Never again in the Third Reich', as Kershaw has observed, 'was such striking criticism at the heart of the regime to come from such a prominent figure' (Kershaw, I, 1998: 510). Initially Papen intended to resign in protest over Goebbels' censorship of his speech, but he was persuaded by Hitler to delay this step. Had he acted quickly, Hindenburg might just have been persuaded to dismiss Hitler and declare martial law. Even so, when Hitler did go to see the President at his estate, at Neudeck, on 21 June he was bluntly told to control Röhm. Blomberg even informed him that if he was unable to do this, Hindenburg would hand over power to the army.

Hitler now had little choice but to eliminate Röhm but he was also determined to have his leading critics on the Right killed as well – Jung was arrested as early as 25 June. He left it to Himmler, the commander of the Bavarian police and Heydrich, the chief of the **SD** the Security Service of the SS, to produce bogus evidence that would show that the SA had plans for an insurrection, and would give him the excuse to unleash the purge. When Hitler arrived at Munich at dawn on the 30 June, accounts of SA protest demonstrations, caused by rumours of Röhm's imminent dismissal, persuaded him to have the SA leaders arrested and shot while they were still in their hotels. In what became known as the **'Night of the Long Knives'** not only the SA

SD (Sicherheitsdienst)
Security service of the SS. It was created in 1932 and in July 1934 became the sole political intelligence agency of the Reich. In September 1939 the SD, Gestapo and Reich Criminal Police Department were amalgamated into one agency – the Reich Security Head Office (RHSA).

'Night of the Long Knives'
The name given to the murders beginning in the night of 29–30 June 1934, which were carried out on Hitler's orders. In Wiessee, near Munich, Röhm and six other SA leaders were seized and shot. Throughout the Reich Hitler settled old scores. Schleicher and Gregor Strasser were also eliminated. At least 85 people were killed; only 50 of these were SA men.

leaders, but two key conservative monarchists in Papen's office, Herbert von Bose and Edgar Jung, as well as other political enemies of Hitler such as Schleicher and Gregor Strasser, and an unknown number of lesser figures were all liquidated. Surviving police files show that at least 85 people were executed, but the 'white book' published in Paris by German *émigrés* claimed that the true total was 401. Whatever the precise number of those murdered Hitler in fact carried out a 'double coup' – against both the SA leadership and his conservative critics.

Although Hitler's popularity in the nation as a whole probably declined sharply, he was nevertheless able to consolidate his power without difficulty. On the day Hindenburg died (1 August) he combined the offices of Chancellor and President, a step which was confirmed by plebiscite on 19 August. As head of state Hitler now automatically became the titular Supreme Commander of the Armed Forces, which voluntarily swore an oath of loyalty to him. The populist wing of the Nazi Party was for the time being decisively checked, and both the SA and the economic *Mittelstand* radicals had no alternative but to accept Hitler's opportunist interpretation of the Nazi revolution. The SA became a mere propaganda arm of the party, unable to compete with the army. Hitler had indeed defeated Röhm's primitive revolutionary threat, but Germany was now to experience the bewildering yet all-pervading Hitlerian revolution imposed from above, which in time was not even to spare the army.

4

State, party and *Führer*: the
government of Nazi Germany, 1933–39

When 'a group of personal failures animated by a desire to destroy
liberalism and pluralism in Germany and grouped around a
fanatical, charismatic and unstable leader took over the reins of
one of the most sophisticated governmental structures in Europe' (Orlow, II,
1973: 17) the consequences were bound to be chaotic and to defy any rational analysis. Despite the veneer of efficiency that so impressed the majority
of contemporary observers, in retrospect it is clear that the Third Reich was
a bedlam of rival hierarchies, competing centres of power and ambiguous
chains of command. There were four distinct centres of power: the single
party monopoly of the Nazi Party, the SS, the central government machine
and the personal absolutism of Hitler. The Nazi Party failed to dictate policy
in the way the Bolshevik Party was able to in Russia, although it was
nevertheless a considerable power in the state that could not be ignored. The
traditional civil service and the ministries initially retained much of their
influence and the subsequent rivalries created by the ambiguous dualism of
party and state could only be resolved by Hitler himself.

MINISTRIES AND 'SUPREME REICH AUTHORITIES', 1933–38

Despite attempts by individual Nazi leaders to develop a coherent overall
strategy, Hitler had no immediate blueprint for constructing a specifically
Nazi state in 1933. When he became Chancellor he relied on the precedents
set by the use of Article 48 to promote the emergency decrees of 28 February
and 23 March (see pages 22 and 24). Hitler merely took over the existing state
and either occupied the key national and local positions with Nazis or ensured
they were in reliable hands. There was no major purge of the civil or the
diplomatic services and no new revolutionary constitutional organs comparable

to the Russian soviets were introduced. Initially, the key area where it looked as if Hitler could be contained by the conservative elites was the Reich Cabinet where, apart from Hitler, only two ministers were members of the Nazi Party. Over the next two years the Nazi presence was strengthened by the addition of Goebbels, Darré, Hess and Kerrl, but until the winter of 1937–38 seven important departments, which included Finance, Economics and Defence, were still in conservative hands. Up to March 1933 the Cabinet met regularly, but once the Enabling Act was passed Hitler's powers as Chancellor were greatly strengthened. By Article 3 he was now given the right to prepare and execute laws independently of both the legislature and the Reich President. The number of Cabinet meetings rapidly declined until there were only six in 1937 and the final Cabinet meeting took place on 5 February 1938.

Both the Enabling Act, which strengthened the central government in Berlin, and the ending of the independence of the *Länder* initially increased the authority of individual ministries at the expense of the party. Schacht at the Ministry of Economics, for instance, was able to defeat efforts by the party to control the banks in 1934, while Franz Seldte could strengthen the Ministry of Labour by taking over the previously independent Unemployment Insurance Authority. At the Defence Ministry it was only in December 1935 that Blomberg allowed his civil servants to join the party. To Frick, at the Ministry of the Interior, fell the insoluble tasks of attempting to devise a satisfactory relationship between the party and state, drafting a new centralised Reich constitution as well as trying to contain the growth of the SS within some sort of legal structure.

Alongside the ministries there grew up a series of Reich organisations, combining both party and state responsibilities under specially selected deputies or leaders who reported directly to Hitler. Secure in the *Führer*'s support, they were able to conduct policy independently of the cabinet. Despite opposition from the Ministries of the Interior, Finance and Transport, Dr Fritz Todt, Hitler's road-building expert, was given a completely free hand to complete his *Autobahn* programme. His organisation formed 'an element of direct *Führer* authority (for particularly urgent *ad-hoc* measures) alongside the normal state government and administration' (Broszat, 1981: 266). The Labour Service under Konstantin Hierl was another example of the evolution of such an authority. Hierl's attempts to make the National Socialist Labour Service independent of the Ministry of Labour met with opposition from Frick, who argued that this would 'splinter' the Reich administration (Broszat, 1981: 267). He was consequently nominally made subordinate to the Interior Ministry, but in practice this did not stop him from running the Labour service independently. Hitler also insisted on setting up a supreme Reich Authority to run the Hitler Youth, so that its leader, Baldur von Schirach, could become independent of the Ministry of

Education. Financially, however, the Hitler Youth remained dependent on a budget drawn up by the Finance Ministry.

Another feature of the Nazi governmental system was the accumulation of responsibilities and positions by individual Nazis. Göring, for instance, built up an immense position of power. In May 1933 he took on the Reich Aviation Ministry as a supreme Reich Authority as well as remaining Prussian Minister President and Minister of the Interior, and in September 1936 he became a 'Minister Supremo' when he was put in charge of the Four Year Plan (see page 50). Himmler, by building up the SS into a 'state within a state', also created an independent sphere of authority which combined both party and state responsibilities.

HIMMLER AND THE SS STATE

The SS had been formed in 1925 under the overall control of the SA to provide guards for leading Nazis. Once Himmler became Reich Leader of the SS in 1929, its membership expanded rapidly from 280 to 52,000 by 1933. Under Himmler, the SS became all that the SA was not: a loyal, highly disciplined elite with strict rules of admission based on race and political loyalty. Himmler intended it eventually to form the basis of a 'new aristocracy' for a German-dominated new racial order in Europe (Kirk, 2007: 138).

Himmler had considerable success in developing the SS as the Nazi Party's main intelligence section and internal police force. In 1931 the SS helped put down a revolt led by Walter Stennes in Upper Silesia and a year later was made responsible for the party's intelligence and espionage section. To carry out this task Himmler set up the SD under Reinhard Heydrich. In the spring of 1933 Himmler was appointed Acting Chief Commissioner of Police in Bavaria. He was determined from the very beginning to extend the control of the SS over the Bavarian political police, and appointed Heydrich as his deputy to carry out this task. Heydrich tellingly observed: 'Now we no longer need the Party. It has played its role and has opened the way to power. Now the SS must penetrate the police and create a new organization there' (Noakes and Pridham, II, 1991: 500). During the winter of 1933/34 Himmler managed to extend his control to the political police forces of all the *Länder* except Prussia and Schaumberg Lippe. Then in April 1934 Göring, wishing to have Himmler as an ally against Frick and the SA, appointed him Inspector of the Prussian Secret Police – the **Gestapo** (*Geheime Staatspolizei*).

Himmler's power was helped by the elimination of Röhm in the 'Night of the Long Knives' (see page 31). As a reward for its loyalty, the SS was

Gestapo (*Geheime Staatspolizei*) The Secret State Police. During the Weimar Republic, Department 1a of the Berlin Police *Praesidium* ran the Prussian political police. In April 1933 Göring, as acting Prussian Interior Minister, set up a new Secret State Police Office (*Gestapa*). In November 1933 he created the Gestapo and appointed Himmler its Inspector in April 1934. Its task was to maintain discipline in the factories and keep political and ideological opponents of the regime under surveillance.

Totenkopfverbände
Literally   meaning
'Death's-Head   Units',
were   the   SS   units
responsible for adminis-
tering the concentration
camps in the Third Reich.
The first unit was formed
to guard Dachau in June
1933, which became the
training centre for the
Totenkopfverbände.

made independent of the SA and responsibility for administering the concentration camps was transferred to it. The notorious Death's Head Units (**Totenkopfverbände**) were created to police them. By 1937 the smaller camps, previously run by the SA, had been concentrated into three large camps, Dachau, Sachsenhausen and Buchenwald, and in the following winter two SS economic enterprises had been set up to profit from the prisoners' forced labour.

However, Himmler's ultimate control of the police forces in Germany was the 'crucial precondition' (Broszat, 1981: 270) for the growth of the SS state. In June 1936 Himmler's appointment as Chief of the German Police confirmed his dual command over the SS and all the police forces in the Reich, even though, purely nominally, he was made subordinate to the Ministry of the Interior. Himmler rapidly used his new powers to create a new Security Police (*Sicherheitspolizei*), which controlled both the Gestapo and the criminal police (*Kripo*) under the command of Heydrich, who also continued to run the Security Service. The uniformed police formed a separate branch under the SS *Obergruppenführer*, Karl Daluege. Increasingly the police became more integrated with the SS. There was, for instance, a regular interchange of personnel. Essentially, they had now become an instrument of 'Führer power' (Noakes and Pridham, II, 1991: 515).

Apart from control of the concentration camps and the police a third pillar of SS power was formed by the armed regiments based on the SS squads which had operated together with the SA as a 'revolutionary strike force' in the early months of the take-over of power. By the winter of 1933–34 the SS possessed three such formations, which were responsible directly to Himmler. Military resistance to further increases was overcome in 1938 with the resignation of Fritsch and Blomberg (see page 40). The officer corps of the SS was to prove particularly attractive to the aristocracy, who composed 25 per cent of its generals.

Himmler's growing empire was the most important of the new supreme Reich Authorities. It was based on the traditional Nazi leader–follower structure and adhered to the National Socialist pattern of creating a chain of new posts and agencies which, in Broszat's words, 'tended repeatedly to generate new positions having a "direct" relationship with Hitler and to encourage these in turn to strive for a separate existence, like some permanent process of cell division' (Broszat, 1981: 276). The fusion of the SS and police also enabled fanatical SS leaders, who were imbued with the revolutionary Nazi spirit of the pre-1933 party, to build themselves an impregnable position within the state. They could now use the bureaucratic police apparatus to launch an effective and brutal campaign against the enemies of the Third Reich, and especially the Jews.

THE CENTRALISATION OF THE REICH

The Law for the Reconstruction of the Reich of 30 January 1934 appeared to mark a radical change in German constitutional history. The *Länder* assemblies were abolished and their governments were firmly subordinated to the Reich. Frick went as far as to observe that 'a centuries' old dream has been fulfilled. Germany is no longer a weak federal state but a strong national centralized country' (Broszat, 1981: 112). How accurate was this observation? Certainly the new ministries and agencies created by the Nazis, such as the Reich Ministry for Information and Todt's Inspectorate for the German Highway System, were given powers on a national basis, while in 1935 a national Ministry of Justice was set up in Berlin. The Prussian Ministries of the Interior, Economics, Agriculture and Labour were amalgamated in 1934 with the corresponding Reich departments, which led paradoxically to the Prussification of the Reich as hundreds of former Prussian civil servants transferred to the new ministries. Frick had hoped to gain Hitler's acceptance for transferring the powers of the *Länder* governments to the Reich Governors, but at that point Hitler began to back away from a logical centralised administrative system and in the 'Second Law concerning the Reich Governors' in January 1935 conceded only the 'possibility' that the posts of Reich Governors and **Ministerpräsidenten** might be amalgamated. The last major constitutional reform was the municipal code of 30 January 1935, whereby local mayors were given dictatorial powers and appointed by the state from a list supplied by the party. Finally, in March 1935, Hitler abruptly announced that 'all written or spoken public discussion of the reform of the Reich, particularly of questions concerning territorial reorganization, must cease' (Broszat, 1981: 117). He was partly taking note of the rivalries and jealousies of the *Gauleiter*, who in their roles as Reich Governors tenaciously defended the traditional boundaries of the *Länder* and had become 'renaissance-like Gauprinces' (Peterson, 1969: 103). Once Röhm had been eliminated, and with him the threat of a second revolution, Hitler had no wish to strengthen the bureaucratic reach of the Ministry of the Interior.

Ministerpräsident The head of a state government in the German states. Invariably these officials, even when they were Nazis, resented the power and the claims of the newly appointed Reich Governors, who were usually the senior local *Gauleiter*. Party–state relations at this level were therefore in a state of permanent conflict.

THE CIVIL SERVICE

The incoming Nazi regime had conflicting attitudes towards the civil service. On the one hand, to many of the Nazi veterans, like Röhm, the civil service with its bureaucratic traditions of orderly government was an object of deep mistrust. On the other hand, Frick envisaged an authoritarian National Socialist state run by an elite 'Führer civil service' (Broszat, 1981: 257). In the short term, his view seemed to prevail, and was, indeed, reinforced by the inefficiencies of many Nazi functionaries who were given administrative posts in early 1933. The Law for the Restoration of the Civil Service of 7 April 1933 confirmed the principle of a professionally trained civil service. It purged the service of Jews (with the exception, until 1935, of those who had fought in the First World War), Communists, Social Democrats and other known opponents of the Nazis. This purge of a mere 2 per cent of the 1,500,000 civil servants in the Reich enabled it to escape for the time being a more radical restructuring.

With the ending of the independence of the *Länder*, Frick was anxious to draw up a new uniform civil service code for the whole Reich. It was completed in 1934 but its publication was delayed until January 1937 by arguments with the party over the question of the political loyalty of the civil servants. Again, for the most part, the civil service managed to defend its independence. Attempts by Hess to insist that all civil servants needed to complete a course on National Socialism were defeated and the hierarchic principle of the civil servants' obedience to their office superiors was preserved. Nevertheless, it was made clear in Article 71 that a civil servant could be prematurely retired if 'he can no longer be relied upon to support the National Socialist state at all times' (Broszat, 1981: 252). Finally, in February 1939, party membership became an essential condition for any new entrant to the civil service. The civil service survived intact until the end of the Third Reich, but increasingly it became the object of attack from the party and was excluded in 1938–39 from playing a major role in the newly annexed and occupied areas of Austria, the Sudetenland and Bohemia (see pages 40–41).

THE PARTY

By the spring of 1933 the future role of the NSDAP was far from clear. Röhm believed, for instance, that it should create a rival centre of power outside the state, while Goebbels, Göring and many of the *Gauleiter* built up empires for themselves by accepting key positions within the state. There was also disagreement about what sort of party the NSDAP should become. Should it

cadre party Political group or party which formed a core unit for later mass expansion.

become a **cadre party**, which would supply the future leaders of the regime, or merely a large depoliticised mass movement? During the first few months after the take-over of power Hitler was determined to stop the party from exerting any influence on the government and developing into a centre of power which could challenge his own position. To that end he appointed Hess, the *Führer*'s deputy for party affairs, whose lack of a popular base in the party ensured that he would never become a challenge. From the summer of 1933 onwards, however, Hitler began to consider how the party, including the SA, could be integrated into the state. He briefly considered setting up first of all an SA Ministry and then a National Socialist Senate, comparable to the Fascist Grand Council in Italy, but in the end feared that they might challenge his own position as *Führer*. In a paradoxical statement in July 1933 he observed that the party had 'now become the state' and that all power lay with the Reich government (Noakes and Pridham, I, 1998: 171). In the Law to Ensure the Unity of Party and State of 1 December 1933 some attempt was made to regularise party–state relations: the party was declared to be 'the bearer of the concept of the German state' and to be 'inseparably linked with the state' (Noakes and Pridham, II, 1991: 233), but there was no real attempt to define what this meant in constitutional terms. As both the Deputy *Führer* and the Chief of the SA were to join the Reich Cabinet and the party was to be made a **public corporation** with the right to claim subsidies from the state, it seemed as if the party was to be firmly subordinated to the state.

> **public corporation** A corporation created to perform a governmental function or to operate under government control.

At the conference of *Gauleiter* on 2 February 1934 Hitler stated that the main task of the party was to carry out propaganda and indoctrination on behalf of the government's measures and in general 'to support the Government in every way' (Noakes and Pridham, II, 1991: 234). However, in the aftermath of the Röhm purge, most likely in an attempt to bolster the party's morale, Hitler appeared to contradict this when he told the Party Congress that '[i]t is not the state which commands us but rather we who command the state' (Noakes and Pridham, II, 1984: 236). It became clear over the following year that Hitler was in fact not going to allow the party to decline into a mere propaganda organisation. He needed it as a counterbalance to the bureaucratic state and consequently at Nuremberg in September 1935 he warned the civil service that 'whatever can be solved by the state will be solved through the state, but any problem which the state through its essential character is unable to solve will be solved by means of the movement' (Noakes and Pridham, II, 1984: 237).

In fact, however, party influence over the state remained relatively weak until 1938. Although there was a personal union of party and state at some ministries, these ministers, especially Frick at the Ministry of the Interior, vigorously defended their departments from party interference. Provided that the expressed will of the *Führer*, as far as it could be assessed, was not flouted, it was frequently possible to check the growth of party influence by a series of procedural wrangles, and it has been argued by Orlow that civil servants initially learned to see 'the party as a rival but not necessarily as an invincible one' (Orlow, II, 1973: 135).

Until 1937 it did seem that 'Party and state appeared to have settled down to an uneasy coexistence' (Orlow, II, 1973: 193). However, 1938 was a year of increasing radicalisation, which marked the beginning of a more aggressive foreign policy as well as a more intensified campaign against the Jews (see pages 75 and 84). The year also witnessed a series of key organisational changes which seriously undermined what was left of the independence of the Foreign Office and the Ministries of Defence and Economics.

In February 1938 Joachim von Ribbentrop was appointed to the Foreign Office to break the grip of the traditional diplomats. He rapidly gave the department a new 'Nazi look' (Broszat, 1981: 298) by granting honorary SS titles to senior diplomats and forcing officials to join the party. He also brought in leading members from his former 'bureau', which has been called 'the incubator of Nazi foreign policy' (Schoenbaum, 1967: 212), as 'experts'. These were to play a key role in the *Anschluss* and the declaration of an independent Slovakia in 1938–39 (pp. 86 and 88). Within the Foreign Office he set up the 'German Division', which had close contacts with the party and the SS and was later to involve the Foreign Office in racial policy in eastern Europe. The Foreign Office increasingly became divided: under Ernst von Weizsäcker, the State Secretary, the majority of the traditional diplomats still remained at their posts, but beside them grew up the new offices, staffed by Nazis, who actually carried out Ribbentrop's policies.

Even the army was unable to preserve its original position of being a 'state within a state'. In the aftermath of the 'Night of the Long Knives', Blomberg had already committed the army to taking a personal oath of loyalty to Hitler. In February 1938 its independence was irreparably damaged when Hitler, exploiting the Officer Corps' reaction to Blomberg's marriage to a former call girl and the allegations that Fritsch, the Commander-in-Chief of the army, was a homosexual, abolished the post of War Minister and took over the command of the armed forces himself. He also retired a further 16 high-ranking officers. The Defence Ministry was replaced by the newly created High Command of the German Armed Forces (OKW), which reported directly to Hitler. The army was now no longer able to prevent the expansion of the armed SS units, which Hitler sanctioned in the summer of 1938.

In November 1937 the Economics Minister, Hjalmar Schacht, resigned, as his attempts to maintain the strength of the German currency and the export capacity of German industry ran counter to Hitler's plans for rearmament and the greatest possible self-sufficiency in raw materials (see page 50). The Ministry of Economics was then downgraded in importance to being just the 'Executive Organ of the Commissioner for the Four Year Plan' (Broszat, 1981: 301) by Göring, who had already turned the organisation of the Four Year Plan into a super-ministry that could dictate policy to the Ministries of Economics, Agriculture, Labour and Transport.

The *Anschluss* of Austria and the annexation of the Sudetenland also increased the power and influence of the party. In Austria, the Nazis seized power effectively by conquest and therefore did not have to make the

Anschluss The incorporation of Austria into Germany, which had been the aim of many Germans and Austrians since 1918. It was, however, prohibited by Article 80 of the Treaty of Versailles. Italy was particularly hostile to the prospect of an *Anschluss*, but after the rupture with Britain and France caused by his conquest of Abyssinia, Mussolini abandoned his opposition and accepted the *fait accompli* of the *Anschluss* on 13 March 1938.

concessions to the old elites that had been necessary within Germany in 1933. Consequently, Josef Bürckel, the former *Gauleiter* of the Palatinate, whom Hitler appointed Commissioner for the reunification of Austria with the German Reich, was able to divide Austria into seven *Gaue* without any interference from the traditional authorities. Six months later a similar policy was implemented in the Sudetenland. The increased stature of the party in both areas had a knock-on effect within the old Reich and gave the party a new lease of life. The Office of Deputy *Führer* interfered more vigorously in Church affairs and judicial reform, and pressed for more vigorous measures to be taken against the Jews.

THE ROLE OF HITLER

The only arbiter between the mass of conflicting agencies which composed the Third Reich was Hitler himself. In theory, Hitler was all-powerful. He combined in his position as *Führer* 'the functions of supreme legislator, supreme administrator and supreme judge', and was also 'the leader of the Party, the Army and the People' (Neumann, 1942: 74). There was no effective institution, not even a Supreme Council of the Nazi Party, which could depose him in an emergency. The Cabinet met only rarely after 1934, the *Reichstag* was reduced to the role of a rubber stamp and the post of the Presidency was combined with the Chancellorship. Yet Hitler did not play a prominent part in day-to-day government. Peterson has described him as a 'remote umpire handing down decisions from on high' (Peterson, 1969: 4), when his subordinates could not agree among themselves, and was surprised by the paucity of documents that bear his signature.

Hitler hated paper work and delegated as much of it as possible to his subordinates. He disliked the mental effort required to come to a decision and usually preferred to let events take their course rather than intervene [**Doc. 12, p. 154**]. He often made little more than vague declarations of intent, which were almost impossible to translate precisely into clear laws and unambiguous directives. Consequently, one of the main problems for his ministers was to obtain decisions from him, especially when he was in his remote chalet in the Berghof. Carl Schmitt, a leading constitutional lawyer, and the diplomat Ernst von Weizsäcker recalled after the war that

> Ministers . . . might for months on end and even for years, have no opportunity of speaking to Hitler. . . . Ministerial skill consisted in making the most of a favourable hour or minute when Hitler made a decision, this often taking the form of a remark thrown out casually, which then went its way as an order of the *Führer* (Noakes and Pridham, II, 1984: 197).

Because of this lack of clarity officials on the ground often had little option but to interpret Hitler's vague and elastic decisions themselves. Consequently, leading Nazis and government departments vied with each other to provide their own interpretation, often coming to diametrically opposed conclusions (see page 75). Werner Willikens, the State Secretary in the Prussian Agriculture Ministry, called this process of interpreting Hitler's will 'working towards the *Führer*' [**Doc. 13, p. 155**].

While there is a consensus among historians that the administration of the Third Reich was a chaotic system of rival and overlapping areas of responsibility, opinions differ sharply on the reasons for this. The intentionalists, or those who believe that Hitler's aims or intentions should be taken seriously, such as Bracher (1973), Hildebrand (1991) and Jackel (1984), stress that Hitler deliberately encouraged rivalry among his supporters to safeguard his own position, while the structuralists, such as Broszat and Mommsen, argue that the administrative chaos was rather the inevitable consequence of Hitler's unstable, charismatic rule (Kershaw, 1993).

This chaos at the heart of the Nazi regime can give an impression of weakness. Neumann, writing as far back as 1942, was convinced that Hitler's policies were compromises dictated by the big four power blocs in the Third Reich: the army, the party, the bureaucracy and big business. He called the Third Reich a Behemoth or 'a nonstate, a chaos, a situation of lawlessness, disorder and anarchy' (Neumann, 1942: 375). Hans Mommsen came to the much-quoted conclusion that Hitler was 'reluctant to take decisions, often uncertain, concerned only to maintain his own prestige and personal authority, and strongly subject to the influence of his environment – in fact, in many ways, a weak dictator' (Hildebrand, 1991: 137).

Was Hitler really so weak? There is little evidence that Hitler wanted to be involved in the day-to-day domestic policy. Indeed, his charismatic system depended on his very aloofness from such matters (see page 68). In some ways, as Peterson has argued, he could be compared to a feudal monarch who mediated between the claims of his rival barons, all of whom had sworn complete loyalty to him (Peterson, 1969). As with all politicians, there were very definite limits to Hitler's powers. He was, for instance, particularly subject to pressure from the party rank and file on his policies for solving the Jewish 'problem' (see pages 73–75), and there were certain intractable economic difficulties, such as the recurring balance of payments deficits, which defied easy solutions. Yet Hitler was no weak dictator. In a negative sense he did control Germany, in that he had broken most potential centres of opposition to his regime. In those areas of policy in which he was interested, particularly foreign policy (see Chapters 8 and 9) and rearmament (see Chapter 5), he was also able effectively – at least in the short term – to implement his policies. Perhaps his weakness, if it can be described as such, depended rather on the inherent instability of the regime he had created.

5

The economy, 1933–39

The Hitler government faced massive economic problems in January 1933: the German economy was virtually bankrupt, with an official unemployment rate of well over 6 million which was in reality nearer 8 or 9 million [**Doc. 15, p. 156**]. Industrial production had in the meantime fallen to the levels of the 1890s, while the volume of German trade was halved. The devaluation of the dollar and the pound added to Germany's woes by effectively pricing Germany out of the markets of the British Empire and the United States. In his first broadcast to the German people Hitler had promised a Four Year Plan to help the peasantry and to overcome unemployment. He also went out of his way to stress that he would not devalue the *Reichsmark* (RM) and so risk inflation and weakening the German currency. Although, in the short term it was vital to reduce unemployment and avoid the risk of further social unrest, it was rearmament that was the real priority. He informed the Cabinet committee on work creation on 9 February that 'the future of Germany depends exclusively and alone on rebuilding the armed forces'. As Adam Tooze has shown, Hitler consistently argued that sustainable economic recovery could not occur until Germany was in a position to conquer new *Lebensraum*. Otherwise Germany would remain at best 'a medium-sized workshop economy, entirely dependent on imported food' and the goodwill of Britain, France and the USA, which all too easily could be withdrawn (Tooze, 2006: 169).

WORK CREATION AND ECONOMIC RECOVERY, 1933–35

By the winter of 1932–33 there were tentative signs that the worst of the Depression was over. Industrial production was beginning to increase, while from January onwards the number of registered unemployed slowly declined. To create work, Hitler's government was ready to apply on a far greater scale many of the policies used by Papen and Schleicher, who had attempted to channel government spending into creating employment, while rigorously controlling prices and wages. The Nazis pursued, as a Labour Ministry memorandum observed in December 1934, 'a multitude of inter-related measures' to create work and rebuild the German economy (Overy, 1995: 5). Rearmament, traditionally seen as 'kick starting' the German economic recovery, was only one of the reasons why Germany recovered so fast after 1932.

On 1 June 1933 the Law for Reducing Unemployment unveiled by Fritz Reinhardt, Secretary of State at the Finance Ministry, made a billion *Reichsmarks* available for public-works schemes such as road- and canal-building and the repairs of bridges. It had most impact on the rural areas. In East Prussia, for instance, more that a hundred thousand men and women were put to work bringing wasteland back into cultivation and building homesteads. The labourers were paid in kind by tokens which could be exchanged for food and goods at specially designated shops, while companies carrying out this work were paid by work-creation bills which were cashed by a group of state-affiliated banks.

By September 1933 unemployment had fallen nationally to below four million (**Doc. 15, p. 156**), but the Reich Labour Ministry feared that the onset of winter as in 1932 would see a sharp increase in unemployment. To combat this a second Reinhardt Programme was launched which made available some 500 million *Reichsmarks* to subsidise building repair and a further 300 million to encourage house construction.

Strenuous efforts were made to remove as many young people as possible from the labour market. In 1933–34 nearly half a million unemployed young people joined the Voluntary Labour Service, which had been founded by Brüning, and the new labour schemes such as the Land Service set up by the Nazis. At the same time the government reduced the length of the working week in order to spread work opportunities more widely and attempted to squeeze women out of the labour market through such devices as the marriage loan. This was offered to newly married couples as long as the woman gave up her job and stayed at home, unless her husband's monthly pay fell below 125 *Reichsmarks* (see pages 61–2).

Reichsbank The German central bank, which was responsible for currency issue. Hitler re-appointed Schacht to its Presidency in March 1933 where he developed the means for financing rearmament through the *Mefo* bills.

To be effective these measures had to be accompanied by a revival in business confidence. This had already started in 1932 when the Reich's credit structure was stabilised and tax rebates were introduced to help potential growth industries. Hitler promised businessmen that there would be no 'wild experiments' and stressed that 'the economy must be treated with extraordinary cautiousness' (Overy, 1995: 56). Hjalmar Schacht, the **Reichsbank** president, was put in charge of a newly created commission to ensure that job-creation schemes did not result in inflation. In this he was helped by the destruction of the unions and the introduction of controls, which fixed wage rates at their lowest level in 1932 [**Doc. 27(A), p. 165**].

Increased industrial activity was further encouraged by government subsidies for house construction and the renovation of dilapidated buildings. The motor industry too was assisted by a series of wide-ranging tax concessions. Fuel tax was abolished, which reduced the costs of running a car by 15 per cent, and firms were allowed to claim tax allowances when new vehicles were purchased. Not surprisingly, car sales improved dramatically in 1933 and doubled again in 1934. The effects of this rippled through the economy and increased employment in the components industries. Overy has argued that '[i]f there is a single industrial sector that helped to drag the German industrial economy out of recession during 1933 and 1934 the motor industry has a good claim' (Overy, 1995: 63). In 1934 its expansion was further encouraged by the *Autobahn* programme for the construction of 7,000 kilometres of motorway, which, besides appealing to the national imagination and providing employment, also stimulated a wide range of subsidiary industries.

Thanks to these measures, unemployment declined steadily until the summer of 1934, when for the next 12 months it stabilised at 2.5 million and was only brought down to 1.7 million in the autumn of 1935 by the introduction of military conscription and increasing investment in rearmament. With the introduction of the Four Year Plan and the move to a much more ambitious rearmament programme in 1936 its decline accelerated, until in 1938 full employment was achieved [**Doc. 15, p. 156**].

AGRICULTURE

The urgency of the unemployment problem was only rivalled by the plight of the peasantry, who made up 29 per cent of the working population. By 1932 German agriculture was in a desperate situation. The government's tariff policy discriminated against the farmers in favour of the urban population. It placed high import duties on fodder and feeds for animals, but tolerated a flood of cheap imports of dairy products and processed foods from Holland and the Scandinavian countries in order to keep down the price of food for the industrial workers. Peasants were caught between the 'scissors' movement of high prices for industrial goods and low prices for their agricultural produce and inevitably many were driven into bankruptcy. Between 1927 and 1932 the number defaulting on their debts and suffering foreclosure rose from 2,554 to 6,200. In January 1933 the Reich Agrarian League attacked the 'pillaging of agriculture' and claimed that its decline had reached levels 'which were not even deemed possible under a Marxist Government' (Hiden, 1996: 158). As initial measures of relief, Alfred Hugenberg, who was initially both Minister for Economics and Food, placed a moratorium on peasants' debts until the end of October 1933, increased tariffs on selected imported foodstuffs, and helped dairy farmers by ordering the compulsory addition of butter to margarine. He also established a central purchasing agency which guaranteed minimum prices to all food producers.

In June 1933 he was succeeded by Darré, the Director of the Nazi Party's Food Organization. Driven by the belief that the very future of the Germanic race was dependent on a prosperous agriculture, he radically reorganised German agriculture in the autumn by setting up the Reich Food Estate and introducing the Reich Entailed Farm Law. The law for establishing the Reich Food Estate was announced on 13 September. The estate was an independent **corporate body** which was responsible for all aspects of food production, and farmers, farm cooperatives and agricultural wholesale dealers were compelled to join it. Through a series of marketing and supervisory boards it controlled crop prices and its staff office was entrusted with the future planning of German agriculture. Altogether it controlled 6 million independent producers and 40 per cent of the total German workforce, and was 'the largest building block of the German economy' (Tooze, 2007: 188). After an initial honeymoon period its interventionist and bureaucratic policies became extremely unpopular with the peasantry.

Of all the economic policies introduced by Hitler in the early period of his government the Reich Entailed Farm Law of 29 September 1933 'was the measure marked most distinctively by specifically Nazi ideology' (Tooze, 2006: 184). It sought to retain 'the peasantry as the blood-spring of the German nation' and gave the small farmer security of tenure by ruling that farms between 7.5 and 125 hectares were both indivisible and inalienable. They were to remain the permanent property of the original peasant owners and consequently could not even be offered as **collateral** against a loan. However, the peasant had to be of 'German or similar blood' (Farquharson, 1976: 110) and to be both efficient at his job and 'honourable'. In the event of any doubt about either of these qualities, a special court could dispossess him in favour of his heir. Although the law only applied to about 35 per cent of the agricultural land in Germany, it was a reactionary measure which attempted to fix the German peasantry 'like a fly in amber at the current stage of its development' (Farquharson, 1976: 69). It hindered intentionally the development of large-scale modern farming units and thus militated against achieving the very self-sufficiency for which the government was aiming. Darré did not hesitate to stress that there was no room for 'grain factories in Germany' as the overriding issues in the Third Reich were blood and race.

corporate body A body such as a company which has its own legal identity.

collateral Pledge made by a borrower of specific property to a lender, to secure repayment of a loan. The collateral serves as protection for a lender against a borrower's default.

The Hugenberg–Darré reforms in the short term restored the confidence of both the great estate owners in the east as well as the peasantry. The combination of protection from foreign competition, tax cuts and favourable interest rates initially encouraged greater profits and output. In 1938–39 productivity was 25 per cent higher than a decade earlier and Germany was 83 per cent self-sufficient, although there was still a serious shortfall in fats. From the summer of 1935 onwards, however, price controls on food began to operate against the farmers as they were prevented by the Reich Food Estate from benefiting from food shortages. It was no surprise then that the peasantry incessantly grumbled about low prices and ceaseless administrative interference.

THE *MITTELSTAND*

No major aid package was devoted to the *Mittelstand*, although initially Hitler could not avoid making some concessions in its direction. In May 1933, for example, the Law for the Protection of the Retail Trade forbade any extension of the much-hated department stores [**Doc. 3, p. 148**], and two months later further ordinances prohibited them from offering a whole range of services, such as baking, haircutting and shoe-repairing, which now became the monopoly of the small corner shop. Yet, significantly, the government could not afford to close the department stores down, and in July 1933 it loaned over 14 million RM to the Jewish-owned Herman Tietz Stores in a successful attempt to prevent their collapse, which would then have thrown thousands out of work. However, the loan was conditional on the resignation of the company's Jewish owners, and the stores were renamed Hertie to signify that they were no longer owned by Jews.

Hitler had little interest in implementing the radical *Mittelstand* socialism of the party programme, as he needed the expertise of big business and the bankers to plan rearmament and to help bring down unemployment, while simultaneously avoiding a financial crash [**Doc. 9, p. 153**]. In June 1933 the 'fighting organizations of the industrial middle classes' were dissolved and their members absorbed into the newly created Estate for Handicraft and Trade, which in its turn was reduced by Schacht, when he became Economics Minister, 'to the status of a mere organization under the control of big business' (Schweitzer, 1964: 146). In open contradiction to the original Nazi programme [**Doc. 3. p. 147**], the years 1933–36 saw the steady growth of cartels and the influence of big business over the economy. Between July 1933 and December 1936, for example, over 1,600 new cartel arrangements were signed.

SCHACHT AND THE FINANCING OF GERMAN REARMAMENT

Despite the initial priority Hitler gave to job-creation projects in 1933, he never lost sight of his intention to rearm Germany as quickly as possible. He thus needed both to save **foreign exchange** to pay for imported raw materials and to raise the necessary money within Germany to finance rearmament. On 16 May 1933 Hitler prepared the way for a more flexible policy by replacing the President of the *Reichsbank*, the orthodox financier Luther, with Hjalmar Schacht, whose first task was to control the outflow of foreign exchange. In June 1933 Schacht announced that German debts incurred to foreign creditors before July 1931 were now to be paid only in *Reichsmarks*, although for the time being repayments in foreign currencies of the loans which had been raised abroad under the Dawes and Young Plans continued, but in 1934 they, too, were stopped.

Schacht expanded schemes for **deficit financing**, which had only been tentatively experimented with by his predecessors, and introduced new methods for financing rearmament. Government procurement agencies paid industries awarded with military contracts credit notes, or '*Mefo* bills', which were issued by a 'dummy organisation' of four large private companies and two government ministries disguised as the *Metall-Forschungs AG* (Metal Research Co – abbreviated to *Mefo*), the debts of which were underwritten by the government. The *Reichsbank* was ready to exchange *Mefo* bills for cash, thereby ensuring the prompt payment of companies. As they were valid for a period of up to five years, the government also tapped a considerable amount of money that was lying idle by offering them, rather as if they were bonds, at 4 per cent per annum on the money market as an investment and by compelling both commercial and private savings banks to invest 30 per cent of their deposits in them.

The pace of German rearmament was bedevilled by recurring balance of payments and foreign-exchange crises. Work-creation projects, rearmament and the growing recovery of the domestic economy resulted in a steep rise in imports. At the same time Germany found it particularly hard to increase its exports, since Schacht refused to devalue the *Reichsmark*, and most other countries had raised their tariffs. By May 1934 export earnings were some 20 per cent lower than they had been 12 months earlier. This in turn led to an acute shortage of foreign currency which was vital to pay for imports. By June 1934 the *Reichsbank*'s currency holdings were reduced to less than 100 million *Reichsmarks*, which was scarcely enough to finance a week's imports, even at minimal levels.

Adam Tooze argues that between 'March and September 1934 the Nazi regime suffered the closest thing to a comprehensive socio-economic crisis in

foreign exchange Foreign-currency holdings in the Reich

deficit financing When the expenditure of a government is greater than its tax revenues, a deficit in the government budget is created. In a depression an increase in government expenditure can help revive the economy.

its entire twelve year history' (Tooze, 2007: 69). The Third Reich stood at an economic crossroads. It could accelerate rearmament at the cost of the rest of the economy by controlling imports and establishing a command economy or apply the breaks, devalue the *Reichsmark* to facilitate exports and either impose a programme of rigorous discipline, as the Reich Finance Ministry urged or, as Schmitt, the Economics Minister, advised, raise consumer demand by cutting social-insurance contributions and the subscriptions to the German Labour Front. Both options were dismissed by Hitler, the generals and Schacht, and Schmitt was forced to resign after collapsing from a heart attack during a speech.

In July Schacht was appointed Economics Minister and given full dictatorial powers in the economic sphere. In September 1934 he introduced the New Plan, which set up the necessary controls for the government regulation of imports and currency exchange. These effectively controlled the access of German firms to vital raw materials. A series of business groups was set up to act as a channel between individual firms and the Reich Economic Ministry. By the end of the 1930s some 18,000 officials were employed in the currency-control section alone.

Schacht also saved vital foreign exchange by negotiating a series of bilateral trade agreements, mainly with the Balkan and South American states. German purchases in these countries were paid for in German currency which could only then be used to buy German goods or to invest in the construction of plants which would later produce goods required for the German economy. Nothing was imported into Germany that could be produced domestically, which effectively ensured that foreign-manufactured goods were excluded from the German market.

THE FOUR YEAR PLAN

Although Schacht was one of the key architects of German rearmament, he had planned its expansion within strict limits, but by the winter of 1935–36 the army's demand for weapons and raw materials were already breaking through this ceiling. For 1936, for instance, the **Wehrmacht** was demanding almost twice as much oil, rubber, metal and iron ore as it had been allocated in 1935. The pressure of foreign-currency reserves was also intensified by Darré's emergency request to import large quantities of butter, vegetable oil and fodder. Schacht rejected this, arguing instead that rationing should be introduced, but with Hitler's consent he was overruled by Göring, who feared the public's reaction to rationing. In December 1935 Schacht informed Blomberg that there was now not enough currency to pay for the doubling

Wehrmacht In 1919 the German army was reduced to 100,000 men. Hitler rebuilt and expanded the armed forces, and in March 1935 he reintroduced conscription. The *Reichswehr* changed its name to *Wehrmacht*, a term which also included the navy and air force. From February 1938 onwards Hitler took over the ultimate command of the *Wehrmacht*. In December 1941 he appointed himself Commander-in-Chief of the army and assumed responsibility for military operations.

of copper imports needed urgently for the rearmament programme. He argued that the only way to pay for rearmament was to increase the volume of exports – a solution which met with support from commerce and the more export-orientated coal, iron and steel industries.

Hitler was not prepared to allow economic arguments to slow down the rearmament programme. In April 1936 he began to by-pass Schacht by appointing Göring Commissioner of Raw Materials and Currency. As a temporary measure to pay for imports Göring ordered all foreign assets to be seized. He then commissioned Carl Goerdeler, the former Price Commissioner, to weigh up the economic options facing the Reich. Goerdeler advocated devaluation and liberalisation of foreign-exchange movements, which would then enable Germany to export more freely to the British Empire and the USA. In effect he advocated the return of Germany to the world economy. A precondition of this, however, was to control the rate of military expansion. Göring dismissed the memorandum as 'cheek' and 'nonsense' (Tooze, 2007: 219), but in the final analysis only Hitler could decide on the future tempo of German rearmament.

In August, in a memorandum which is 'one of the basic documents of the Third Reich' (Noakes and Pridham, II, 1984: 280) [**Doc. 16, p. 156**], Hitler ignored Goerdeler's advice and introduced the Four Year Plan, for the implementation of which Göring was again made responsible in October 1936. Its ostensible aim was to make Germany as independent as possible of both industrial and agricultural imports, either by increasing production or by inventing substitutes. Within four years both the German economy and the army were to be ready for war. The key to the Four Year Plan was to increase production in synthetic rubber, fuel oil and iron ore. To administer the plan, Göring set up six offices with special responsibilities for the production of raw materials, their distribution, the labour force, agriculture, price control and foreign exchange. During the winter of 1936–37 he was successfully able to prise responsibility for the economy and rearmament away from the Ministry of Economics and the army. Schacht was forced to resign as Economics Minister in November 1937 (see page 40). The Four Year Plan marked, as Overy has put it, 'the point at which the armed forces' conception of recovery of defensive strength gave way to Hitler's conception of large-scale preparations for aggressive imperialism over which the armed forces were to have less and less say' (Overy, 1995: 186)

The most immediate problem facing Göring and the bureaucrats of the Four Year Plan in the autumn of 1936 was the shortage of steel. In the short term there was no alternative but to impose steel rationing and to freeze army procurement at 1936 levels. Only in November 1937 after a meeting with the senior members of the armed forces with Hitler, were these restrictions removed. Göring hoped that the steel shortage would eventually be solved by mining the extensive low-grade German iron ore deposits at Salzgitter, but this was opposed by the Ruhr iron and steel magnates since it was much cheaper to import high-grade ores from Sweden and it made more sense to rationalise and use existing plants. In July 1937 Göring summoned the representatives of the German steel industry to Berlin and announced the nationalisation of German iron ore deposits and the construction of the huge state-owned steel plant at Salzgitter, the *Reichswerke* Hermann Göring. The *Reichswerke* expanded steadily and began to absorb smaller concerns like the *Rheinmetall-Borsig* armaments firm. It also took over the major Austrian iron, steel and machinery firms after the *Anschluss* (see page 84) and, six months later, the Skoda works in the Sudetenland. By the early 1940s it had become one of the largest industrial conglomerates in the world.

THE INDUSTRIALISTS AND THE FOUR YEAR PLAN: WINNERS AND LOSERS

Robert Brady, writing in 1937, described the Nazi regime in orthodox Marxist terms, as the dictatorship of monopoly capitalism (Brady, 1937). Up to June 1934, big business appeared to exert considerable influence over the regime, as the defeat of the Nazi radicals and the appointment of Schacht seemed to show, but it never dominated the state. It arguably became a partner of the state and army in rearmament, but as Schweitzer pointed out, the price it had to pay for the profits of this partnership was obedience to the market regulations imposed by the government (Schweitzer, 1964). The introduction of the Four Year Plan emphasised that capitalism could only continue to thrive in Germany provided it was ready to subordinate itself to the Nazi government. The chemical industry welcomed the plan and subsequently prospered, whereas the steel industry was more critical. Both Schacht and the heavy industrialists in the Ruhr saw the construction of the *Reichswerke* as a challenge to private enterprise, but Göring was not deterred. In protest at the growing state intervention in private industry Fritz Thyssen, one of the leading Ruhr industrialists, left Germany. He later remarked that '[s]oon Germany will not be any different from Bolshevik Russia . . . the heads of enterprises who do not fulfil the conditions which the Plan sub-scribes will be accused of treason and shot' (Overy, 1995: 110).

This was certainly an exaggeration. Hitler had no intention of expropriat-ing private industry as long as it was useful to him. Indeed, while the Four Year Plan enormously increased the potential of the state, it also strengthened the tendencies towards the concentration of monopoly power by such firms as IG Farben, the large chemical combine. Even state-owned plants like the

Hermann Göring Steelworks were organised along traditional capitalist lines and raised capital by selling some of their shares on the open market. Big business remained a partner of the Nazi regime, but it was a partnership that could be terminated by the Nazi Party in the event of a clash of interests.

REARMAMENT AND THE GERMAN ECONOMY, 1937–39

In 1959 the American historian Burton Klein, basing his views on statistics produced by the United States Strategic Bombing Survey in September 1945, argued persuasively that the 'scale of Germany's economic mobilization for war was quite modest' and pointed out that the production of consumer goods increased by over 30 per cent between 1936 and 1939 (Klein, 1959: 78). Klein's interpretation was seized upon by A.J.P. Taylor to support his arguments that Hitler had no plans for war (Taylor, 1961b), while Alan Milward argued that he was planning a series of brief *Blitzkriege* that would not strain the economy (Milward, 1965). However, both these arguments play down the fact that by 1938 17 per cent of Germany's gross national product was spent on rearmament, which was a sum far greater than any other European power was spending on armaments [**Doc. 18, p. 159**]. Richard Overy has challenged Klein's conclusions and shown that the Four Year Plan really was 'a decisive step towards preparing Germany for total mobilization' (Overy, 1995: 185), which also severely cut investment in the consumer industries. It provided the economic substructure for the later expansion of the armaments industries. Overall, according to Overy, 'consumption as a share of national income declined from 71 per cent in 1928 to 58 per cent in 1938' (Overy, 1995: 192), and between 1936 and 1939 armaments and preparations for war absorbed over 60 per cent of all capital investments made. Consumer industries came right at the bottom of priorities in allocating raw materials. In the summer of 1938 further plans were drawn up for creating a fleet of 16,000 fighter planes, while in January 1939 an ambitious naval building programme involving six battleships, four aircraft carriers, eight heavy cruisers and 233 submarines was drawn up. Obviously Hitler hoped for a brief war, as he told his generals in May 1939, but he simultaneously stressed that 'the government must . . . also prepare for a war of from ten to fifteen years duration' (Overy, 1995: 190).

Inevitably, rearmament at this pace created economic problems. There were production bottlenecks, red tape and competing claims from the armed services, as well as labour shortages and difficulties in raising foreign exchange to pay for the imported materials that were still needed [**Doc. 17, p. 158**]. It

Blitzkrieg Literally, a lightning war, which would, in Hitler's words, 'defeat the enemy as quick as lightning'. These tactics had been first practised by the *Reichswehr* in the 1920s in western Russia, where the Soviet government had allowed it to organise manoeuvres which could not be monitored by Anglo-French officials. Later, economic historians came to see the *Blitzkrieg* as a means for waging war without making massive demands on the German population. In fact, while Hitler clearly welcomed quick victories, Germany was being prepared for a long war of 10–15 years.

also became clear by 1938 that in the production of steel, synthetic fuel and gunpowder the Four Year Plan was way behind schedule. A new version of the Four Year Plan was approved by Göring. To remedy the shortfall in high-explosive production a temporary emergency programme, the *Schnell Plan* (named after Colonel von Schnell), was launched to ensure that the output levels of 1918 were achieved by the end of December 1939. Inevitably the accelerated tempo of rearmament created growing inflationary pressures. Between September 1937 and 1939 the volume of money in circulation had doubled. When Schacht warned of the dangers inherent in this, he was dismissed from his post as *Reichsbank* president and in June 1939 the statutes of the bank were revised to allow the expansion of the money supply. 'The path was now cleared for unfettered military spending' (Tooze, 2007: 299).

The seriousness of the economic problems caused by rearmament and their consequences for German policy are disputed by historians. Tim Mason, for instance, argued that a deteriorating trade balance, a financial crisis and labour shortages were producing irreconcilable 'domestic pressures and constraints', which were causing 'acute social and political tension' (Mason, 1981: 39). Consequently in a desperate effort to keep the lid on the simmering crisis in Germany, Hitler embarked on what he hoped would be a brief victorious war of plunder against Poland (see pages 89–91) which would enable him to maintain living standards and allow further rearmament.

This apocalyptic view of the German economic crisis is not shared by one of the leading economic historians of the Third Reich, Richard Overy. He argues on the contrary that while in the medium term the German economy did face economic problems, if anything, the situation in the summer of 1939 was more under control than it had been a few months earlier. Walther Funk, Schacht's successor at the Economics Ministry, had produced the New Finance Plan for financing rearmament over the next three years, which proposed that all firms working on state contracts would receive 40 per cent of their payments in tax certificates (not unlike the *Mefo* bills of five years earlier), a proportion of which could only be cashed after 37 months. Similarly, labour shortages were being alleviated by recruiting foreign workers from southern and central Europe, as well as the introduction of labour conscription in Germany and large-scale retraining programmes. By 1939 the German economy was the second strongest in the world and much less vulnerable to world pressure than either the French or British economies. Overy trenchantly argues that '"crisis" is an inappropriate characterization of the German economy in the months before the war' (Overy, 1995: 223).

Adam Tooze, too, argues, that while the pace of German rearmament was frequently interrupted by raw material and currency shortages and certainly did not reach Hitler's over-ambitious targets, 'in 1939 there was no crisis in the Third Reich, either political or economic' since 'the means of coercion and control developed since the near crisis of 1934 (see pages 28–32) were too effective for that' (Tooze, 2007: 321–22). Yet, at the very least, as Tooze himself has so graphically shown, there were some worrying inflationary trends and growing tension between the demands of the rearmament programme and the availability of resources. It was, however, the diplomatic rather than economic situation that determined the timing of the war in 1939, but, nevertheless as Kershaw has pointed out, 'the mounting economic problems fed into the military and strategic pressures for expansion' (Kershaw, II, 2000: 163).

6

The People's Community: German society and the Third Reich, 1933–39

The Nazi concept of the **Volksgemeinschaft**, or 'People's Community', drew on the 'spirit of 1914', which had momentarily unified all classes behind the German government at the beginning of the First World War (see page 11). It appealed to those nostalgically longing for national unity after the divisive years of the Weimar Republic and was part of the attractiveness of Nazism for so many German voters in the period 1930–33 [**Doc. 6, p. 151**]. For Hitler, the task of the *Volksgemeinschaft* was to create nothing less than a new social order. Unlike liberalism with its emphasis on the individual and Marxism with its call for class war, the *Volksgemeinschaft* would unify the Germans in the service of the nation and was primarily a way of mobilising the population for war and turning it into a 'fighting community'. Through propaganda, masterminded at every level by Goebbels' Reich Ministry of Popular Enlightenment and Propaganda, a new mentality and ethos was to be inculcated into the German population [**Doc. 8, p. 152**]. At the heart of these new ideas lay the Nazi and Social Darwinist doctrines of racial purity and perpetual struggle. Only the racially 'pure', the hereditarily healthy, the industrious and ideologically reliable could be members of the *Volksgemeinschaft*.

Volksgemeinschaft
Literally, 'People's Community'. This was to be brought about by unifying the population primarily on the basis of nationalism. Hitler believed that fusing nationalism with some elements of socialism would end class conflict and enable him to create a new national community based on race.

THE WORK OF THE REICH MINISTRY OF POPULAR ENLIGHTENMENT AND PROPAGANDA

The main responsibility for fostering the spirit of the *Volksgemeinschaft* lay with Goebbels, who was appointed head of the Propaganda Ministry when it was created on 13 March 1933 [**Doc. 8, p. 152**]. His mission was 'to transform the very spirit itself to the extent that people and things are brought into a new relationship with one another' (Noakes and Pridham, II, 1984: 397). To achieve this Goebbels set up within the ministry departments covering propaganda, the press, film, theatre and 'popular enlightenment'. Both Hitler and Goebbels grasped the potential of the radio for influencing public opinion. In April 1934 regional radio stations were taken away from the control of the *Länder* and formed into the Reich Radio Company, whose director had close links with Goebbels, while the news programmes were subordinated to the ministry's press department. The government did all it could to encourage radio ownership. Millions of cheap radios were produced and special local radio wardens were appointed to encourage *Volksgenossen* (national comrades) to buy them and to listen to programmes. They were constructed with a limited range so that they would be unable to pick up programmes beyond the Reich borders.

Similar care was taken over the written word. All socialist and Communist papers were rapidly closed down and the remaining newspapers were controlled by the Reich Press Chamber, directed by the Nazi publisher Max Amann. In October 1933 the Editors' Law ensured that editors became puppets whose task was accurately to record the views and opinions of the regime in their newspapers. In April 1935 papers were forbidden to appeal to any 'confessional, vocational or special interest groups', and corporate businesses were banned from purchasing newspaper titles for commercial reasons (Noakes and Pridham, II, 1984: 391).

The Propaganda Ministry also laid down strict guidelines for the arts. They were, as it declared in the Theatre Law of 15 May 1934, a 'public exercise' subject to 'police supervision' and state guidance (Noakes and Pridham, II, 1984: 397). Consequently, Goebbels ensured that the public was fed a suitable cultural diet which conformed to Nazi ideology. In music and art, for instance, experiments in modern art forms were condemned, while in literature, books on war, the 'heroic' early days of the Nazi movement, Germany's historic mission in the east and similar topics were the approved themes. Hitler, as an 'artist manqué' (Noakes and Pridham, II, 1984: 398), paid particular attention to art. He dismissed modern art as 'degenerate' and favoured instead pastoral scenes showing virile peasants or compositions depicting heroic warriors. To exhibit such works, the House of German Art was opened in Munich. All modernist art was removed from the galleries and exhibitions mocking 'degenerate art' were shown in several German cities.

Modern music was also condemned. The work of the Russian experimental composer Igor Stravinsky met with particular ridicule and hostility. Jazz, too, as an African-American art form, was condemned as degenerate and banned. Even the great German classics were subject to restrictions. For instance, in three Mozart operas the libretti had been written by Lorenza da Ponte, who was by birth Jewish. These had now to be rewritten in German translations. Felix Mendelssohn's work could still be heard but because he was Jewish his name never actually appeared on a concert programme.

In the theatre there was an attempt to create a new Nazi art form, the *Thingspiel*, which Grünberger has called 'open-air medleys of "Nazi agit-prop", military tattoo, pagan oratorio and circus performance' (Grünberger, 1974: 459). However, the most popular entertainments were those that allowed people temporarily to escape from the importunate demands of the *Volksgemeinschaft*. Goebbels recognised this when he insisted that more emphasis should be put on light music and entertainment in radio programmes. Similarly, only one-quarter of the films produced between 1933 and 1934 had a political content, although admittedly no costs were spared in their production. The rest were comedies, love stories, musicals and thrillers. On the other hand the news feature *Weekly Review* (*Wochenschau*), which was in effect a vehicle for Nazi propaganda had to be included in every Nazi programme.

EDUCATION AND YOUTH

The control of the educational system was vital for the inculcation of Nazi ideology. The traditional structure of the German educational system remained largely unchanged, even though in May 1934 it was put under the centralised control of the new Reich Education Minister, Bernhard Rust. From 1936 onwards, attempts were made to amalgamate Catholic and Protestant schools to create new 'community schools' in order to encourage national unity, and annual local referenda were held in which parents were subjected to considerable pressure to vote yes to such proposals. Only in the Rhineland were the Catholic clergy initially able to organise an effective opposition and maintain confessional education. However, the pressure continued to grow on both private and denominational schools; tax concessions were removed and civil servants and members of the armed forces were forbidden to send their children to these schools. Finally in 1938 all the remaining private or denominational elementary schools were closed, and all children between the ages of 6 and 14 were legally obliged to attend state *Grundschulen* (primary schools).

Educational syllabuses were radically revised in the light of Nazi racial, political and social prejudices. Special emphasis was placed in the school curriculum on history, biology, geography and German as the subjects which were particularly effective vehicles for Nazi propaganda [**Doc. 19, p. 160**]. 'Racial science' was introduced as a compulsory subject in September 1933. Jewish teachers were dismissed and the law 'Against the Overcrowding of German Schools and Universities', of 25 April 1933, ensured that the number of Jewish schoolchildren in any one institution did not exceed 1.5 per cent, which it was claimed was the proportion of Jews to German gentiles in the

Reich. The Jewish children who remained were often forced to sit at separate desks and were stopped from playing with 'Aryan' children during the breaks.

A key to the new priorities was given by Hitler's observation that 'the racial state must build upon its entire educational work . . . not on the pumping in of empty knowledge but on the development of healthy bodies. Only in the second place comes the training of mental facilities' (Brady, 1937: 107). Consequently, sport became a major subject, and 'games masters advanced from the periphery of the teaching body almost to the very centre' (Grünberger, 1974: 365). There was also a marked reduction in the number of girls in the grammar schools (*Gymnasien*), and those who remained were encouraged to specialise in domestic science or languages.

The universities did not outwardly change, but their courses, particularly in German and history, were brought into harmony with Nazi prejudices. Even the apparently apolitical science of physics could become metamorphosed into 'German physics', which, among other things, entailed the root-and-branch rejection of Einstein's 'Jewish' Theory of Relativity. Of course scientific research did continue but it was conducted within the framework of the Four Year Plan and devoted to armaments. The prestigious historical periodical *Historische Zeitschrift* also deemed it wise to open a special section on the Jews. As in secondary education, students were compelled to join in organised games run by the National Socialist Students' Association. Initially, the number of women students declined. In December 1933 the total number of girls at university was not to exceed 10 per cent of all the students, but full employment and the economic demands of the Four Year Plan pushed their number up, contrary to all earlier statements by the Nazi ideologues, to a record 20 per cent of the whole student population in the autumn of 1939.

The potentially most radical educational innovation introduced by the Nazis was the creation of a small number of special schools and institutions which were entrusted with the task of producing the future elite of Germany, the *Napolas* (National Political Educational Establishments), the Adolf Hitler Schools and the pseudo-medieval *Ordensburgen*. Relatively small numbers of these schools were actually set up. By December 1938, 21 *Napolas* had been founded, although a further 20 were created during the war. Only ten Adolf Hitler Schools and three *Ordensburgen* were established. The *Napolas* were given the status of grammar schools, and in 1936 fell under the control of the SS. They were intended particularly to help the rural and more impoverished sections of the population and also to offer an educational alternative in Catholic-dominated regions. Entrance to the Adolf Hitler Schools was reserved for 'outstanding' graduates of the **Deutsches Jungvolk** (see below). *Ordensburgen* were to be the party universities, and according to Robert Ley were supposed to open 'the door to political leadership to the man in the street' (Schoenbaum, 1980: 270). All these institutions, however, signally

Deutsches Jungvolk The junior section of the Hitler Youth, for boys between the ages of 10 and 14.

failed to produce a new Nazi elite, because the grammar schools and universities were still seen by the professional classes to be the best road to secure and well-paid careers.

While few chances were missed to brainwash the mass of children in school, the main responsibility for carrying out Hitler's exhortation, 'Be hard, German youth, and make yourselves hard' (Baynes, I, 1942: 547), was borne by the Nazi Youth Movement. In January 1933 only 55,000 young people belonged to it, but in July Hitler gave its leader, Baldur von Schirach, the responsibility for controlling all youth activities under the supervision of the Ministry of the Interior. By early 1934, the Hitler Youth had absorbed all other youth groups, with the single important exception of the Catholic ones, and two years later 60 per cent of all young people were members. Increasing pressure on the Catholic Church led to the dissolution of its own youth organisations in 1939, the year in which service in the Hitler Youth became compulsory. From the age of 10 to 14 boys joined the *Jungvolk* and then for the next four years the Hitler Youth itself, where they were subjected to the familiar mixture of sport, war games and indoctrination. There were parallel organisations for girls in the **Jungmädel-Bund** and the League of German Girls where, however, there was greater stress on teaching traditional female domestic skills. In Claudia Koonz's words, they 'prepared girls for a lifetime in the second sex' (Koonz, 1987: 196).

Jungmädel-Bund The junior section of the League of German Girls, for girls aged between 10 and 14.

Hitler boasted that the Nazi movement had 'sown seeds that have sunk deep' (Baynes, I, 1942: 616). In many ways, the Hitler Youth was the most successful of all the Nazi mass movements. Its activities and sense of belonging appealed to many young people. In 1935 socialist observers were shocked when they heard some young workers remark that '[t]he People's Community is better than belonging to the lower classes' (Aycoberry, 1999: 182). Similarly, Christa Wolff, who later became one of East Germany's leading authors, recalled how it meant 'the promise of a loftier life' (Koonz, 1987: 193), far removed from the cramping duties and discomforts of her home [**Doc. 20, p. 161**]. By the end of the 1930s the movement was so strong that it could withdraw children for as much as two and half days a week from school. In one Westphalian school 870 pupils lost out on nearly a month of teaching in this way in the 1937–38 academic year. It was no wonder that employers and the *Wehrmacht* began to register a decline in pupils' knowledge.

By the late 1930s the Hitler Youth had become a large bureaucratic organisation whose leaders were ageing. Also, as a result of its membership having become compulsory, it had to absorb a large number of unwilling teenagers, and inevitably, almost as many young people became bored by the tedium of drill and often badly organised games as were fired by patriotic enthusiasm. Indeed, Peukert argues that 'the second half of the 1930s reveals a growing crisis in the Hitler Youth' (Peukert, 1989: 152), which during the war years escalated into open opposition (see pages 128–29).

THE PEASANTRY

Outside the classroom and the make-believe of Hitler Youth manoeuvres Nazi dogma clashed painfully with economic reality. Nothing illustrates this more clearly than the Nazis' failure to stop the accelerating urbanisation and industrialisation of Germany, despite the fact that the peasant was seen as the backbone of society. David Schoenbaum has described support for the peasantry, together with anti-Semitism, as 'one of the few consistent premises of Nazi life' (Schoenbaum, 1967: 161), but the regime was unsuccessful in its efforts to combine rearmament with the preservation of a pre-industrial peasant class. In practice, the need to rebuild German industry after the Depression, and then to prepare for war, ensured that the interests of the rural population came second to those of the proletariat who worked in the factories. Ultimately Hitler held that the agricultural question could only be solved effectively by the conquest of *Lebensraum* in Russia.

In addition to economic assistance and the Reich Entailed Farm Law (see pages 45–47), the Nazi government attempted to protect the peasantry in a number of ways. The Reich Food Estate (see page 46) aimed to restore the peasants' self-confidence by reviving what was in most cases defunct or bogus peasant folklore and impressing on them at every opportunity their role as 'responsible carriers of German society renewing its strength from blood and soil' (Farquharson, 1976: 212). The regime also attempted to stem the migration from the countryside to the towns. During the period 1929–34 migration had all but died out as a result of the slump, but as soon as the economy began to expand, it resumed its rapid tempo. In May 1934 labour exchanges were authorised to stop land workers accepting jobs in industry, and they were liable, like escaped slaves, to be returned to their farms, although in practice this rarely happened. Legislation was in fact powerless to prevent what amounted to a mass exodus from the countryside. The rural population voted with its feet against poverty, poor housing and the back-breaking nature of unmechanised farm work. Between 1933 and 1938, for instance, the number of paid farm labourers fell by nearly 20 per cent. The boom in construction work acted as a magnet for unskilled farm labourers. The construction of the **Westwall**, particularly, was blamed for creating severe labour problems in western Germany. As the pace of rearmament quickened, agriculture again sank back into its role of the Cinderella of the German economy.

Westwall Defence system stretching more than 630 km (390 miles) with more than 18,000 bunkers, tunnels and tank traps. It went from Kleve on the border with the Netherlands, to the Swiss border.

Darré and the Nazi Agrarian Office also met with failure in their plans for resettling peasants in the frontier regions of the Reich, particularly in the east, where, as one Nazi put it, the aim was to build 'a living wall against the Slavs pressing forward' (Farquharson, 1976: 144). Darré intended to break up the estates of the Junkers and so release land for new settlements, but rapidly these ambitious schemes ran into political and economic opposition. The Junkers appealed through Hindenburg to Hitler and successfully used their influence in the *Wehrmacht* to keep their estates. The army also argued with some justification that the big estates were indispensable for producing the staple foods of rye and potatoes. Hitler was curiously lukewarm about settlement on the eastern frontiers because he was convinced that land would be ultimately found in Russia. Thus by 1938 only 20,408 new settlements were created along the Reich's frontier regions.

WOMEN AND THE FAMILY

Central to Hitler's policy for the 'Thousand Year Reich' was the need to increase dramatically the German population so that it could people the territories of eastern Europe that were to be conquered for *Lebensraum*. The primary importance of women to the Nazis was their role as childbearers and home-makers [**Doc. 21, p. 161**]. Consequently, they were to be discouraged where possible from full-time work or embarking on academic courses which would lead to professional careers. To prepare them for their domestic duties they were to learn domestic science, and the preservation of their health was a matter of public policy. To train women for motherhood and marriage, the regime set up two women's organisations, the National Socialist Womanhood (NSF) and the German Women's Enterprise (DFW).

Before 1929 labour trends indicated that the number of women employed in industry, the professions and commerce would rapidly increase, but the Depression interrupted this pattern and severely restricted the opportunities open to women. Under Brüning, a campaign had already started to ease married women out of work, particularly where their husbands were still earning, so that unemployed males could take their places. Hitler developed this programme more vigorously to persuade as many women as he could to return to the home. Professional women were hardest hit by his measures. Soon after the seizure of power married women in the higher ranks of the civil service and in medicine were dismissed, and in 1936 the higher legal posts were completely barred to women, who were also excluded from playing any part in politics. It seemed at first as if it was only in those sections of the party's organisation which dealt exclusively with women that they could enjoy what Mason has called a certain degree of 'surrogate emancipation' (Mason, 1976: 101), yet by the end of the decade this was not quite the picture.

The Hitler government attempted to ease women out of industry and commerce by making motherhood an attractive financial proposition through a series of grants, loans, tax-relief schemes and the introduction of family allowances. In the Law for Reducing Unemployment, of 1 June 1933, there were two clauses which particularly affected women: tax concessions were granted to those employing female domestic servants, and interest-free loans were given to newly married couples, provided the wives withdrew from the labour market. Loans could, however, be refused 'if one of the partners was suffering from a hereditary or mental or physical illness, which renders their marriage undesirable to the whole national community' (Burleigh and Wippermann, 1991: 46). Women who helped their husbands on the land or in small businesses were not eligible for this loan as their labour was seen as indispensable, a view which 'was hardly in line with the Nazis' obsession with encouraging the growth of a healthy peasant class' (Stephenson, 1975: 86).

The significant increase in the German birth rate between 1933 and 1939 [**Doc. 22, p. 162**] may marginally have been assisted by Hitler's financial inducements, although the discouragement of birth-control methods and the crack-down on backstreet abortionists may arguably have played an equally important role. However, the rise in the population was more a result of the end of the Depression and improvements in the economy. Marriage rates would almost certainly have risen anyway as the younger generation of men, which had not been decimated in the First World War, grew into adulthood. Mother's Day, which was actually an American custom, was celebrated on a national scale with much pomp and propaganda, and a special medal, the Mother's Cross, was awarded to women who had four children or more.

Despite its rhetoric, the government did in reality accept that women would compose a significant part of the workforce once the economy picked up. A women's section was set up in the German Labour Front in July 1934 under Gertrud Scholtz-Klinik. Apart from ensuring the political loyalty to the Nazi regime of the 7 million women under its control, Scholtz-Klinik saw her main tasks as devising measures to protect women's childbearing capacity and preparing the younger women for their role as future mothers. Thus, working women were encouraged to attend courses on domestic science and childcare in their spare time. To stress that their real duty was to produce children, women were advised to reject make-up and give up smoking. The government also issued a series of laws restricting the number of hours women could work in factories and prohibiting them from undertaking heavy work in certain industries. By 1937, at a time of growing labour scarcity, women were recruited to work in many of the new plants set up under the Four Year Plan. Once again the ideology of the Nazi government 'found itself in head-on collision with a long-term process of social and economic change' (Mason, 1976: 93) when, in November 1937, it was compelled to relax its ruling that only unemployed married women were eligible for the marriage loan. By May 1939, 12.7 million women were in employment and comprised 37 per cent of the German workforce. Increasingly, the government was even ready to consider encouraging half-time employment of housewives with children. The welfare benefits available to women were advanced for their time. Pregnant working women, for instance, were granted six weeks of leave with full pay both before and after the birth of their child, and free holidays were also provided for mothers with children.

In the late 1930s, as the labour market tightened, women also joined the professions in greater numbers. The *Völkische Beobachter* went so far as to observe as early as September 1936 that 'today we can no longer do without the woman doctor, lawyer, economist and teacher in our professional life' (Stephenson, 1975: 172). The number of women doctors actually increased from 5 per cent in 1930 to 7.6 per cent in 1939, and in 1937 girls were once again encouraged to enter teaching. In 1937, despite opposition from Martin Bormann and Rudolf Hess, the Ministry of the Interior managed to persuade Hitler that women could, in exceptional cases, be appointed to senior posts in the civil service which dealt with the administration of welfare. Adroit exploitation of this concession by the ministry managed to extend this ruling also to the departments of education and health.

The Nazi regime regarded the family as the 'germ cell' (Koonz, 1987: 178) of the nation, yet in many ways the concept of the family as an oasis of peace and privacy from the public sphere was undermined by the way the government's racial laws and eugenic policies intruded on private decisions relating to marriage and children. Similarly, the growing pressure for children to join the Hitler Youth undercut the authority of the parents [**Doc. 20, p. 161**]. Claudia Koonz has argued that Nazi policy was 'deeply revolutionary because it aimed at the creation of a family unit that was not a defence against public invasion as much as the gateway to intervention' (Koonz, 1987: 180). In other ways Nazi policy towards the family facilitated divorce. In 1938 a new law made adultery, refusal to have children, venereal disease, a three-year separation, mental illness, racial incompatibility and eugenic weakness all grounds for ending a marriage.

If it came to the choice, the Nazi priority was not so much the family as the procreation of healthy 'Aryan' children. Hitler was quite specific that 'it must be considered reprehensible conduct to refrain from giving healthy children to the nation' (Stephenson, 1975: 61). On the one hand, this led to banning abortion in May 1933, but on the other it made possible some improvement in the status of the unmarried mothers, even though opinion in both the Reich and the party was conservative on this issue.

The unmarried mother's greatest champion was Himmler, who argued that as a contributor to the birth rate she should be 'raised to her proper place in the community, since she is, during and after her pregnancy, not a married or an unmarried woman but a mother' (Stephenson, 1975: 64). Provided children born of single mothers were 'racially and hereditarily valuable', Himmler was, where necessary, ready to offer them 'legal guardianship'. He set up the *Lebensborn* homes for pregnant and nursing mothers whose partners were or had been SS men and 'other racially valuable Germans' (Grünberger, 1974: 314).

THE WORKERS

Hitler's most controversial claim was that his government had 'broken with a world of prejudices' [**Doc. 23, p. 162**] and created a genuine people's community, where there was equality between the 'workers of the brain and fist'. To evaluate this assertion it is necessary to assess the fate of the industrial proletariat in the Third Reich. This class was, of course, far from homogeneous as it embraced not only the 'Third Reich's aristocracy of labour' (Grünberger, 1974: 244), the metal and high-tech workers who were employed in the armaments industries, but also relatively underprivileged groups who worked in the consumer-goods industries and in small businesses employing under ten wage earners.

Hitler justified the dissolution of the trade unions and the political parties of the Left by claiming that he had liberated the workers from their bureaucratic and corrupt Marxist leaders and given them a more respected place in society. Bereft of union protection, the workers were forced to join the Labour Front, to have their wages fixed by the Trustees of Labour and to witness the enhancement of the authority of their employers, who now were officially called 'plant leaders'. In all factories where there were more than 20 workers, Councils of Trust were set up. These councils were elected annually from lists compiled by the employers and the representatives of the NSBO, but after 1935 no more elections were held because the workers, despite all precautions to the contrary, were electing politically 'unreliable' candidates. For instance, at Krupp's in 1934–35 voting slips were either left blank or crossed out, or else the least reliable candidate on the list in the eyes of the Labour Front officials was voted for. A Council of Trust could theoretically take an employer to the specially created Courts of Social Honour if the local Labour Trustee was convinced that he was maltreating his employees, but this only rarely happened – as is shown by the fact that between 1934 and 1936, out of a labour force of over 20 million, only 616 cases were brought against employers. These courts were a poor substitute for trade-union power!

The Labour Front could not afford to be merely an instrument of oppression. It had both to encourage and to exhort the workers while offering them 'an objectified appearance of socialism combining the promises of an emancipation with an extensive depoliticization of industrial relations' (Rabinbach, 1976: 50). It was in some ways a force for economic rational-isation, welfare reform and the 'nurturing of human relations' (Prinz, 1991: 300). It was essential for it to be seen to be putting into operation what Hitler called 'socialism of the deed' [**Doc. 26, p. 164**]. The Labour Front thus evolved two key departments which owed much to the experiments in welfare capitalism in the 1920s. The 'Beauty of Work' scheme, run by Albert Speer, aimed with considerable success to persuade employers to modernise and humanise their factories by installing, for example, modern lighting, swimming baths and canteens. By 1939, 67,000 firms had become associated with the movement. The Labour Front's leisure organisation, 'Strength through Joy' (KDF), existed mainly to give the workers the opportunity to refresh themselves before making even greater efforts for the *Führer* and Fatherland. According to Robert Ley, the head of the Labour Front, it was an attempt to dispel boredom, as from it 'sprang stupid, heretical, yes, in the end criminal, ideas' (Burleigh, 2000: 250). Concerts and plays were held inside the factories and golf, sailing and skiing clubs, which had hitherto been the preserve of the wealthy, were now opened up to the workers for a modest subscription fee. The workers were also afforded the chance of cut-price cruises or holidays in the German countryside. By 1938 a growing number of hotels and even the passenger services of the national railways were becoming economically dependent upon their patronage. Potentially the most popular policy of the KDF was the launching of the *Volkswagen* (people's car) project. The foundation stone of the plant was laid in the summer of 1938 and a savings scheme was opened, which, unlike traditional hire purchase agreements, only provided for delivery once the last payment had been made. Nevertheless, by 1940 300,000 purchasers had already signed up, although the war stopped production and not a single car was handed over.

The achievement of full employment was arguably Hitler's 'sole gift to the masses' (Neumann, 1942: 431), but it did create increasing problems for the regime and gave the workers a real economic power which they started to exploit, with the consequent danger of rising wage costs and crippling labour shortages in the less well-paid industries. The number of workers giving notice rose dramatically. In eastern and central Germany, for example, major employment problems were created when miners from the Silesian coal pits and building workers from Saxony and Thuringia gave up their low-paid work and migrated to the new IG Farben factories in Leuna and the Hermann

Göring Steelworks in Salzgitter. With the accelerating tempo of work and the extension of working hours after 1936, absenteeism and go slows increased, and there were also lightning strikes, which usually lasted for only a few hours. In 1936, for instance, there were 179. The regime therefore began to take steps to check the situation. In November 1936 employers were ordered to obtain permission from the labour exchange before taking on more than ten extra men, and workers who left their jobs in breach of contract were threatened with the temporary loss of their work books, which were vital for their further employment. In June 1938, the Trustees of Labour were given power to set wage levels in key industries and simultaneously labour conscription was introduced. By August 1939 some 300,000 men had been conscripted to work on the *Westwall*, the fortifications in western Germany, or on the construction of new factories in central Germany. The employers' reactions to the new problems caused by full employment varied. Some, like Siemens and Krupp, for example, attempted to negotiate a consensus with their workers and use new technology to save labour. Others resorted to repression and the use of force. On the *Autobahn* construction sites 'bullying compounded by inadequate lodging, poor food, and lax safety created a detestable atmosphere' (Aycoberry, 1999: 164), while at Daimler-Benz the management set up an elaborate policing apparatus based on surveillance by heads of sections and agents. Ultimately, of course, in the background there loomed the terror of the Gestapo and 'the camps of education for work', which were almost as brutal as the concentration camps [**Doc. 25, p. 164**]. All this, however, failed to stop wages, especially in the armament industries, from rising. Deprived of the power of trade-union collective bargaining, the workers, either individually or in small groups, managed to exploit the novel situation of full employment and gain concessions from the employers, which Peukert called a 'sort of "do-it-yourself" wage system' (Peukert, 1989: 112) [**Doc. 24, p. 163**]. This was also made much easier by the introduction of piece-work rates. Skilled workers in the armaments industries could be remarkably successful. An electrician in Siemens, for instance, could, together with bonuses and overtime, earn as much as a salaried employer. Those in the consumer industries did much less spectacularly, and on balance average wages did not reach their 1929 level until 1941 [**Docs 27(A) and 27(B), p. 165–66**].

Mason initially interpreted the absenteeism and work stoppages of the late 1930s as 'the stubborn, despairing refusal of the working classes to become the selfless servants of the regime' (Mason, 1966: 137), and regarded them as marking a return to class warfare. Later he modified this analysis and accepted that he had exaggerated the importance of these incidents. He adopted the view that the workers were isolated from all other social groups and, in the words of the former SPD trade-union leader Wilhelm Leuschner, 'imprisoned in a great convict prison. To rebel would amount to suicide, just as if prisoners were to rise up against their heavily armed overseer' (Overy, 1995: 224). Yet, while a working-class culture did manage to survive and '[r]esistance by workers formed the most significant component of the German resistance movement' (Peukert, 1989: 118), there was, as Kershaw has stressed, 'some penetration of Nazi values' (Kershaw, 1993: 145). Younger workers, particularly, responding to the chance to maximise their earnings, took advantage of retraining possibilities and transfers to new jobs [**Doc. 24, p. 163**]. Sometimes, too, the Hitler Youth gave them chances of upward mobility. Material benefits like longer holidays and low heating and lighting costs did, of course, help buy the workers' acquiescence, and many admired Hitler for his successful foreign policy [**Doc. 14, p. 156**]. Oral history projects have, not surprisingly, shown that in the immediate post-war period many workers looked back on the years 1934–39 as a period of 'work, adequate nourishment, KDF and the absence of disarray' (Bessel, 1987: 97). Yet this nostalgia was not directed at party values but rather at a system of full employment where, if one was lucky and skilful, it was possible to live one's own life and retreat into the family – rather like the 'niche society' in the GDR some 30 years later.

POLICING THE *VOLKSGEMEINSCHAFT*

The defence of the *Volksgemeinschaft* was in the hands of the *Gestapo*, the Criminal Police (*Kripo*) and the uniformed police. Together all three forces under the overarching control of Himmler (see page 36) waged war against both the political and '**asocial**' enemies of the state. In the words of Werner Best, the legal expert at the Gestapo headquarters, the task of the police was to watch over 'the health of the body politic', to recognise 'every system of sickness' and destroy all 'destructive cells' (Gellately, 2001: 41). The role of the police as the defenders of the *Volksgemeinschaft* was given prominence in the local press and considerable efforts were made to imply that the guilty criminals were Jews, Communists or 'asocials'.

asocials People such as tramps and the homeless who did not conform to the normal rules of society.

As Richard Evans has written, 'the Gestapo . . . quickly attained an almost mythical status as an all seeing, all knowing arm of state security' (Evans, 96: 2006) but in reality it was a relatively small organisation consisting of only about 20,000 officials of whom 3,000 were members of the SS. Many spent most of their time in their offices updating card indexes in which the particulars of 'deviants' and Jews were kept. The *Gestapo* was dependent on informers for most of their information. These could be committed Nazis or merely those hoping to get even with difficult neighbours or colleagues. The

Nazi block wardens, who were allotted some 50 flats or houses to keep under surveillance, were one of the Gestapo's most reliable sources of information. Those prepared to denounce someone would usually make their accusation to the block warden first.

THE HITLER MYTH AS A FACTOR OF INTEGRATION

Hitler, or rather the popular image of Hitler, was also a major integrative factor in the Third Reich. After the take-over of power in 1933, a key task for Nazi propaganda was the virtual deification of Hitler. He was above all, as Ian Kershaw has pointed out, the personification of the nation and the unity of the '"National Community"' and the 'selfless exponent of the national interest' (Kershaw, 1987: 253). The economic, diplomatic and military successes of the Third Reich were all attributed to him. He was also seen as the upholder of popular justice or as the voice of common sense and also as the bulwark against Communism. Amongst the party faithful he was above all regarded as Germany's defence against the 'insidious machinations' of the Jews. An important strand of the Hitler myth was that Hitler, unlike many of the party hacks and fanatics, was personally sincere and often unaware of the excesses of his Nazi followers.

Although the Hitler myth met with only partial success in penetrating socialist, Communist and Catholic subcultures, and was received with considerable scepticism by the German elites, it made deep inroads into the Germans of the middle classes. To achieve this, Nazi propaganda exploited the longing of many Germans for national unity and a single charismatic ruler, who could sweep away the discredited pluralist policies of the Weimar Republic and resurrect Germany as a powerful nation state. Through nationalism, economic recovery and, beginning with the remilitarisation of the Rhineland, an impressive string initially of diplomatic successes and then of military successes, the Hitler myth as an integrative factor was largely successful, at least until the battle of Stalingrad (see page 97).

7

The racial state

Race pervaded every aspect of Nazi policy [**Doc. 28, p. 166**]. As we have seen in the last chapter, the *Volksgemeinschaft* was to be based on a racially homogeneous 'Aryan' people, whose health and racial purity it was vitally important to preserve. The corollary of this new racial unity was the determination by Hitler and his subordinates ultimately not only to eliminate what they regarded as alien racial minorities within Germany, such as the Jews, the **Sinti** and **Roma**, but also the mentally ill or incurably handicapped 'Aryan' Germans.

Sinti and **Roma** Minority ethnic groups generally known as 'Gypsies'.

NAZI HEALTH AND EUGENIC POLICIES

As with so much else in the Third Reich these policies were to a great extent a development of contemporary ideas and practices. Charles Darwin himself had been worried about the degenerative consequences of modern civilisation for humankind, while the German zoologist Ernst Haeckel, in the *Riddle of Life*, published in 1904, advocated euthanasia. In the early 1920s surgeons in the Zwickau district of Saxony were already quite illegally sterilising the mentally handicapped. The Depression, which simultaneously drove up welfare costs at a time of falling tax receipts, also lowered 'the ethical threshold of politicians' (Burleigh and Wippermann, 1991: 34), and in July 1932 the Prussian government had actually drafted a Sterilisation Law and sent it to the Reich government for further consideration.

Once Hitler came to power these ideas were developed further. Several different agencies were set up, and the subsequent interdepartmental rivalry and bureaucratic chaos only served to radicalise and drive forward more rapidly Nazi health, racial and eugenic policies as each tried to outbid the other in 'working towards the *Führer*' [**Doc. 13, p. 155**]. The Committee of Experts for Population and Racial Policy was created in the Ministry of the

Interior in June 1933, and a year later an attempt was made to set up a centralised public-health administration, but its remit was challenged at every turn by the rival party agencies. The Reich Labour Front, for instance, claimed responsibility for industrial health, while Himmler, in his role as head of the police and SS, showed a growing interest in racial and eugenic policies and established the Reich Central Office for the Combating of Homosexuality and Abortion (for healthy Aryan women only of course!).

In the end many of the key decisions were made by small *ad-hoc* committees created by Hitler. A series of laws progressively discriminated against those Germans who were judged to be of 'lesser racial value'. They could not, for example, be the recipients of marriage loans (see page 62) or receive travel concessions and tax allowances which were normally given to those with large families, and, after October 1935, all prospective marriage partners had to be in possession of a fitness certificate. By the Law for the Prevention of Hereditarily Diseased Progeny, which came into force in January 1934, both alcoholics and those with hereditary diseases could on medical advice be sterilised.

The logical development of these policies was euthanasia, which Hitler had originally planned to implement in wartime on the grounds that hospital beds would be urgently needed for wounded service personnel, but the first steps towards realising this programme began in the winter of 1938–39. In response to a petition by a father to allow his deformed son to be killed (the **Knauer case**), Hitler eventually authorised the setting-up of a committee chaired by his physician and Philipp Bouhler, the head of the *Führer* Chancellery. Their task was essentially to decide which unfortunate children would have to be killed as a result of their 'congenital deformities'. In the first stage of this programme, 5,200 children were murdered.

Knauer case Herr Knauer, the father of a severely handicapped child appealed to Hitler for permission to have the child killed. The appeal reached Hitler through his private Chancellery, and was approved.

In the summer of 1939, again on Hitler's explicit instructions, the euthanasia programme was extended to adults, although great care was taken to ensure that his involvement in this never became general knowledge. In 1940, after the German asylums and clinics had been ordered to fill in forms on their patients' health, selection for those to be killed began. They were transferred to specially selected asylums, equipped with small gas chambers set up by the SS. The news leaked out and growing public criticism, which came to a head with the dramatic sermon by the Bishop of Münster, Clemens August Count von Galen, in August 1941, persuaded Hitler to call a temporary halt (see page 126). Another reason for the pause was that the euthanasia programme, which had gassed 70,273 people and killed a further 23,000 by other means, had released sufficient hospital beds for the time being.

The programme soon recommenced. The asylums, which had been involved in the original programme of euthanasia, were now used to 'free' the concentration camps of Jews, Communists and other 'deviants'. New extermination centres were also opened in Germany where patients were not only the mentally sick but foreign workers suffering from severe physical illnesses, 'racially inferior' babies of eastern European women, sick or unruly prisoners from the German prisons and even sometimes German soldiers suffering from incurable shell shock. These were all killed either through starvation or lethal injections. Simultaneously, efforts were made to win over public opinion by such films as *I Accuse*, in which a doctor initially opposed to euthanasia came round to accepting it when his wife was struck down with multiple sclerosis.

THE 'ASOCIALS' AND HOMOSEXUALS

The Nazis were convinced that criminal and 'asocial' behaviour and sexual deviancy were not the result of individual choice or the environment but rather of genetic factors. Consequently, society could only be ultimately protected from these perceived threats by having the relevant individuals sterilised or ultimately killed. The Law against Dangerous Habitual Criminals in November 1933 thus allowed the compulsory castration of certain types of criminal, and in January 1937 the same principle was extended to the punishment of young people. Increasingly both the punishment meted out to the person concerned and his or her treatment in prison was determined by biological-racial criteria.

No comprehensive law on the status of the 'asocials' was ever drawn up, but the campaign against both them and homosexuals intensified when Himmler was appointed chief of the German police in June 1936. In December 1937 the Ministry of the Interior authorised the arrest of 'beggars, tramps, Gypsies, alcoholics with contagious diseases, particularly sexually transmitted diseases, who evade measures taken by the public health authorities' (Burleigh and Wippermann, 1991: 172). Over the course of the following year more than 10,000 people in these categories were arrested by the police, incarcerated in concentration camps and forced to work in SS-owned quarries where the majority perished. A similar fate awaited homosexuals. Between 1937 and 1939 25,000 of them were arrested and possibly as many as 15,000 were sent to the concentration camps.

GYPSIES, PART-AFRICANS AND THE SLAV MINORITIES

While the fate of European and German Jewry under the Third Reich has been comprehensively researched, Nazi policy towards the other much smaller ethnic minorities has been, until recently, largely ignored. Compared to the half million Jews these were very small groups indeed: there were about 30,000 Sinti and Roma, a few hundred mixed-race children who had been fathered by French-African troops during the Rhineland occupation of 1919–30 and about 70,000 Wenden or **Sorbs**, who were of Slav descent and lived along the Silesian–Saxon borderlands (see Map 1). The Nazi regime inherited a legacy of policies from the Weimar Republic, which had harassed the Gypsies, considered sterilising the mixed-race children in the Rhineland and had regarded the Sorbs, whose leaders had petitioned the Allies in 1919 for the creation of an independent Sorbian state, as a potential fifth column in Germany.

Sorbs A distinct racial group living in south-eastern Germany in an area originally called Lusatia. In 2000 there were still some 80,000 Sorb speakers.

The Nazis' policies for eliminating these minorities, which they saw as a threat to the racial hygiene of the nation, evolved during the period 1933–40 [**Doc. 29, p. 167**]. The sterilisation laws were extended to cover the mixed-race Rhineland children in 1937. However, plans to deport them were cancelled for fear of alienating world opinion. Initially, many of the Sinti and Roma were driven from their caravan sites on private land and forced to camp on unhealthy wasteland. In 1935 a research unit, financed by the SS, was set up in the Ministry of Health to classify them racially. It came to the conclusion that 90 per cent were of mixed race and were therefore predisposed towards being criminal and asocial, and should be sterilised as a consequence. In September 1939 Himmler decided to have all 30,000 Gypsies forcibly removed to the **Generalgouvernement** (occupied Poland), but in the summer of 1940, after only 2,500 had been transported, the programme was stopped to give priority to the Jews. It was resumed again in December 1942, when Himmler ordered their despatch to Auschwitz, although the nature of their itinerant lives enabled many to evade arrest in the Reich.

Generalgouvernement Government-General. The area of Poland which was not annexed by the Reich but was directly controlled by a German civil administration in Cracow.

Initially, the vulnerability of German minorities in Poland and Czechoslovakia forced the Nazi government to adopt a relatively tolerant policy towards the Sorbs for fear of retaliation, but with the dismemberment of Czechoslovakia in 1938–39, Sorb leaders were put in concentration camps. In May 1940, Himmler was planning to move the Sorbs to the *Generalgouvernement*, as they were classified as 'the same racial and human type' as the Poles (Burleigh and Wippermann, 1991: 135), but these plans were never implemented and the small Sorb population managed to outlive the Nazi regime.

THE JEWS

Of all the minority groups persecuted by the Nazis, the Jews suffered the most. Although there were only 500,000 Jews in Germany in 1933, most of whom were fully integrated into German society, they were perceived by the

Nazis to be the embodiment of evil, the real power behind Bolshevism and thus a major threat to the racial state. [**Doc. 30, p. 168**]. In the succinct formulation of Noakes and Pridham, they 'formed a propaganda stereotype, a collection of negative attributes representing the antithesis of the qualities of a true German' (Noakes and Pridham, II, 1984: 521). For most Nazis, the Jews were virtually mythological figures, upon whom they focused their anxieties about the modern world.

As in so many other areas of government, Nazi policy towards the Jews after the seizure of power was often hesitant and contradictory. The intentionalists, particularly Dawidowicz (1986), Hildebrand (1991) and Bracher (1973), argue that Hitler consistently planned the mass murder of the Jews, even though events might at times have forced him to make tactical retreats. The structuralists, on the other hand, the most prominent of whom are Broszat (1985), Mommsen (1986) and Schleunes (1972), seek rather to find the ultimate cause of the Holocaust in the fragmented and chaotic way in which policy was made in Nazi Germany. Government departments and Nazi leaders, they argue, vied with one another to formulate anti-Semitic policies, and thus set in motion a spiral of ever more radical policies. Both positions, as Michael Burleigh and Wolfgang Wippermann argue, 'have a number of merits and demerits' (Burleigh and Wippermann, 1991: 96). Structuralists put Nazi anti-Semitic policy firmly into the context of the *structure of the Nazi state* with its chaotic decision-making process and the system of 'working towards the Führer'. Understandably, such attempts to depersonalise the responsibility of what ultimately ended in the Holocaust are bitterly resented by the intentionalists, who see such an approach as initiating a new 'cycle of apologetics' in German history (Dawidowicz, 1986: xxvi). In fact to understand the Nazi persecution of the Jews neither the structuralist nor the intentionalist approach can be excluded.

After the seizure of power there were no directives issued from the Nazi Party on the Jewish question. Only when independent action by the SA against individual Jews and their property threatened to escalate uncontrollably and damage his reputation as a responsible statesman did Hitler seek to channel and control the violence by entrusting Julius Streicher, the *Gauleiter* of Franconia, with organising a boycott of Jewish shops. The boycott, which occurred on 1 April, was both unpopular in Germany and sharply criticised abroad, particularly in America, and it also risked damaging the German economy as a whole. Hitler therefore sought to deflect the party's anti-Semitism to less politically and economically sensitive targets. In April 1933 all Jews, with the exception of those who had served or had suffered bereavement in the First World War, were expelled from the civil service and excluded from the universities. Their ejection from journalism was foreshadowed by the setting up of the Reich Chamber of Culture and the Press Law of October 1933 (see page 56).

Intentionalists and structuralists disagree profoundly on Hitler's role in the formulation and execution of these policies. The structuralists argue that Hitler essentially responded to grass-roots pressure, while the intentionalists emphasise his role as 'stage manager' or 'skilful tactician waiting until the time was ripe before making his next move' (Bankier, 1988: 4–5). Most historians, however, agree that over the next two years economic and political realities forced Nazi Jewish policy into a relatively moderate mould. For instance, in August 1933 the Foreign and Economic Ministries could only avert a world-wide boycott of German trade planned by international Jewish organisations by negotiating with the Anglo-Palestine Bank, which was responsible for the finances of the Zionist movement, an agreement whereby the money of German Jews intending to emigrate to Palestine could be used to purchase imported German goods. Up to the spring of 1935 the Nazi government dis-couraged the renewal of overt racial violence and even allowed, for instance, Jewish textile businesses to tender for military contracts.

By the summer of 1935 a mixture of aggressive confidence, fostered by the return of the Saar to the Reich and by the provocative announcement of the German rearmament programme, and of frustration at Hitler's apparent lack of radical drive in domestic policy led to further outbursts of anti-Semitism by party activists. Again the Nazi government responded by seeking to divert anti-Semitic violence into more legal channels. In July 1935 Frick, the Minister of the Interior, circulated a memorandum to the state governments informing them of plans to prohibit marriages between 'Aryans' and 'non-Aryans'. These were announced suddenly and unexpectedly by Hitler on 15 September. Originally Hitler had intended to speak on foreign policy to the members of the *Reichstag*, who had been specially summoned to Nuremberg where the annual party rally was taking place. When the speech was cancelled on the advice of Konstantin von Neurath, the Foreign Minister, the notorious Law for the Protection of German Blood, forbidding marriage or sexual intercourse between Jews and German gentiles, and the Reich Citizenship Law, depriving Jews of their German citizenship, gave Hitler something of substance to announce. Predictably, however, these two laws disappointed many of the hard-liners, who suspected that Hitler had again compromised and accepted the advice of his civil servants rather than of his party activists.

For the next two years Hitler took no further steps to clarify his anti-Semitic policy, although at the Party Congress of Labour in 1937 he blamed the rulers of 'Jewish-Bolshevism in Moscow' for fomenting global turmoil (Friedländer, 2009: 67). Leading Nazis and government departments competed with one another to fill the vacuum by proposing their own solutions to the Jewish 'problem', each quoting Hitler as their ultimate source of authority. At one inter-ministerial meeting of 17 November 1935, for example, an official from the Ministry of the Interior claimed that Hitler wanted all Jewish emigration halted and the Jews kept as potential hostages in the event of war, while Hess, again quoting Hitler, employed diametrically opposed arguments and insisted that Hitler wished them to emigrate from Germany as quickly as possible.

By the spring of 1938 the tempo of anti-Semitism was again accelerating. Schacht's resignation from the Economics Ministry in November 1937 (see page 50) ensured that there was now no restraining hand on Göring, when in his role as Commissioner of the Four Year Plan he pressed for the rapid economic expropriation of the Jews. Against the background of the triumphalist mood unleashed by the *Anschluss* of Austria and the growing threat of war with Czechoslovakia, the spring and summer of 1938 witnessed a series of decrees ranging from measures forcing Jews to adopt what the Nazis regarded as the specifically Jewish forenames Sarah or Israel, to having their wealth and property registered as a preliminary for expropriation by the state.

The opportunity to instigate a full-scale pogrom came in November 1938, when Ernst von Rath, a minor diplomat in the German embassy in Paris, was assassinated by Herschl Grynszpan, a 17-year-old student whose parents had recently been expelled to Poland from Germany. Goebbels seized the chance to organise what were portrayed to the outside world as spontaneous attacks on synagogues and Jewish-owned businesses. Hitler had agreed that such demonstrations were not to be 'discouraged if they originated spontaneously' (Noakes and Pridham, II, 1984: 553). Some 25 million *Reichsmarks'* worth of damage was done and nearly 100 Jews were killed, while a further 30,000 were put into concentration camps.

Goebbels' tactics were a direct challenge to both Göring and Himmler, who each had their own plans for solving the Jewish 'problem'. However, *Reichskristallnacht* did mark a fresh stage in Nazi policy towards the Jews. With Hitler's support, Göring coordinated all initiatives on the Jewish question through his office and began to implement measures for the total expropriation of Jewish property. Not only did the Jews have to pay a collective fee of 1.25 billion *Marks*, but they were also forced out of the retail trade, skilled labour and management posts. In April 1939 their remaining wealth was confiscated. Decrees, inspired by Goebbels, also barred them from public places, such as theatres and beaches, and the few remaining Jewish children still in state schools were expelled.

In January 1939 the role of the SS within the various Nazi agencies dealing with the Jews was decisively strengthened. Göring delegated to Heydrich, the Chief of the Security Police and the SD, responsibility for setting up an organisation modelled on the Central Office for Jewish Emigration, which Eichmann had already established in Vienna, to supervise the emigration of

Reichskristallnacht
Literally 'Night of Broken Glass': the wave of anti-Semitic violence of 9 November 1938.

the remaining 214,000 Jews in Germany. Paradoxically, the very success of Göring's expropriation policies made Jewish emigration more difficult to achieve, as no state was willing to accept a large number of impoverished refugees. Heydrich's task was further complicated by the German occupation of Bohemia in March 1939, which increased the number of Jews at the mercy of the Nazis by more than 100,000.

Although on 12 November 1938 Hitler apparently instructed Göring both by telephone and through his Chief of Staff, Bormann, that 'the Jewish question be now once and for all co-ordinated and solved one way or another' (Noakes and Pridham, II, 1984: 558), he remained, in public at least, aloof from the numerous anti-Semitic policies initiated in the aftermath of *Reichskristallnacht*. Nevertheless, on two occasions in January 1939 he was quite specific about the future fate of the Jews. He informed the Czech Foreign Minister of his intention to 'destroy the Jews', and shortly afterwards in the *Reichstag* made his notorious prophecy that the outbreak of war would lead to the 'annihilation of the Jewish race in Europe' [**Doc. 31, p. 169**]. To the intentionalists these threats are unambiguous evidence of Hitler's ultimate aims, but the structuralists remain sceptical. They caution historians against interpreting Hitler's words too literally. Mommsen, for instance, stresses that Hitler 'considered the "Jewish question" from a visionary political perspective that did not reflect the real situation' (Mommsen, 1986: 112), and argues that Hitler was in fact invoking a ritual hatred of the Jews, rather than expressing definite plans for their murder. The structuralists are almost certainly correct that Hitler's horrific threats were not precise plans for the Holocaust, but it is hard not to see them as expressions of intention, however vague and unformulated. As Dawidowicz observed about an earlier speech of Hitler's, 'in the post Auschwitz world' his words carry a 'staggering freight' (Dawidowicz, 1986: 43).

Within a few weeks of the outbreak of war the persecution of the Jews in Germany intensified. First they had to hand in their radio sets, then in the following months they were forbidden to buy chocolate, cocoa, shoes and leather goods. In May 1940 they were also forbidden to go shopping after 3.30 in the afternoon. They were also increasingly corralled into ghettos as a result of the law of 30 April 1939, which had banned Jews and non-Jews from living in the same block of flats. In September 1941 all German Jews were forced to wear the Star of David.

The Nazi government was determined to drive the Jews out of the Reich, but initially the number of Jews expelled was small. Poland, after its defeat by the Germans in September 1939, was the obvious destination (see page 100), but largely because of the chaos in the Generalgovernment and the lack of any clear-cut decisions in Germany, it was not until 1942 that large-scale deportations to the death camps in Poland began. Out of some 185,000 Jews who still remained in the Old Reich in September 1939, only 31,807 remained by March 1943 (see pages 104–7).

THE GERMANS AND THE JEWS

Ian Kershaw, writing on public opinion in Bavaria during the Third Reich, came to the conclusion that 'Dynamic Jew haters were certainly a small percentage of the population; but active friends of Jews formed an even smaller proportion' (Kershaw, 1984: 275). Nazi propaganda probably had most impact on the age cohorts which passed through the Hitler Youth. For most Germans the demands of everyday life left little time for concern over the government's Jewish policy. However, if this policy became too overt and violent, public opinion did become more hostile, although this often took the form of hostility towards the party rather than an active sympathy for the Jews.

It was, however, *Reichskristallnacht* that confronted the Germans with the reality of the Nazi terror. While inevitably some fully supported it and even joined in, the majority were appalled by the damage to property, the negative message it sent to foreigners abroad and by its sheer violence. There were also many instances of spontaneous acts of kindness and mercy particularly towards elderly Jews. However, this widespread feeling of revulsion against the regime soon died down, as it lacked any structure and focus. Unlike the opposition to the 'euthanasia action' in 1941, the Churches provided no leadership (see pages 70 and 126). Nevertheless, it is possible that the reaction of public opinion to the *Reichskristallnacht* persuaded Hitler not to stage a repeat pogrom inside Germany.

The secrecy that shrouded the 'Final Solution' (see pages 104–7) is also evidence that the Nazi leadership felt that it could not rely on the anti-Semitism of the German population. In fact, of course, the murder of the Jews in Poland was by 1942 'an open secret' (Evans, 2009: 560). The deportation of the remaining Jews from the Reich could not be hidden, and rumours of what was occurring behind the German lines in the USSR and in the death camps in Poland were spread widely by soldiers on leave, railway personnel and German officials in the occupied territories. What was the reaction of the German population? Again there were instances of kindness and sympathy and some concrete assistance to individual Jews [**Doc. 46a, p. 180**], but the majority of the Germans was more preoccupied with surviving the nightly air raids and the increasing demands of total war.

8

Foreign policy, 1933–39

Despite the fierce rivalry between the various Nazi agencies over domestic affairs and Hitler's frequent failure to offer a definite lead, there is little doubt that most historians now agree with Rauschning that in foreign affairs it is 'in the last resort Hitler who decides and . . . does indeed "lead"' (Rauschning, 1939: 195). By 1937 at the very latest, neither the Foreign Office nor the armed services were able to exercise any decisive influence on Hitler. On the other hand, Hitler's policy was not, of course, immune from domestic pressures. Indeed, structuralist historians argue that the development of Nazi foreign policy was primarily influenced by domestic policy. Hans Mommsen, for instance, insists that it was largely an opportunist exercise aimed at enhancing Hitler's image and satisfying the Nazi Party's demand for instant action (Mommsen, 1979). It is certainly true, as Orlow has shown, that in 1938 Hitler's foreign-policy initiatives were particularly welcome to the Nazi Party, which was becoming increasingly impatient of its inability to change German society more rapidly, but then Orlow goes on to stress that there was no 'direct and obvious connection between the radical ferment of the Nazi Party and the foreign-policy initiatives of the German Government' (Orlow, II, 1973: 230). Similar objections can be applied to Mason's argument that by the end of 1937 the German economy was facing grave financial and labour problems, which could only be solved in the context of a victorious war (Mason, 1966 and 1971). Even if one conceded that there was an economic crisis in 1938/9 (see page 53), the historian is still hard put to pin-point 'any causal relation between Hitler's awareness of [it] and the gathering pace of German foreign policy after 1937' (Carr, 1972: 65).

Inevitably much of the debate on German foreign policy during the Third Reich is concentrated on the aims and motives of Adolf Hitler. Rauschning's thesis that Hitler's ultimate aim was simply the 'maximum of power and dominion' (Rauschning, 1939: 284) was powerfully endorsed by Alan Bullock in his biography of Hitler, when he observed that 'Hitler had only

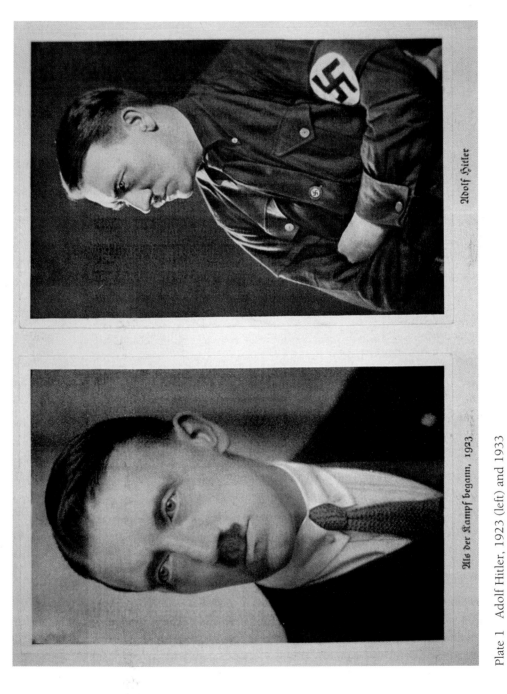

Plate 1   Adolf Hitler, 1923 (left) and 1933
Source: German Photographer (20th Century) Private Collection/ Peter Newark Pictures/ The Bridgeman Art Library

Plate 2   Anti-Jewish poster for Nazi propaganda film "The Eternal Jew", 1937

Plate 3   Polish cartoon on the Nazi-Soviet Pact, 1939
Source: Polish School (20th Century) Private Collection/ Peter Newark Military Pictures/ The Bridgeman Art Library

Plate 4 SA Brown Shirt cutout figures for children, c.1935

Plate 5 German sentries on the ramparts of the Ehrenbreitstein Castle, 1936

Source: German Photographer (20th Century) Koblenz, Germany/ Peter Newark Military Pictures/ The Bridgeman Art Library

Plate 6 Russian POWs captured by the Germans, 1941

Source: German Photographer (20th Century) Private Collection/ Peter Newark Military Pictures/ The Bridgeman Art Library

Plate 7 German victims of the Allied bombing of Mannheim, 1943

Plate 8 Hitler's new Autobahn system, 1934

one programme, power without limit, and the rest was window dressing'
(Bullock, 1962: 448). This view of Hitler as a 'manic expansionist' was
rejected by Trevor-Roper, who argued that *Mein Kampf* was 'a complete
blueprint of his intended achievements and in no significant point different
from its ultimate actual form' (Trevor-Roper, 1953: viii.). He stressed that
Hitler was a systematic thinker, whose ideas must therefore be taken as
seriously as Bismarck's or Lenin's, and drew the conclusion that the conquest
of *Lebensraum* in Russia was the overriding aim of Hitler's foreign policy
[**Doc. 32(a), p. 169**]. Thus up to 1960 the great majority of historians
did not doubt that Hitler intended war. The only debate was the scope of
his aims.

However, in 1961, Taylor, in his seminal study on the origins of the
Second World War, attempted to demythologise Hitler by arguing that 'his
foreign policy was that of his predecessors, of the professional diplomats at
the Foreign Ministry and virtually all Germans' and was aimed at making
Germany 'the greatest power in Europe from her natural weight' (Taylor,
1961b: 68). He categorically dismissed the possibility that Hitler was a
system-maker 'deliberately preparing . . . a great war which would destroy
existing civilization and make him master of the world' (1961b: 68–69), and
insisted that Hitler was a pragmatist whose foreign policy was to a great
extent a reaction to the initiatives of other powers.

Taylor's views unleashed a passionate debate which still reverberates. His
most radical critics have been among the German historians of the 'programme
school' led by Andreas Hillgruber (1965) and Klaus Hildebrand (1973), who
argue that Hitler's foreign policy was formulated in the mid-1920s and
remained 'remarkably consistent . . . in spite of his flexible approach to
details' (Hillgruber, 1974: 7). They claim that Hitler's 'programme' consisted
of two main phases: the continental phase, which would involve the defeat
of France and the conquest of European Russia, and then the global phase,
which would establish Germany as a world power through the annexation of
colonial territories, the construction of a large navy and the defeat of the
United States of America. In the first phase Britain and Italy were to be allotted the key role of allies, whereas in the second phase Hitler realised that he
might well have to face British hostility, although he apparently hankered
after a global partnership with the British Empire. The programme thesis
depends primarily on a close reading of *Mein Kampf* and *Hitler's Secret Book*
(T. Taylor, 1961). In both books Hitler outlined his plans for the conquest
of *Lebensraum* [**Doc. 32(a), p. 169**] in Russia after the defeat of France, which
he hoped to achieve with the assistance of a British and Italian alliance
[**Doc. 32(b), p. 170**]. But Hillgruber, by emphasising Hitler's tacit assumption that the new Germanic super-race would inherit the earth and his
criticism of Wilhelmine foreign policy [**Doc. 32(c), p. 170**], argues, not always

convincingly, that 'contrary to the opinion of many historians, the essentials of the idea of overseas expansion were already covertly indicated in *Mein Kampf*' (Hillgruber, 1974: 10).

Taylor and the proponents of the programme thesis have adopted diametrically opposed interpretations, both of which in their turn have been subjected to considerable criticism. Although Taylor forced historians to rethink the causes of the Second World War, he is nevertheless open to the criticism that he ignored Hitler's obsession with gaining *Lebensraum*, which was crucial to his plans for the future of the racial state. The precise arguments of the programme school also lose some of their credibility when it is remembered that in domestic affairs the Nazis so often carried out the opposite of what they preached. Hans Mommsen is therefore fully justified in questioning 'whether National Socialist foreign policy can be considered an unchanging pursuit of established priorities' (Mommsen, 1979: 177). However, as with the racial policy of the Third Reich the clash between intentionalist and structuralist views can be seen, as Alan Bullock put it, as an 'unnecessary polarization not required by the evidence' (Bullock *et al.*, 1998: 448). In the short term, Hitler could be remarkably flexible in his aims, yet he never forgot his ultimate objectives. To quote Alan Bullock again, Nazi foreign policy was only comprehensible if it was seen as combining 'consistency of aim with complete opportunism in method and tactics' (Bullock, 1971: 193).

HITLER'S PRIORITIES, 1933–37

Hitler's immediate priorities in 1933, apart from safeguarding the new Nazi regime from foreign intervention, were to destroy the Versailles settlement, rearm, dismantle the French alliance system in eastern Europe, and escape from isolation by securing alliances with Britain and Italy. Only then would he be able successfully to confront France and gain a free hand against Russia. In 1933 Germany was both economically and militarily weak, but the realities of world politics in fact favoured a revival of German power: the world slump confirmed American isolation, France had never properly recovered its nerve after failing to coerce Germany in the Ruhr in 1923 and Britain, menaced by Japan in the Far East and weakened by the incipient break-up of its empire, was ready to make concessions in Europe. Hitler also had the luck to come to power at a time when the serious revision of the Versailles settlement had already begun. In 1929–30 Britain and France evacuated the Rhineland, and in 1932 German reparation payments were effectively cancelled at the Lausanne Conference.

Since February 1932 the world disarmament conference had been in session in Geneva. Hitler was anxious to avoid becoming enmeshed in multilateral disarmament agreements or regional pacts which would perpetuate German military weakness. In October 1933, with minimal risks, he was able to exploit Anglo-French differences and walk out of both the disarmament conference and the League of Nations. To avoid provoking retaliation, he consistently stressed his desire for peace, and in June had even signed the four-power pact proposed by Mussolini, which had been intended to achieve a peaceful but modest revision of the Versailles settlement, gambling correctly that French opposition would ultimately prevent its ratification.

As Kershaw has pointed out, '[i]n the decision to leave the Geneva disarmament conference and the League of Nations, not much more than the timing was Hitler's' (Kershaw, 1993: 117), since both Papen and Schleicher had also favoured withdrawal as soon as it was possible. However, in reversing his country's traditional hostility towards Poland, Hitler played a more decisive role in formulating foreign policy. In January 1934, against the advice of the Foreign Office, he achieved a considerable diplomatic success with the signing of the ten-year non-aggression pact with Poland. It was a major breach in the French alliance system in eastern Europe and freed Hitler from pressure on his eastern frontiers while Germany was still vulnerable. Nevertheless, Hitler made it clear to Hermann Rauschning, President of the Danzig Senate, that the agreement had 'a purely temporary significance'. He added, 'I have no intention of maintaining a serious friendship' (Williamson, 2009: 80).

The pact inevitably aroused suspicions in both Rome and Paris. The Italians feared that a German–Polish understanding would lead to the annexation of Austria, and the French perceived it to be a temporary measure, which would provide Hitler with security from an attack on two fronts while Germany was rearming. It thus accelerated a Franco-Russian and Franco-Italian *rapprochement* and made an Italian–German alliance seem increasingly unlikely. German–Italian relations again deteriorated sharply when the Austrian Nazis, with tacit backing from Berlin, staged an unsuccessful coup in Vienna in July 1934, and Mussolini retaliated by moving troops up to the Austrian frontier. In January 1935 France and Italy signed the Rome Agreements which committed them to act together in the event of German unilateral rearmament or threat to Austrian independence.

As early as April 1933 Hitler had indirectly begun to approach the British about an alliance. No progress was made until February 1935 when Britain, responding to reports on the growth of the **Luftwaffe**, began to sound out Germany about joining an Anglo-French air pact, which would set mutually agreed limits to the size of national air forces. The British had no desire for an alliance but hoped to moderate German rearmament by agreement rather than by coercion. Hitler had thus little to fear when he announced the

Luftwaffe The German Air Force. Under the Treaty of Versailles Germany was forbidden to possess an air force, but in 1933 Hermann Göring was appointed Reich Aviation Minister with the brief to build up in secret a strong air force.

reintroduction of conscription in March 1935, even though the western powers met at Stresa and condemned the German action. In May the French signed the Franco-Soviet Treaty, but this was not as threatening to Germany as it looked, since it was not accompanied by military staff talks, and was really aimed more at dissuading Stalin from attempting to draw closer to Nazi Germany.

Hitler countered these moves by assuring the powers of his peaceful intentions and offering to conclude bilateral disarmament pacts with his neighbours. The British government seized on the chance to negotiate a naval convention which limited the German navy to 35 per cent of the strength of the Royal Navy. Their unilateral action broke up the unity of the Stresa front and, by implying British approval of German rearmament, 'set in motion the momentous chain of events that prevented a possible anti-Hitler coalition and freed the Third Reich from the threat of isolation' (Bracher, 1973: 369). It was also a triumph for Ribbentrop, who led the German delegation to London. British and German interpretations of the convention differed markedly: to Hitler it was a first step towards an alliance, whereas the British cabinet saw it primarily as a means of taming Hitler and ultimately drawing him back into the League of Nations.

Mussolini's attack on Abyssinia in October 1935 and his subsequent break with Britain and France, which had reluctantly imposed sanctions approved by the League of Nations, on Italy, provided Hitler with the chance to take the vital step of remilitarising the Rhineland. Until January 1936 Hitler carefully maintained a neutral position and even sold arms to the Ethiopians. However, to avoid complete isolation, Mussolini was driven to approach Hitler and to secure his goodwill by intimating that Italy would not prevent Austria from becoming, in due course, a German satellite. Hitler was therefore able to extract assurances from Mussolini in February that he would not oppose the remilitarisation of the Rhineland. Dismissing advice from the Foreign Office, which believed that this could be achieved peacefully at a later date through a diplomatic settlement, Hitler insisted that the favourable international situation provided by the Abyssinian war should be immediately exploited. He gambled correctly on Anglo-French inaction and, using the ratification of the Franco-Soviet Treaty of 27 February 1936 as a justification, reoccupied the Rhineland on 7 March with a weak military force, which would almost certainly have been withdrawn had French troops immediately intervened. The remilitarisation of the Rhineland has been described as 'a real turning point in the inter-war years which marked the beginning of a shift in the balance of power away from Paris and back to Berlin' (Carr, 1979: 126–127). It deprived France of its main strategic advantage over Germany and showed that neither Britain nor France had the will to defend the **Locarno** and the Versailles Treaties. It was, too, a major victory for Hitler.

Locarno Treaties Signed in December 1925, the most important of which was the treaty guaranteeing the inviolability of the Franco-German and Belgo-German frontiers and the demilitarisation of the Rhineland.

His boldness was in stark contrast to the timidity and caution of the soldiers and diplomats, who shared his aims but feared to act.

Despite the virtual collapse of the Versailles system by 1936, Germany's military weakness prevented Hitler from making any further major advances in the immediate future. His intentions were, however, made clear in August 1936 when he refused to let the acute balance-of-payments crisis slow down the tempo of rearmament, and personally intervened to set up the Four Year Plan with the expressed intention of preparing both the army and the economy for war against the USSR within four years. It is quite possible that the tone of Hitler's memorandum was influenced by the need to overcome Schacht's opposition to accelerated rearmament (see page 49), but it was also a clear expression of his ultimate aims and of his ideological hatred of Bolshevism [**Doc. 16, p. 156**].

Anti-Bolshevism was also one of the reasons for Hitler's decision to intervene in the Spanish Civil War. In response to requests from General Franco, the leader of the rebel Nationalist forces, Hitler first provided a fleet of 20 planes to airlift his troops from Spanish Morocco to the mainland in July, and then in October he agreed to the dispatch of a small task force, the Condor Legion, consisting of 6,500 troops supported by fighter and bomber planes. He again took this decision contrary to advice from the Foreign Office because he feared that a Republican victory would result in a Communist Spain. This would influence the situation in France, where a left-wing popular front government had just been established, and might possibly result in the creation of a Franco-Spanish 'Bolshevik bloc'. There were, of course, other benefits to be had from assisting Franco. A Nationalist victory would give Germany access to Spanish iron ore and tungsten, while a lengthy struggle, as long as it ended eventually in Franco's victory, would distract the western powers and the USSR and enable Germany to rearm and strengthen its position in central Europe.

The war rapidly became an ideological conflict between Left and Right and exacerbated mutual suspicions between Britain and France on the one hand, and Soviet Russia on the other, and so hindered the building up of a firm anti-Nazi front. Britain and France tried to localise the war by setting up the Non-Intervention Committee, while Stalin sent aid and advisers to assist the Republicans. As both Hitler and Mussolini gave military assistance to Franco, the war cemented German–Italian cooperation, which was given more precise form in the October Protocols (1936). By these the two dictators agreed to work together to neutralise Communist propaganda and acknowledge Franco as the legal head of the Spanish government. Hitler also recognised the Italian empire and its interests in the Mediterranean.

In November Hitler again overrode professional advice from the Foreign Office and signed the Anti-Comintern Pact with Japan, which was aimed against the Comintern rather than Soviet Russia. The professional diplomats, as well as Schacht and the leading industrialists, regarded China, which since July 1937 was locked into a steadily escalating war with Japan, as a far more important trading partner in the Far East. Hitler, however, insisted that Japan was a potential ally in the fight against Bolshevism [**Doc. 16, p. 157**], and in November 1937 the pact was further strengthened by Italy's accession.

By the end of 1937 Germany's diplomatic position had improved dramatically, while the divisions and distractions among its potential enemies had greatly increased. However the shortage of steel threatened the armaments' programme of the Four Year Plan (see page 50) and forced Hitler to intervene. On 5 November he called a secret meeting at the Reich Chancellery on 5 November, which was attended by Neurath the foreign minister and the heads of the armed forces. Hitler stressed that his overriding aim was to acquire *Lebensraum* within Europe rather than colonies in Africa, at the latest by the period 1943–45, by which time Germany's lead in rearmament would be eroded by the efforts of her enemies. He warned specifically that Germany would have to reckon with two 'hate filled antagonists', Britain and France, to whom a German colossus in the centre of Europe was a thorn in the flesh' [**Doc. 33, p. 170**]. However, he indicated that he would move against Czechoslovakia and Austria before this date if France were distracted either by a civil war or hostilities with Italy.

How significant was this meeting? It was claimed by the Allies at the Nuremberg trials in 1946 and by the immediate post-war generation of historians that Hitler had produced a complete blueprint of his aims at this meeting. In 1961, however, Taylor 'stirred up a hornets' nest' (Wright, 2007: 9) by arguing that Hitler's exposition was for the most part 'day dreaming, unrelated to what followed in real life', and that the meeting was called primarily for domestic purposes (Taylor, 1961b: 132). The meeting was certainly triggered by the steel crisis, but, as William Carr observed, 'the consensus still favours the view that Hitler was serving notice on Blomberg and Fritsch that a more adventurous and dangerous phase in foreign policy was imminent' (Carr, 1979: 128). Significantly On 22 November the decision was taken decision to raise the production of Germany's raw iron 'to the limit of capacity' (Tooze, 2007: 241) and on 7 December General Jodl, the Chief of the Operations Staff, drew up plans for an offensive rather than defensive war against Czechoslovakia.

THE *ANSCHLUSS*

As an Austrian and a pan-German, Hitler assumed that the future of Austria lay in union with the Reich. He had made a bad mistake when, in July 1934, he had supported the bungled coup carried out by Austrian Nazis. This had severely damaged Italian–German relations, but the outbreak of the Abyssinian war and the subsequent rupture between Italy and Britain and France forced Mussolini to look towards Berlin. Mussolini was still opposed in principle to an *Anschluss*, but he now advised Schuschnigg, the Austrian Chancellor, to negotiate a general settlement with Germany. The subsequent agreement of 11 July 1936 was a considerable success for Hitler, as it clearly showed that German rather than Italian influence was now paramount in Vienna: Austria's foreign policy was to be more closely harmonised with Germany's while the two states were to cooperate closely economically and culturally.

The opportunities to annex Austria were presented to Hitler both more quickly than he envisaged and in a diplomatic situation that differed markedly from the scenario he had outlined at the meeting of 5 November 1937. The *Anschluss* was a 'striking example' of Hitler's ability to combine 'consistency in aim, calculation and patience in preparation with opportunism, impulse and improvisation in execution' (Bullock, 1971: 204). In January 1938, although Göring, as head of the Four Year Plan, was anxious to gain control of Austria's raw material resources, Hitler had no immediate plans for action. It was Schuschnigg, who was inadvertently to act as a catalyst for the *Anschluss*. Hoping to divide the Austrian Nazis and appease Berlin, he had offered Arthur Seyss-Inquart, a 'moderate' Nazi sympathiser, a post in his cabinet. He then sought an interview with Hitler in an attempt to persuade him to curb Nazi agitation within Austria.

Hitler readily agreed to a meeting, particularly since a success in Austria would provide a distraction from the embarrassing Blomberg–Fritsch crisis (see page 40). Schuschnigg travelled to the Berghof on 12 February where Hitler dictated a series of conditions which would effectively turn Austria into a German satellite: not only was there to be an end to all restrictions on the Nazi Party, but Seyss-Inquart was to be appointed Minister of the Interior with control over the police, while another Nazi, Glaise-Horstenau, was to take over the War Ministry. It was only Schuschnigg's desperate attempt on 9 March to regain a measure of independence from Hitler by asking his countrymen to vote in a referendum for a 'free and German, independent and social, Christian and united Austria' that prompted Hitler to drop his policy of gradual absorption and order a military occupation of Austria. Hitler secured Mussolini's agreement by reassuring him that he would respect the Brenner frontier. On 12 March German troops moved into Austria, but the army was so ill-prepared that many of its vehicles broke down. It was perhaps fortunate for the *Wehrmacht* that in his resignation speech on the radio Schuschnigg announced that the Austrian army would offer no resistance! Later that day Hitler himself crossed the border. Faced with a tumultuous reception at Linz, he quickly abandoned his original idea of installing a satellite government under Seyss-Inquart, and instead incorporated Austria into the Reich.

The *Anschluss* was a tremendous success for Hitler. Contrary to the cautious advice of the army and the professional diplomats, he had again achieved in his own way what the vast majority of both the Germans and Austrians wanted. Yet the *Anschluss* was also a 'watershed for Hitler and for the Third Reich' (Kershaw, II, 2000: 83). British and French passivity had convinced him that he could now move more quickly to build up the Greater German Reich.

THE DESTRUCTION OF CZECHOSLOVAKIA

However, before this could be achieved Czechoslovakia would have to be dismembered. Czechoslovakia occupied a strategic position in central Europe and inevitably looked to Paris and Moscow for protection against Germany. Not surprisingly, Hitler regarded it as a hostile aircraft carrier in the middle of Europe. It possessed a well-equipped army and an efficient armaments industry, but its potential strength was undermined by its internal divisions. Not only was there tension between the Czechs and Slovaks, but there were also hostile Hungarian, Polish and Ruthenian minorities. Its unity was, above all, menaced by the 3 million Sudeten Germans who wished to be included in the Third Reich.

Until late May 1938 Hitler had no immediate plan for attacking Czechoslovakia. He may have been waiting for the kind of international distraction in the west, which he had forecast at the meeting on 5 November 1937, or for the conclusion of a definite military pact with Italy before committing himself. On 28 March 1938 Konrad Henlein, the Sudeten German leader, was instructed by Hitler to formulate demands for Sudeten home rule, which would appear reasonable to outside observers, but which the Czechs could not accept without risking the break-up of their state. On the weekend of 20–21 May the Czech government completely surprised Hitler by partially mobilising its army in response to inaccurate rumours of an imminent German attack. When Britain, France and Russia made clear that they would not tolerate such an attack, Hitler proclaimed his innocence, but paradoxically their intervention, far from deterring him, persuaded him to set 1 October as the deadline for 'smashing Czechoslovakia'. Taylor dismisses this as mere bluff, arguing that 'Hitler did not need to act. Others would do his work for him' (Taylor, 1961b: 152). It is of course correct that in response to Hitler's threats Neville Chamberlain, the British prime minister, did come forward with proposals for the cession of the Sudetenland, but now few historians doubt that Hitler was ready to destroy Czechoslovakia by force. Throughout the summer of 1938 Hitler continued to encourage not only Sudeten separatism, but he also tried to orchestrate similar demands from the Polish and Hungarian minorities, so that Hungary and Poland would support his efforts to eliminate Czechoslovakia.

On 12 September Hitler's anti-Czech campaign moved into a new phase when, at Nuremberg, he bitterly attacked and demanded self-determination for the Sudeten Germans. This provoked increasing unrest in the Sudetenland. Both in Germany and Europe as a whole there was a feeling that war was imminent. To avert unilateral German action the British Prime Minister Neville Chamberlain flew to Berchtesgaden for talks with Hitler. Hitler grudgingly agreed to Chamberlain's proposition that, subject to agreement with the French, Czechoslovakia should be persuaded to cede to Germany all areas which contained a German population of 50 per cent or over. After consultations with the French and the Czechs, Chamberlain would return to Germany for further talks. In the meantime Hitler agreed to take no military action, which was not a difficult concession to make, as the German army needed two more weeks before it was ready to occupy Czechoslovakia.

Chamberlain met Hitler again at Bad Godesberg on 22 September, after both Britain and France had forced the Czechs to agree to cede the Sudetenland. The only concessions made to Prague were that there would be an Anglo-French guarantee of the new border, which would be mapped out by an international commission, and a Czech–German non-aggression pact. Hitler, however, referring to attacks on the Sudetens which he had done his best to encourage, rejected these terms outright and presented Chamberlain with what was in effect an ultimatum. He demanded that the German occupation of the Sudetenland should be speeded up so that it would be completed by 28 September. Only on the following day (23 September) did he reluctantly agree to postpone it to 1 October. Taylor argues that Hitler was merely attempting to procrastinate in order to give the Hungarians and Poles the chance to formulate their own territorial demands on Czechoslovakia, thereby giving himself an admirable pretext for intervening as 'a peace-maker to create a new order' (Taylor, 1961b: 179), but the weight of evidence indicates that he was initially determined to advance into the Sudetenland and, if necessary, risk war with the western powers.

Hitler's rejection of Chamberlain's peace package led to the scenario he had contemplated. The Czechs refused to agree to Hitler's ultimatum and there appeared to be no other option but war. When the British and French began to mobilise, Hitler was at first determined to press ahead with the occupation of the Sudetenland, but then 'the unthinkable happened' (Kershaw, II, 2000: 119). The obvious desire of his generals, and indeed of the German people as a whole, to avoid war, combined with the willingness of Britain and France still to find a compromise, finally persuaded Hitler on 28 September to consent to negotiations. His retreat was masked by his acceptance of Mussolini's offer to mediate and the subsequent proposal of a conference to meet at Munich the following day. There it was agreed that Germany should occupy the Sudetenland in stages between 1 and 10 October 1938, and later an international boundary commission would map the boundary line. Germany, Britain, France and Italy would then guarantee what was left of Czechoslovakia. Hitler also consented to sign a declaration which affirmed the intention of Britain and Germany 'never to go to war against one another again'.

Although Winston Churchill's damning criticism of Munich is hard to fault, Chamberlain had at least succeeded in stopping unilateral German action and in securing a four-power guarantee for rump-Czechoslovakia. Hitler interpreted the conference as a diplomatic defeat which cheated him of his war against Czechoslovakia and as a sign that Britain, despite its willingness to appease, would not allow Germany a completely free hand in eastern Europe. Significantly, on 21 October 1938 the German army was told to draw up plans for the final defeat of Czechoslovakia, and on 1 November the navy was ordered to accelerate its construction programme, which became known as 'Plan Z', as quickly as possible. There were both cogent economic and strategic reasons for Hitler's desire to destroy Czecho-Slovakia, as it was now called. Czech industry, military equipment, raw materials, gold reserves and foreign currencies were urgently needed to boost the Four Year Plan, while strategically the occupation of Czecho-Slovakia would strengthen Germany's southern defences, open the road to the Balkans and facilitate negotiations with Poland over the status of Danzig and the Corridor.

Hitler used the separatist demands of the Slovaks as his Trojan horse to provoke the break-up of the Czech state. While it is true that the actual timing of the crisis in March 1939 may again have taken Hitler by surprise, he speedily exploited the situation which he had done so much to provoke. In early March 1939 the tension between the Czechs and Slovaks came to a head when the central government in Prague deposed the regional Slovakian cabinet. The former Slovak Prime Minister, Jozef Tiso, was invited immediately to Berlin where, on 13 March, he was told by Hitler to declare Slovakian independence unless he wished to risk being overrun by Hungary. A Slovak National Assembly was called the following day and, after a German naval flotilla had been sent down the Danube to Bratislava, it duly asked for German 'protection'. In a desperate attempt to preserve some independence, the Czech President, Hacha, then travelled to Berlin where he was ruthlessly bullied into agreeing to the German occupation of Prague and the creation of an independent Slovakia, which was in fact little more than a German satellite state.

Within ten days Hitler achieved two further successes. On 22 March, Memel was returned to the Reich by Lithuania and a far-reaching economic treaty was signed with Romania, which gave Germany access to its oil fields.

THE POLISH CRISIS AND THE OUTBREAK OF WAR

In early 1939 it could be said that Hitler 'had lost his bearings' (Carr, 1979: 132) and momentarily did not know where next to turn. In December 1938 he had started to cultivate good relations with France by abandoning German claims to Alsace-Lorraine in the hope that France would give up her interest in eastern Europe. In January, and again in March, Ribbentrop unsuccessfully sounded out the Polish government on the return of Danzig and a German road and rail link through the Corridor in return for eventual Polish gains in Ukraine. Polish support would have facilitated an attack on the USSR, but also have freed him to turn westwards should he decide to knock out France and Britain first. The Poles were ready to make minor concessions, but not run the risk of becoming a client state of Germany.

The occupation of Prague, followed by the absorption of Memel and the Romanian Treaty, brought about a sea-change in the policies of Britain and France. Their foreign policy switched now from appeasement to deterrence. On 31 March 1939 the British government, backed by Paris, announced that it would guarantee Poland against external attack. This had an immediate and dramatic impact on German diplomacy and concentrated Hitler's attention on the destruction of Poland. Hitler hoped to isolate Poland, but if he failed, he was ready simultaneously to fight Britain and France. He did not want to run the risk of another Munich, that is of Britain and France again conjuring up a compromise settlement that would prevent the destruction of Poland. On 3 April orders were issued to the army to be ready for a military attack on Poland by 1 September. The talks which had resumed on Danzig and the Corridor in March 1939 were abruptly cancelled and for the rest of the summer determined attempts were made to isolate Poland and bring pressure to bear on the western powers to abandon it to its fate. Links were also tightened with Italy through the Pact of Steel in May, which committed both powers to assist each other in the event of war, although Ribbentrop, quite deliberately, led Mussolini to believe that it was still five years away. Broadly successful efforts were made to secure the neutrality of the smaller European states, but Ribbentrop failed to turn the Anti-Comintern Pact into an anti-western alliance, since the Japanese, who were already involved in escalating clashes with the Russians along the Mongolian–Manchurian border, declined to be drawn into a war with the western powers.

The key to the coming conflict lay in Moscow where, in the summer of 1939, both the western powers and Germany competed to negotiate an agreement with the USSR. Since 1933 the USSR had made several attempts to improve relations with Berlin, but these had been ignored by Hitler. However, in the summer of 1939 a pact with the USSR was becoming an attractive proposition. To many of the Nazi 'old fighters' it seemed hardly credible that Hitler could negotiate an agreement with the power symbolising all he was pledged to destroy, but the logic of the situation was explained by Ribbentrop to the Italian ambassador: as Poland was the 'immediate enemy' and Britain and France the 'intermediate enemies' who might come to her aid, an alignment with the USSR, which was the 'later enemy' was a sensible step to take (Weinberg, II, 1980: 567). After preliminary economic talks, serious political discussions began in Moscow on 12 August and the Nazi–Soviet Non-Aggression Treaty was signed on 23 August. By securing Russia's benevolent neutrality in return for territorial concessions in eastern Europe, it deprived Britain and France of the only alliance which could have stopped Poland's defeat. In a secret protocol it also outlined the German and Russian spheres of interests in eastern Europe: Finland, the Baltic states, eastern Poland and Romanian Bessarabia would belong to the Russian sphere of interest, while central and western Poland would be within the German sphere of interest.

Hitler was now understandably confident that he had minimised the danger of western intervention and planned to attack Poland on 26 August. On 25 August, however, Britain and France stubbornly ratified their treaties of guarantee, instead of abandoning Poland, and Mussolini announced that he could not go to war without impossibly large deliveries of German armaments and equipment. Hitler reacted to this by postponing the attack. Was he again having second thoughts, as in September 1938? Taylor argues that he was hoping to persuade Britain to repeat its Munich policy and force Poland to make concessions, but a peaceful settlement with Poland was the last thing Hitler wanted. On the contrary, as the deadline for the declaration of war on Poland was 1 September, Hitler was going to use the small margin of time he had, once again, to try to separate Britain and Poland. To that end he first offered Britain an alliance and guarantee of its empire, provided it consented to the destruction of Poland and German hegemony in eastern Europe. When the British government insisted that only after a freely negotiated Polish–German agreement could the future of Anglo-German relations be discussed, Hitler proposed on 29 August that the British should arrange for the Poles to send to Berlin a minister with full powers to negotiate a settlement of the Danzig question and the Corridor by the following day. By way of a compromise, Hitler was apparently ready to offer a plebiscite in the Corridor. The British refused to press the Poles to obey what was in reality an ultimatum and, consequently, on 31 August, at 12.30, Hitler gave the order for war. Taylor insists that the war began because Hitler launched 'on 29 August a diplomatic manoeuvre which he ought to have launched on 28 August' (Taylor, 1961b: 278). Perhaps it is possible that, given more time, he might have driven a wedge between Britain and Poland, but he did not want a compromise settlement with Poland. The terms he was offering to the Poles were for propaganda consumption only. He was aiming to isolate Poland and to manoeuvre it into a position where its 'stubbornness' could be blamed for starting the war [**Doc. 34, p. 174**].

When German troops crossed the Polish frontier at 4.45 am on 1 September, Hitler did not abandon his attempts to keep Britain out of the war. Birger Dahlerus, the Swedish industrialist and friend of Göring, was sent on an unofficial mission to London, while Chamberlain's adviser Sir Horace Wilson was invited for talks to Berlin, but British demands that German troops should first be withdrawn from Poland before any talks could begin were contemptuously rejected. On 3 September Britain and France had therefore little option but to declare war on Germany. Hitler had failed to isolate the Poles.

9

Germany, Europe and the world, 1939–45

Anglo-French military passivity enabled Hitler to destroy Poland in six weeks. Invaded from three sides with an army twice their size the Poles never really stood a chance. Their fate was finally sealed when on 17 September, in accordance with the secret protocol accompanying the Nazi–Soviet Pact (see page 90), Soviet troops occupied eastern Poland. Hitler had now either to attempt to come to terms with Britain and France or defeat them. Initially he kept both options open. On 6 October he proposed a negotiated peace on the basis of a new order in Poland, which would apparently involve the continued existence of a small Polish rump state as a German satellite. When Britain and France rejected these peace feelers, Hitler prepared for an attack in the west. This was scheduled to start on 12 November but, as a result of bad weather, had to be postponed until the spring.

Throughout the winter of 1939–40 Germany received considerable economic assistance from Soviet Russia. Russia's supplies of vital raw materials, the use of its railway system to transport rubber from the Far East and the protection given to German merchantmen all helped neutralise the economic consequences of the British blockade. In exchange for supplies of German naval equipment, Stalin also offered the Germans a naval base near Murmansk. In return, when Russia attacked Finland, which resolutely refused to make concessions to Moscow, Hitler had, contrary to his most deeply held anti-Bolshevik beliefs, to exert considerable pressure on Mussolini to stop him supplying the Finns with aircraft. Hitler feared, however, that Britain, under cover of assisting the Finns, might occupy Norway and threaten German iron ore supplies. To pre-empt this, German forces occupied Denmark and Norway in early April 1940.

On 10 May the German offensive opened in western Europe. Within six weeks Holland, Belgium and France were all overrun and British troops driven off the continent. The sheer scale of these victories at last persuaded Mussolini to take the plunge and declare war on Britain and France on

10 June. Ten days later the Reynaud government was replaced in France by a new administration under Marshal Pétain, which immediately asked for an armistice.

THE BRITISH PROBLEM, 1940–41

To end the war in the west Hitler hoped that Britain would rapidly follow suit and request a cease-fire. Hitler was initially ready to grant relatively generous peace terms to Britain. As early as 13 June he assured the British that it had never been his intention to destroy their empire, and on 19 July he stressed in the *Reichstag* that there was now no reason for the continuation of the war. He suspected that if the British Empire disintegrated, it would be America, Japan and the USSR that would pick up the bits rather than Germany. When his offer was again rejected on 22 July he became increasingly perplexed and vacillated half-heartedly between a number of courses, all designed to force Britain into making peace. On 16 July Hitler issued his first directive preparing for the invasion of Britain. Klaus Hildebrand has argued that he had a 'doctrinaire inclination towards his British enemy', and 'was never absolutely and genuinely prepared to agree wholeheartedly to an invasion' (Hildebrand, 1973: 103). However there were good reasons for caution. Hitler did not have the naval force to undertake a successful invasion of Britain and the failure of the *Luftwaffe* to defeat the RAF in September 1940 in the Battle of Britain forced him to consider instead other options for forcing Britain to make peace.

Admiral Raeder, the Commander-in-Chief of the navy, advised him to attack Britain's lines of communication through the Mediterranean. By seizing Gibraltar, the Suez Canal and by establishing bases in the Azores and off the west African coast, as well as occupying Palestine and Syria, Britain would be fatally weakened. Any American attempts to secure bases in northwest Africa before intervening in the war could then be thwarted. Up to a point Hitler acted on this advice and explored the possibilities of creating an anti-British alliance in the Mediterranean. In the autumn of 1940, in what, according to Norman Rich, 'may have been the most important diplomatic discussions of the war' (Rich, II, 1974: 217), Hitler attempted to persuade Franco and Marshal Pétain, the Minister President of Vichy France (see page 98), to enter the war against Britain. At a meeting with Franco at Hendaye on 23 October 1940 he tried to secure Spain's cooperation in seizing Gibraltar, but Franco refused to abandon neutrality unless he was guaranteed a large part of French North Africa, a request which Hitler could hardly grant if he wished to win over Vichy France. On 24 October Hitler met Pétain at Montoire but, despite assurances that he accepted the principle of collaboration with Germany, Pétain skilfully avoided any actual military commitment. It is possible that Hitler might have won him over, if he had negotiated a generous peace treaty, but he was unwilling to make a final settlement with France until the defeat of Britain, and was also handicapped by having privately assured Mussolini that Nice, Corsica, Tunis and French Somaliland would in due course fall to Italy. Hitler cynically but correctly observed that 'the resolution of the conflicting interests of France, Italy and Spain in Africa is only possible through a grandiose fraud' (Cecil, 1975: 89).

Hitler's difficulties in the Mediterranean were increased by Mussolini's incompetent attempts to emulate Germany's military achievements. Although Mussolini had declared war on Britain and France on 10 June 1940, German and Italian strategy was never effectively coordinated. Mussolini's expressed aim was to fight 'not for Germany but only for Italy alongside Germany' (Noakes and Pridham, III, 1988: 793). Alarmed by the dispatch of a division of German troops to secure the Romanian oil fields (see page 95), Mussolini launched the disastrous Italian invasion of Greece across inhospitable mountains covered with the first snow falls of winter. By the early spring it became clear that German troops were needed to save Italy from defeat. The Italian advance on Egypt also met with disaster and a complete rout was only avoided when German troops under Rommel were sent to Libya in February 1941. Rommel's achievements in the next 18 months were impressive and show what a larger German force could have brought about if it had been dispatched earlier.

Prodded on by Ribbentrop, Hitler also explored the chance of creating an anti-British continental power bloc. On 27 September a Tripartite Pact was signed between Italy, Japan and Germany, in which the three powers not only recognised their respective spheres of interest in Europe and eastern Asia but, in a clause that was aimed at the United States, also undertook 'to assist one another with all political, economic and military means' should one of them be attacked by a power not currently involved in hostilities in Europe or China. Hungary, Romania and Slovakia all joined the pact, but in November 1940 Ribbentrop failed to persuade Molotov to accept what Cecil has called 'a junior partnership in an international crime syndicate' (Cecil, 1975: 107). Molotov, the Soviet Foreign Minister, stressed with an embarrassing clarity that Russia was not prepared to forget its traditional interests in Turkey, south-eastern and central Europe. The Tripartite Pact soon proved to have little real value. It failed to deter the United States from stepping up its naval and economic cooperation with Britain or to dissuade Japan from seriously considering a *rapprochement* with the United States in early 1941.

THE DECISION TO ATTACK SOVIET RUSSIA

While Hitler was preparing for an invasion of Britain and toying with alternatives in the Mediterranean, he had already instructed his generals to prepare plans for an attack on Russia. By early August 1940 a growing number of troops were being transferred eastwards, and on 18 December he finally decided to launch the Russian invasion in the spring of 1941, Operation Barbarossa. His reasons for taking this fatal step at the time he did are by no means clear. Of course, the destruction of Bolshevik Russia was one of his major aims, but by leaving an undefeated Britain increasingly backed by a powerful United States in the west he committed the very strategic error he had sworn to avoid in *Mein Kampf*. Weinberg argued that the 'decision to attack the Soviet Union was Hitler's answer to the challenge of England – as it had been Napoleon's' (Weinberg, 1954: 171). At a conference on 31 July 1940 [**Doc. 35, p. 173**], Hitler sought to convince his generals that the defeat of the Soviet Union would at a stroke deprive Britain of the hope of both a Russian and an American alliance and consequently bring about its capitulation. Although there were certainly formidable obstacles in the way of defeating Britain, it is nevertheless true that Hitler was 'pursuing an indirect approach of a singular kind' (Cecil, 1975: 78). If the defeat of Britain had really been his first priority, he would surely have concentrated on intensifying the naval war and on attacking Britain in the Mediterranean with adequate forces. Perhaps it is therefore more accurate to say that the defeat of Britain was only a 'subsidiary aim of the Russian offensive' (Hildebrand, 1973: 17).

Rich argues that Hitler attacked the Soviet Union because he believed that Stalin would 'never tolerate a definitive German victory in the west' (Rich, I, 1973: 204). It is true that by 1941 Stalin had exploited the Nazi–Soviet Pact to build up the Russian position in eastern Europe and, by annexing northern Bukovina and Bessarabia in June 1940, he was poised to strike next at the Romanian oil fields on which the Nazi war machine depended. Hitler had been sufficiently worried to send troops into the oil fields in September 1940, which in turn prompted Stalin to raise the question of Russian interests in Finland and Bulgaria. Rich also stressed that as the Soviet Union either directly supplied the Nazis with most of their raw materials or allowed them to be transported across its territory, Stalin could at any time strangle Germany economically. However, this argument can be countered by pointing out that the USSR profited from its trade with Germany and had every incentive to keep the peace. In June 1941 there was no evidence that Stalin was planning a war against Germany in the near future.

Hitler's decision to attack Russia cannot be properly understood unless it is seen in the context of Nazi ideology. His belief in his mission to destroy

Bolshevism and to provide *Lebensraum* [**Docs 16, 32(a) and 33, p. 156, 169 and 170**] is the real motivating force behind the invasion. Conquered Russian territory would become, as he was later to put it, 'our India' (Wright, 2007: 176). Alan Bullock's assessment made in 1971 that 'of all decisions it is the one which most clearly bears his own personal stamp, the culmination (as he saw it) of his career' (Bullock, 1971: 218) still remains valid today.

Before Hitler could launch the attack he had to secure his south-eastern flank. Mussolini, contrary to Hitler's desire to keep the Balkans quiet, had attacked but failed to defeat Greece in the winter of 1940–41, and consequently gave the British an opportunity to land and establish air bases which could seriously threaten the southern flank of a German offensive in Russia. In March 1941, when the pro-German regime in Yugoslavia was overthrown in favour of a more Anglophile administration, German forces rapidly over-ran both Greece and Yugoslavia and secured the whole of south-east Europe as a base for military operations against Russia, which were launched on 22 June.

FROM EUROPEAN TO WORLD WAR, 1941–45

Once the *Blitzkrieg* was finally halted by the Russians before Moscow in December 1941, Hitler was faced with the prospect of a long-drawn-out war on two fronts. On 7 December the European war escalated into a world war when Japan attacked the American fleet at Pearl Harbor. The following day Britain and America declared war on Japan. As Japan was the aggressor, Germany was not committed to assist it by the Tripartite Pact, but Hitler seized the chance to declare war on the USA on 11 December and to give Japan every encouragement to tie the Americans down in the Pacific and weaken the British by seizing Singapore. He gambled on the Pacific war preventing the USA from helping Britain in the west and leaving him free to defeat Russia. In the light of Anglo-American cooperation in 1940–41 he saw a declaration of war as merely formalising what in fact existed already. Germany, Japan and Italy undertook not to 'seek an armistice or seek peace' with either Britain or the USA 'without full agreement of each other', and 'after the victorious conclusion of the war' agreed to cooperate 'for the purpose of achieving a new just order on the basis of the Tripartite Pact' (Noakes and Pridham, III, 1988: 835–36). On 18 January the three powers signed a military agreement which divided the world into two military operational zones along the line of 70° latitude. In practice, however, the Japanese fought a separate war in the Far East and refused to become involved in hostilities against the USSR. Indeed, it was in their interests for the Russo-German war to end as quickly as possible so that Germany could redouble the pressure on Britain and America in Europe.

In the early summer of 1942 the Germans renewed their advance into the Soviet Union and by July had reached the Caucasus. For a few months it seemed as if the German–Japanese agreement of 18 January 1942 to divide up the eastern hemisphere would be realised. After defeating the USSR, Hitler intended to turn on the United States and Britain with Japanese help, although there is no doubt that he still had some reservations about the possible dismemberment of the British Empire and even believed a Soviet defeat and Japanese pressure on India might open up the way for a separate peace with Britain.

In the autumn and winter of 1942–43 Hitler finally lost the initiative at Stalingrad and El Alamein and was remorselessly pushed on the defensive in both the east and the west. In July 1943 British and American troops landed in Sicily and Mussolini was deposed in Rome. In September he was rescued by German paratroopers, and with German support the Republic of Salò was established in northern Italy, which was in reality only a German satellite state. The Italian army was interned and over half a million soldiers were sent to Germany as forced labourers.

In June 1944 the Allies landed in Normandy and by January 1945 the Soviet army was only 60 kilometres east of Berlin. Hitler had rejected both the peace feelers put forward by Stalin in 1942 and 1943, and the Japanese attempts to mediate on his behalf with the Russians in September 1944. He continued to pin his hopes on the development of new weapons. At the end of the war he was desperately hoping that a split would develop between the Russians and the Americans that would lead to a separate peace with the west, but these were illusions because the western Allies had already agreed at Casablanca in January 1943 to insist on the unconditional surrender of the Axis powers.

EUROPE UNDER GERMAN OCCUPATION, 1939–44

In the west, Germany annexed little territory outright in 1940, although in the long term Hitler and his advisers harboured more ambitious plans. From Belgium he took Eupen and Malmédy, which had been German up to 1918, and he also integrated Luxembourg, Alsace and most of Lorraine into the Reich. Hitler regarded the Scandinavians and the Dutch as Germanic peoples who would in due course find a permanent place in the Greater German

Reich. When German troops occupied Norway, Denmark and Holland in 1940, Hitler had originally hoped to cooperate with the existing governments and work through them to secure essential German interests, but only in Denmark was this policy initially successful. Both the Norwegian and Dutch monarchs fled to London with their cabinets, and Hitler had to install *Reichskommissaren*, who were, however, able to rule through the existing administrative machinery and only needed a relatively small number of German bureaucrats to assist them. For a time Denmark was the showpiece of Nazi Europe. King, cabinet and parliament appeared to function normally and in March 1943 there was even a general election, but this was in fact only a façade for indirect German rule. Danish economic and foreign policy were both dictated from Berlin, and when the elections produced a large majority against collaboration with Hitler, the German authorities seized the opportunity provided by strikes and sabotage to declare martial law.

Belgium was also deemed to be a Germanic country which would eventually be dissolved into two new *Reichsgaue*, Flanders and Brabant, but up to July 1944 it was administered, together with the two French departments of Nord and Pas de Calais, by a military government as it was an essential base for military operations against Britain. The military government under General Baron von Falkenhausen kept both the Nazi Party and Himmler at arm's length, and the pre-war administration and judicial system were kept virtually intact.

France, of course, was by far the most valuable of Germany's conquests in western Europe. Although Goebbels made no secret of the fact that 'in future France would only play a role as a small Atlantic state' (Mazower, 2008: 108), in practice Hitler was far more pragmatic. He devised what Norman Rich called 'a remarkably clever arrangement' (Rich, II, 1974: 200) to protect German interests in France, by dividing France into the occupied and unoccupied zones. The French government, which remained at Vichy in the unoccupied zone, saved German manpower by administering the whole country, but could at any time be put under pressure by the mere threat of tightening up the border restrictions between the two zones. German troops were spread relatively thinly over the occupied areas, and only a small number of German officials were necessary to coordinate policy with General Pétain. All in all the Germans managed to crown their military victories in France 'with a significant political achievement', which tempered 'ideology with pragmatism' and created a 'more or less nationally accepted government to work alongside them and run the country' (Mazower, 2008: 110).

In Vichy both the French bureaucracy and the police filled the vacuum of power left by defeat and attempted to preserve what was left of the French state by cooperating with the Germans in the arrest of resistance members and the deportation of French Jews to the death camps. When the Allies landed in North Africa in November 1942, German troops moved in to occupy Vichy France. The whole area was put under surveillance by the *Wehrmacht* and SS, and demands for mass repression and round-ups were intensified. The response to this by René Bousquet, the head of police, was to argue this should be left to the French authorities. When several small bombs exploded in the harbour area of Marseilles in January 1943, the Germans insisted that the whole of the old port quarter should be evacuated and dynamited, and sent an SS regiment to accomplish the task. The French, however, managed to persuade Berlin to allow the local police to carry out the task, which involved the transfer of some 40,000 people to camps in the north.

With the Allied occupation of North Africa and establishment of the **Committee for National Liberation** by the Free French leaders in Algiers in 1943, the policy of collaboration with the Germans became increasingly difficult to enforce. In the week after D-Day in June 1944, for instance, nearly a third of the gendarmes in the Auvergne joined the **Maquis**. Once France was liberated in the autumn of 1944, the Vichy government and key collaborators fled to southern Germany.

Committee for National Liberation Formed in Algiers in June 1943. It was committed to an Allied victory and the defeat of Vichy France.

Maquis French resistance movement.

In south-eastern Europe Hitler had few territorial ambitions. Romania, Bulgaria and Hungary were German satellites. After the defeat of Yugoslavia and Greece, Hitler annexed the former Austrian territories in Slovenia, but broke up Yugoslavia into three small countries, Croatia, Serbia and Montenegro, where puppet regimes were installed as façades for German and Italian rule. A weak collaborationist government was tolerated in Greece, which Hitler regarded as primarily within the Italian sphere of interest. Only in 1943, after Mussolini's fall, did German troops take over full responsibility for the occupation of Greece and northern Italy.

Hitler had more ambitious plans for eastern Europe, which he started to implement during the war. After defeating Poland, he annexed the Danzig Corridor, Silesia and a small section of territory bordering on East Prussia. Rump-Poland (now called the Generalgovernment) was handed over to a civilian German administration under the notorious Dr Hans Frank. Then, when the Soviet Union was invaded in 1941, Bialystok province was annexed outright and two vast territories, Ostland and Ukraine, were created and ruled by civilian commissariats. Two further regions, Muscovy and the Caucasus, were planned but owing to the defeat of the German forces were never set up.

Hans Frank may have been called a 'megalomaniac Pasha' (Rich, II, 1974: 85) by his military colleagues, but in fact his power was far from absolute. The army, Göring – as Plenipotentiary of the Four Year Plan – and the Reich Defence Council (see page 108) all had the right to intervene in Polish affairs and issue decrees to protect their particular spheres of interest. Frank's

RKFDV (Reichskommis-sar/Reichskommissariat für die Festigung des Deutschen Volkstums) Himmler was appointed Reich Commissioner of the office of the Commissariat for the Strengthening of the German Race in October 1939. His task was (a) to remove all people of 'alien race' from the annexed territories in eastern Europe, and (b) to strengthen the Germanic element there by transferring ethnic Germans from the occupied territories

greatest rival was Himmler, who, as head of the security forces and of the Reich Commissariat for the Strengthening of the German Race (**RKFDV**), which was responsible for implementing the key policy of German resettlement, was in a powerful position to challenge him. Himmler initially created the greatest difficulties for Frank by using occupied Poland as a dumping ground for Poles, Gypsies and Jews expelled from the newly annexed territories (see page 72) and, in 1942–43, his attempts to Germanise the Lublin area by settling ethnic Germans caused havoc by seriously disrupting local agriculture and driving many of the Polish peasants over to the partisans. [**Doc. 38, p. 175**]

There was a similar pattern of conflict in Ukraine and Ostland. Rosenberg was appointed head of the Reich Ministry for the East, but far from enjoying the powers of a viceroy he was unable to secure acceptance of his policies for winning over minority nationalities in the Soviet Union. He repeatedly and ineffectually clashed with the generals, Himmler and Göring, who all pursued quasi-independent and contradictory policies. Dallin has shown that the chaos which marked German rule in the Soviet Union arose because 'the basic contradiction between long-range objectives and immediate demands was never reconciled'. Thus, 'at the very moment when some pressed for the utmost use of labour in eastern agriculture, others forcibly transported farm hands to work in the Reich. While the Army sought to enrol Soviet prisoners as troops, German factories pressed for their use in labour' (Dallin, 1957: 664). The disastrous effect of these contradictory policies was further exacerbated by the acute shortage of efficient German administrators and by the sheer size of the Russian commissariats. Belatedly, in 1944, Hitler tried to reverse his original policy of destroying the Russian state when he allowed General Vlasov, the captured Red Army general, to set up the Committee for the Liberation of the Peoples of Russia and to organise a congress at Prague where a constitution for a new non-Bolshevik federal Russia was unveiled. However, such concessions, coming after three years of Nazi atrocities, were both too little and too late.

In the first two years of the war the Germans had adopted a crude policy of 'smash and grab' towards the economies of the occupied territories (Wright, 1968: 116). Both in Poland and the Soviet Union the initial policy was to send back anything of value to the Reich, and even in France, where plundering was less blatant, initially 250 train-loads of arms and war materials were transported across the frontier. However, the failure of the *Blitzkrieg* in the winter of 1941–42 compelled the Germans to consider making belated economic concessions to the Russians. In February 1942 the New Agrarian Decree promised to liberate the peasants from 'the tyranny' of the 'Jewish Soviet government in Moscow' (Mazower, 2008: 284) but in reality it did not give the individual peasants back their farms. It merely turned the Soviet **collective farms** into communal farms owned by the peasants themselves – a system not far removed from what in fact existed under Stalin.

The growing demand for munitions also persuaded Hitler to abandon his original policy of de-industrialising the Soviet Union. By July 1942 steps had been taken to rebuild industry in the Donets Basin but, before the Germans were driven out by the Red Army, production had only reached 10 per cent of its pre-war level. In the General Government the pressure of German military and economic needs also produced change. In March 1940 Frank described the area as economically an 'empty shell', but by 1943 it was delivering nearly RM 630 million to Germany. (Noakes and Pridham, III, 1988: 962, 967).

In western Europe the Nazis were more willing to harness local industry to the needs of the German war economy. No attempts were made to dismantle Belgian or Dutch industry, and relatively subtle and semi-legal ploys were used to exploit the French economy and ensure German control of key industries. An arbitrary exchange rate was fixed, and clearing accounts were established in Berlin which enabled the Germans to defer payment for French material until after the war. With government backing, German banks attempted, with some success, to gain control of the French investment banks, and mixed Franco-German companies were set up in which the Germans held a majority of shares.

In the autumn of 1943 Albert Speer, the German Armaments Minister, took a significant step towards building an integrated Franco-German economy. He negotiated an agreement with Jean Bichelonne, the Vichy Minister for Industrial Production, whereby French industry would take over the production of consumer goods for the German market and so enable German factories to concentrate on war production. It was arranged that the French would meet the production quotas set by Berlin in exchange for the ending of labour conscription. However, as was frequently the case in the Third Reich, the clash of personal rivalries and contradictory plans prevented any consistent policy emerging. Fritz Sauckel, the Plenipotentiary for Labour Mobilisation, protested vigorously, and in the end persuaded Hitler to authorise a continuation of labour conscription in France.

In western Europe, German intentions to exploit the economy were to be partly veiled by the veneer of idealistic talk about a united anti-Bolshevik Europe in which there would be, in the words of Otto Dietrich, Germany's press chief, 'equal chances for all' (Wright, 1968: 140). The meeting of the leaders of the Anti-Comintern Pact in Berlin in 1941 was described as 'the first European Congress', and a 'Song of Europe' was even written to celebrate it. The Nazi 'European idea' was based upon both creating a 'European Economic Area' and a seductive myth of European unity which would oppose both Bolshevism in the east and American dollar imperialism in the

collective farms The Soviet collective farm system consisted of a mixture of state-run farms (*Sovkoz*) and farms run by the peasants themselves along cooperative lines (*Kolkhozy*).

Atlantic Charter A statement of fundamental democratic principles for the post-war world issued jointly by Churchill and Roosevelt in 1941.

Waffen-SS Armed or militarised SS. In the aftermath of the 'Night of the Long Knives' Hitler gave permission for the creation of three SS regiments. These formed the nucleus of the *Waffen-SS* – a term introduced in 1940.

west. It was a counter blast to the **Atlantic Charter** of August 1941 and had considerable propaganda potential until it became clear that it was just a camouflage for German domination of Europe.

A more practical expression to European unity was given by the small groups of volunteers from western Europe for the anti-Bolshevik 'crusade', and the expeditionary forces from Finland, Italy, Spain and Romania, which fought on the eastern front. Himmler initially recruited only 'Germanic' volunteers for the **Waffen-SS**, but then, as the German need for manpower grew, enlisted a veritable United Nations of peoples: Frenchmen, Ukrainians, Croatians, and so on. On 8 August 1944 the Free Indian Legion, comprising about 2,300 men, who had been taken prisoners in North Africa, was transferred to the control of the *Waffen-SS*. Himmler also had little difficulty in recruiting a 'Black International' (Rothfels, 1970: 19) drawn from a wide range of European peoples to guard the concentration camps (see page 107).

'ETHNIC CLEANSING' AND SETTLEMENT POLICIES IN EASTERN EUROPE

Poland was the laboratory for Nazi racial policy in eastern Europe. On 7 October Himmler was appointed head of the Reich Commission for the Strengthening of the German Race. Its initial aims were to supervise the repatriation of the *Volksdeutsche* to the Polish territories, which had been annexed to the Reich, whilst simultaneously evicting sufficient Poles and Jews to make room for them. By 1943 the RKFDV had expelled about a million Jews and Poles and brought in roughly 600,000 ethnic Germans, of whom only about half were settled on the land. The remainder spent the war in refugee camps. When it became clear that repatriation was not going to conjure up sufficient settlers, the Nazi regime began to draw up a complex list of groups drawn from the local population. People belonging to the first two were re-categorised as ethnic Germans. The third group was composed of 'state members', which included Germans married to ethnic Poles and people of 'intermediate nationality' such as the **Kashubians**, **Masurians**, **Silesians** and **Water Poles**, while the fourth was made up of 'renegades', that is Poles who looked like Germans and who could be re-educated to act as such! The rest of the Polish population in the incorporated areas were treated almost as badly as the Jews. Many were forced out of the inner cities into the suburbs, forbidden to speak their own language in public, paid lower wages than the Germans and were barred from cinemas, theatres and libraries.

For the 11 million Poles within the area of the *Generalgouvernement*, life was equally brutal. Hitler wished to reduce the Polish population there to

Kashubians West Slavic ethnic group in Pomerelia, north-central Poland. Their language or dialect is Kashubian.

Masurians Ethnic group along the former East Prussian–Polish borders. They are descended from Masovians who migrated to Prussia mainly during the sixteenth century and were largely Protestant.

Silesians Inhabitants of Silesia, who speak a distinctive Slav dialect.

Water Poles Poles in Silesia who speak a dialect composed of Czech, Slovak and German.

a semi-illiterate mass, whose main function would be to serve the interests of Greater Germany, and to allow the economy to deteriorate into what he called 'Polish chaos' (Rich, II, 1974: 86). Much of the Polish elite was rounded up and shot or sent to concentration camps, and there was talk in some Nazi circles of deporting or else simply 'ethnically cleansing' the whole Polish population, while Himmler had long-term plans to resettle the whole of Poland with Germans. Model villages would be built and after five years each settlement would begin to look German 'thanks to the blond girls and lads' everywhere in evidence (Burleigh, 2000: 447). The fortunes of war, however, prevented Himmler from implementing these ideas, apart from a trial expulsion of Poles in the Zamosc region near Lublin in November 1941. Between November 1942 and the summer of 1943 some 100,000 villagers from about 300 villages were uprooted and many sent to the camps at Majdanek and Auschwitz. This in turn led to an escalation of partisan warfare right across the region.

In the Soviet Union Hitler's plans were far more ambitious, even if not immediately realisable. Bolshevism and the Soviet elite were, of course, to be exterminated and large cities like Leningrad, Moscow and Kiev were also to be destroyed. Although the southern Ukraine and Crimea would be the first areas to be settled, he ultimately envisaged building up a population of 250 million Germans in western Russia within a time span of 70 or 80 years. In one of his late-night monologues in July 1941 Hitler even dreamed of pushing the new German frontier 'as far as possible to the east, and if necessary beyond the Urals' (Kershaw, II, 2000: 400). At regular intervals Hitler would elaborate on his plans for the colonisation of Russia. German peasants would live in specially constructed villages, while the German administrators and governors would live in palatial buildings appropriate to their rank. Motorways would link the new settlement to the Reich and the Black Sea would become a German holiday resort. The Russians, deprived of their elites, would become an exploited underclass, which would gradually die out. As Hitler remarked in February 1942 'no vaccinations for the Russians, and no soap to get the dirt off them. . . . But let them have all the spirits and tobacco they want' (Burleigh, 2000: 531).

Shortly before the invasion of the USSR the *Wehrmacht* commanders were ordered to have all Soviet political commissars, who were taken prisoner, shot out of hand. Four SS *Einsatzgruppen*, each composed of between 500 and 1,000 men, were formed to prepare the way for 'the political and administrative organization' of the occupied areas. Their role was to carry out special security police duties, which in practice involved, as Otto Ohlendorf, then a commander of one of the *Einsatzgruppen*, later testified at Nuremberg, 'putting to death all racially and politically undesirable elements among the prisoners' (Buchheim *et al.*, 1968: 62). He had in mind four main groups: Soviet officials, Gyspies, Jews and the so-called 'second-class Asiatics'.

Two days after the invasion of Russia Himmler ordered the Planning Office of the RKFDV to draw up plans for the wholesale resettlement of eastern Europe. In May 1942 it produced the notorious General Plan East, which envisaged a preliminary settlement of Ukraine and the Volga region with a network of frontier marches or settlements populated by tough SS war veterans, who would act as soldier-settlers. These settlements would be defended from native revolts by mobile defence forces. The plan was a long-term one and envisaged only about 3.5 million settlers at the end of the first 25 years and the deportation of about 31 million Slavs into western Siberia. A beginning was actually made at Hegewald in Ukraine in November 1942. Seven villages were cleared of their population and ethnic Germans were moved in from Volhynia, only to be driven away by Ukrainian partisans. The defeat at Stalingrad finally forced Hitler to abandon any further settlement plans.

THE HOLOCAUST

The large-scale settlement plans involving the movement of millions of people and the systematic attempt to destroy the Russian and Polish elites provided the context in which the murder of nearly 6 million Jews took place. The conquest of Poland put between 2–3 million Jews into Hitler's power, while there were a further half million in occupied territory in western Europe and some 3 million in Russia. In the winter of 1939–40 the RKFDV was given a free hand to create Jewish 'reservations' and ghettos in the General Government. There, the Jews from the newly incorporated territories were to be 'resettled'. However, the sheer scale of the logistical problems involved in resettling hundreds of thousands of people in wartime forced Göring, who still had overall responsibility for the Jewish question, to call a halt to the resettlement programme in March 1940.

The unbelievable cruelty of the Holocaust renders it a particularly difficult subject for the historian to analyse dispassionately. The structuralist view that the Holocaust was as much a consequence of muddle and improvisation as of clear planning can all too easily degenerate into an apologia for Hitler and the Nazi regime. Dawidowicz, for instance, accuses the structuralists of a 'mechanistic interpretation' of Nazi Germany, which eliminates personal blame (Dawidowicz, 1986: xxvi). On the other hand, the intentionalists' understandable emphasis on the unique horror of the Holocaust can also inhibit legitimate attempts by historians to subject it to a rational analysis.

The very use of the word 'holocaust', the dictionary definition of which is 'a sacrifice totally consumed by fire or a burnt offering', reflects, according to Marrus, 'an urge not only to distinguish this massacre from all others but also to register the ethereal quality of this terrible episode, its removal from customary discourse' (Marrus, 1987: 115).

Undoubtedly, one of the most difficult problems facing historians of the Third Reich is to pin-point when and by whom the decision was taken to murder the Jews. Their task is made more difficult by the fact that there is no clear documentary link between Hitler and the destruction of the Jews in the death camps. On the whole, intentionalist historians argue that the decision was taken once war broke out in September 1939. John Fox, for example, believes that 'the main purpose and objective of Hitler's war in Europe from 1939 to 1945 was to destroy utterly and totally Russian Jewry followed in turn by European Jewry' (Fox, 1991: 3). The structuralists are, however, less certain. Many have been struck by how 'evolutionary' or 'improvised' Nazi anti-Jewish policy in practice was (Marrus, 1987: 125).

Emigration continued to remain official policy at least up to June 1941, but during this period only about 71,500 Jews managed to leave Reich territory with the official permission of the Nazi government. After the fall of France there momentarily appeared to be a possibility of resettling the European Jewish population in the French colony of Madagascar, but the continuation of hostilities with Britain and Hitler's reluctance to alienate Vichy France (see page 93) ensured that, until Germany had won the war, this scheme was not viable. Does the Madagascar Plan, then, indicate that Hitler had not initially planned to exterminate the Jews? Did later unforeseen events force this action upon him and upon those whom he had made responsible for solving the Jewish 'problem'? Essentially, it is important to grasp that plans for 'resettlement' in Madagascar, or later in Siberia, were not really an alternative to extermination. One German historian, Hermann Graml, has convincingly argued that the Nazi authorities assumed that the great majority of Jews would anyway die from disease on Madagascar and that consequently mass murder would be 'given the appearance of a natural process' (Graml, 1992: 82). In this context it is also worth stressing that Philipp Bouhler, who had been in charge of the euthanasia programme in Germany (see page 70), had been tipped as the first governor of Madagascar.

Given, then, that Germany remained at war with Britain, the RKFDV in the winter of 1940–41 had little option but to revert to its original plan of concentrating the Jews in ghettos in Poland. This, too, ran into insuperable logistical problems as it coincided with the military build-up in preparation for the invasion of Russia. Nevertheless, Hitler was unwilling to stop the deportation programme, although in practice the lack of sufficient transport facilities had conspired to slow it down. In April 1941 he specifically vetoed suggestions from Göring that the Jews in Reich territory should be employed in the local war industries [**Doc. 39, p. 176**].

The real turning point in Nazi policy towards the Jews came with the invasion of Soviet Russia in June 1941. Not only did this bring some 3 million more Jews under German control, but the whole campaign was an overtly ideological struggle fought against Bolshevism, which to the Nazis was merely another manifestation of the Jewish bid for world power [**Docs 16 and 31, pp. 157 and 169**]. Hitler himself made clear to his generals on 30 March 1941 that they were about to embark upon 'a war of extermination' (Noakes and Pridham, III, 1988: 1086). As we have seen (page 103), the German High Command then issued the notorious Commissar Order, whereby all captured Red Army political officers were to be shot, and on Hitler's specific orders special SS *Einsatzgruppen*, or task forces, were given the job of 'mopping up' behind the lines of the invading German army [**Doc. 36, p. 174**]. Although they were officially supposed only to execute Communist Party officials and 'Jews in service of the state' (Noakes and Pridham, III, 1988: 1091), in fact by the spring of 1942 well over a million Jews who had nothing to do with the Communist Party had been murdered. In October 1941, for example tens of thousands of people were machine-gunned to death in the Babi Yar Ravine near Kiev.

Undoubtedly, massacres on this scale marked a new and more deadly stage in Nazi policy. However, historians do not agree on when and how the actual decision was taken to begin the Holocaust or systematic extermination of European Jewry. On 31 July 1941 Heydrich was ordered by Göring to draw up a detailed plan 'for bringing about a complete solution of the Jewish question within the German sphere of Europe' (Noakes and Pridham, III, 1988: 1104). Göring may well have intended Heydrich to draw up a blueprint for the total extermination of European Jewry, but the wording of the document is ambiguous.

The structuralists argue that at this stage the assumption in Berlin was still that the war would soon be over and the Jews would be 'resettled' in Madagascar or perhaps more likely Siberia. They stress that it was the unexpected success of the Red Army in December 1941 which was the crucial factor leading to the Holocaust (Broszat, 1985; Kettenacker, 1986; Mommsen, 1986: 156, 159). Not only did the continuation of the war make Siberia inaccessible to the Nazis, but the constant need to keep the German armies supplied also created enormous logistical problems in Poland and occupied Russia, which could only be made worse by the deportation of further Jews into the area. Arguably, then, a large-scale programme for liquidating the Jews was, in Broszat's words, a '"way out" of a blind alley into which the National Socialists had manoeuvred themselves' (Broszat, 1985: 405). The intentionalists vehemently criticise the implications of Broszat's argument that the Holocaust was, in effect, an accidental consequence of the military situation in eastern

Europe. Dawidowicz, for instance, argues that Hitler 'implemented his plan in stages, seizing whatever opportunities offered themselves to advance its execution' (Dawidowicz, 1986: Intro). This stress on the combination of opportunism and planning in Hitler's thinking is familiar and has already been noted by Bullock in relation to his foreign policy (see page 80). It was certainly the way that Hitler proceeded, but then, as has already been emphasised, the lack of documents linking Hitler directly to key decisions on the Holocaust makes it much more difficult for historians to trace his precise role in these terrible events. Nevertheless, by late 1941 there were so many Nazi initiatives aiming at the eventual extermination of the Jews that it is very probable that 'a green light was coming from the highest level' (Noakes and Pridham, III, 1988: 1136). At the very least, it must have been abundantly clear to Hitler's followers and officials that he favoured such policies. Arguably, this alone was sufficient to guarantee that they would compete with one another to 'work towards the *Führer*' [**Doc. 13, p. 155**] and ensure their implementation. On 11 and 12 December Hitler presided over a series of meetings with his *Gauleiter,* and after surveying both the international and domestic situations, he is recorded in Goebbels' diary as stating that the 'world war is here, so the annihilation of Jewry must be the necessary consequence'. Mazower regards this unambiguously as 'the green light for organizing the mass murder beyond the territories of the USSR' (Mazower, 2008: 376).

In January 1942 an attempt was made at the Wannsee Conference in Berlin by Heydrich and other senior officials in the SS, the Ministry of the Interior, the Justice Ministry, the SS and the General Government to coordinate these various initiatives [**Doc. 40, p. 176**]. Details were worked out for the wholesale conscription of Jews into labour gangs in eastern Europe, where it was chillingly assumed that 'a large number will drop out through natural elimination'. The remainder would then be 'dealt with accordingly' (Noakes and Pridham, III, 1988: 1131). Extermination camps were built in 1942 at Belzec, Sobibor and Treblinka, and a year later two more death camps were opened at Majdanek and Auschwitz. By 1945 nearly 6 million Jews from all over Europe had been murdered.

Mommsen has argued that 'the psychological bridge between the emigration and reservation "solutions" and the Holocaust itself was created by the fiction of *Arbeitseinsatz* or labour mobilization' (Mommsen, 1986: 124). Was the Holocaust inevitable once war broke out in 1939? It is probable, as the structuralists stress, that the exact form it took was largely dictated by events in eastern Europe. The intentionalists are nevertheless correct in stressing Hitler's absolute determination to rid the European states of their Jewish citizens, and that process would not have been gentle. In the course of 'resettlement' in Madagascar or Siberia millions of Jews would almost certainly have died from disease or starvation – or have been murdered.

10

The home front, 1939–45

DISINTEGRATION OF THE *FÜHRER* STATE

For much of the time from June 1941 onwards Hitler was absent from Berlin overseeing military operations either from his headquarters at the Wolfsschanze in East Prussia or from near Vinnitsa in the Ukraine. He immersed himself in the problems of the war and was cocooned from the real world. Only in November 1944 did he move back to Berlin. In December 1941 he took over the post of Commander-in-Chief of the army from General Brauchitsch, which gave him responsibility for both strategy and detailed military tactics. It was an immense workload and made him directly responsible for all the future defeats, which inevitably shattered his charismatic image. For the first three years of the war this image had survived intact, but it never recovered from the German defeat at Stalingrad in January 1943. From that point on, to quote Kershaw, 'the German people's love affair with Hitler was at an end' (Kershaw, II, 2000: 557), even though considerable pockets of support still remained [**Doc. 48, p. 182**].

With Hitler distracted by the military aspect of the war, the government of the Reich became even more dysfunctional. On 30 August 1939 the Ministerial Council for the Defence of the Reich was set up, but it failed to develop into a war cabinet, and after November 1939 no longer met. Another ineffectual attempt was made to coordinate policy by Frick, Funk and Keitel, the Chief of Staff of the High Command of the Armed Forces (OKW), but their proposed committee was never convened. Hitler was determined to prevent the emergence of any committee with real executive powers that might eventually be used to challenge him. He consistently blocked attempts by Lammers, the Head of the Reich Chancellery, to reintroduce regular cabinet meetings and even stopped ministers meeting unofficially. The only way to gain a decision was, of course, to go straight to Hitler. Goebbels, Himmler, Göring and later Speer were able to do this, but as Hitler became ever more bogged down in operational details, clear-cut decisions became almost impossible to obtain. Increasingly, too, Martin Bormann, in his pivotal position as Chief of the Party Chancellery at the *Führer* headquarters, which he assumed after Hess's flight to Scotland in May 1941, controlled access to Hitler and so played a key role in determining policy. Bormann was always at Hitler's side and jotted down even his most casual remarks in case they needed to be converted to *Führer* decrees.

To counter this, Lammers proposed in early 1943 the creation of a small committee composed of himself, Keitel and Bormann, which, under Hitler, would formulate policy. This 'committee of three', as it was called, did actually meet 11 times before it withered away in the autumn of 1943, but again Hitler safeguarded his power by ensuring that it had no independence or autonomy. It also aroused the jealousy of Funk, Ley and Goebbels, who seized on a suggestion by Speer to resurrect the Ministerial Council with the brief to take responsibility for the home front, while Hitler concentrated exclusively on military affairs. Goebbels, worried about Hitler's lack of leadership and absence from Germany, spoke openly of a 'leader crisis'. He was convinced that Hitler was being manipulated by Bormann. Yet, whenever they tried to confront Hitler with their proposals, their courage failed. In reality the regime was not re-formable as it 'was both the inexorable product of Hitler's personalised rule and the guarantee of his power' (Kershaw, II, 2000: 573).

THE INCREASING POWER OF THE NAZI PARTY AND THE SS

In the war years the power and political influence of the Nazi party and the SS significantly increased. Arguably it marked the 'second stage of the Nazi revolution' (Mazower, 2008: 226).

The SS not only continued to develop into a 'collateral state', but began to undermine and even dissolve the existing state institutions (Fest, 1979: 180). In September 1939 Himmler set up the Reich Security Head Office under Heydrich which brought together the police and the SS under a single directorate. It was a vast organisation, which was independent of the state and responsible solely to Hitler. It consisted of seven departments all dealing with various aspects of security both in the Reich and the occupied territories. It organised the dispatch of task forces into both Poland and Russia and was supposed to coordinate security right across Nazi-occupied Europe. The power of the SS was further strengthened by the appointment of Himmler as Commissioner of the RKFDV (see page 102). This gave him the key responsibility for organising the resettlement of ethnic Germans and eliminating 'the harmful influences of such alien parts of the population as constitute a danger to the Reich and the German community' in the occupied and incorporated territories (Broszat, 1981: 319). Both theses bodies with their numerous subordinate offices could act independently of the state and the party and their creation marked the beginning of the metamorphosis of the SS into a state within a state.

The control and administration of the concentration camps gave the SS access to a large pool of labour which could be used exclusively in its industrial undertakings. In February 1942 the task of administering the concentration camps was given to its Main Administrative Office for Business and Commerce. By 1944 the economic empire of the SS comprised about 150 firms organised together into one large trust, the *Deutsche Wirtschaftsbetriebe GmbH*, the activities of which ranged from quarrying, mining and the production of foodstuffs and mineral waters to the manufacture of armaments and textiles.

With the *Waffen-SS* Himmler was also able to provide the Nazi regime with a committed and fanatical National Socialist army, which expanded rapidly from a mere 18,000 in 1939 to 140,000 in November 1941. In the last two years of the war the armed (*Waffen*) SS was expanded up to a point where it nominally consisted of 35 divisions. In Himmler's eyes it was 'an institution not of the German people, but of the Germanic race' (Evans, 2009: 503), even though as the war progressed it increasingly had to fill its ranks with eastern Europeans, Croatians and renegade Indian troops captured in North Africa (see page 102). After the failure of the attempt on Hitler's life on 20 July 1944, Hitler ordered Himmler, who was appointed Commander of the Reserve Army to form 15 new divisions. He was determined to make these the core of a new National Socialist People's Army, but before such an army could be raised and indoctrinated, Germany had lost the war.

By 1944 Himmler was theoretically the most important man in the Reich after Hitler. Besides his power base in the SS, he was appointed Reich Minister of the Interior in 1943, and in 1944 in quick succession first Commander-in-Chief of the Rhine Army Group in December 1944 and then of the Vistula Army Group in January 1945. But paradoxically, while Himmler's power reached unprecedented heights in the Reich, his influence on Hitler was quietly and doggedly undermined by Bormann, who lost no chance to strengthen the influence of the party at the expense of the SS.

The war also presented the Nazi Party with numerous opportunities to extend its growth and influence at both central and local levels. The majority of the *Gauleiter* were appointed Reich Defence Commissioners in September 1939, and in 1942 were authorised to take complete charge of the civil authorities within their *Gaue* in the event of an invasion. The *Gaue* became Reich defence zones and increasingly the key administrative units throughout the Reich. When Hitler created the **Volkssturm** in September 1944, which was in effect a party-controlled citizen militia, it was organised on the territorial basis of the *Gaue* under the overall control of Bormann. In their roles as Defence Commissioners the *Gauleiter* behaved like barons in a period of feudal anarchy. For instance, they jealously hoarded labour so that they could keep industry in their own *Gaue* functioning, and in the last six months of the war did not hesitate to commandeer for local use vital coal trains *en route* to supply industries elsewhere.

At the start of the war the party was assigned the task of maintaining the morale of the civilian population. The military successes in Poland and western Europe fuelled the party's ambition to engineer the social and racial revolution which had been denied it in the 1930s. In the first half of 1941 Nazi activists attempted to take advantage of the wartime emergency to break the hold which the Churches still had over the population. They were supported by Bormann who, in a circular in June 1941 to the *Gauleiter*, bluntly stated that Christianity was incompatible with National Socialism and that the party should attempt to destroy its power and influence. Christian magazines and publications were banned, while the welfare activities of the Catholic nuns were replaced by 'the brown sisters', a Nazi organisation, and feast days were moved from weekdays to the nearest Sunday to avoid interference in the war effort. In some areas monasteries and convents were closed down to accommodate evacuees or make space for party offices. Adolf Wagner, the local education minister and *Gauleiter* of Munich and Upper Bavaria, angered local Catholics by ordering the removal of crucifixes from schoolrooms.

Facing articulate opposition from Galen, the Bishop of Münster, on euthanasia (see page 70) and mounting fury in Bavaria, Hitler ordered the *Gauleiter* to stop their campaign against the Churches. Yet in the *Reichsgau* Wartheland (the newly incorporated area of the West Prussian province of Posen), where Hitler had personally ordered that all responsibility for the Churches should be given to the Reich Governor, *Gauleiter* Greiser, rather than to the Reich Minister for the Churches, 94 per cent of the churches and chapels in the diocese of Posen-Gnesen were closed and 11 per cent of the clergy murdered. This 'clearly showed the face of the future' and, had Germany won the war, the Churches would almost certainly have faced renewed persecution (Kershaw, II, 2000: 428).

The party was able to use the war to tighten its grip on education. In 1940 an ambitious operation code-named 'sending the children to the countryside' was started. Officially, the aim was to protect children from the danger of possible air raids, but it also presented a marvellous opportunity for removing children from the influence of their parents and more traditional teachers. Somewhere between 800,000 and 2.5 million children were moved to

Volkssturm A conscript home guard created in September 1944. The Nazi Party was made responsible for its organisation, although Himmler was to decide how it should be deployed. All males between 16 and 60 were liable for service. Most of the *Volkssturm* units served locally, although initially some were posted to the front.

evacuation camps throughout both the old and new Reich. There they were taught by their teachers for six hours a day, and for the rest of the time they were in the hands of the Hitler Youth leaders, who inevitably gave greater priority to military rather than academic disciplines. The Nazi regime also insisted in September 1941 that political reliability rather than academic success should be the key to entering teacher-training colleges. Thus it was no longer necessary to have passed the high-school leaving exam, *Abitur*, to train to become a teacher.

The last vestiges of the independence of the judiciary were destroyed when in April 1942 a *Reichstag* 'Resolution' gave Hitler complete power to remove from office 'judges who clearly fail to recognize the mood of the hour' (Broszat, 1981: 341). This opened the way to direct Nazi interference in the legal process. In August 1942 Bormann and the Party Chancellery ensured that Otto Thierack, an SA *Gruppenführer* and President of the People's Court, was appointed Minister of Justice, while the top officials at the ministry were replaced by more pliant bureaucrats. From now on it became the practice for the public prosecutors to interfere in the actual course of justice by indicating to judges beforehand what their verdicts should be.

After Stalingrad, the army, too, was increasingly permeated by the party. By the end of 1943 party officials participated in the selection and training of new officers, and in the aftermath of the 20 July plot (see page 133) the traditional military salute was replaced by the Nazi salute. Goebbels also set up a special post-office box address to which any soldier in the ranks could write, if he felt that his officers were not sufficiently conscientious in introducing the new Nazi education programmes.

In the occupied and incorporated territories the party enjoyed unprecedented opportunities to assert its authority. Newly created *Gaue* did not have any of the anachronisms of the old Reich where Reich Governors and *Land* Minister Presidents often coexisted. Instead, they were administrative units in which there was an exact overlap between state administration and party jurisdiction. The Reich Commissioners were theoretically state officials, but were in reality party functionaries whose task was not to create an orderly administration but rather to carry out the ideological racial policy of the Nazi movement.

THE WAR ECONOMY

When the Allies analysed the impact of bombing on the German economy in 1945, it appeared that until early 1942 the German economy was not mobilised for a total war. The argument was then developed by Klein, Mason and Milward (see page 52) that Hitler had deliberately planned for a series of *Blitzkriege*. Milward described the *Blitzkrieg* as a 'system of warfare best suited to the character and institutions of Hitler's Germany' (Milward, 1965: 31), since it did not entail full mobilisation of all economic resources, thereby putting the civilian population under strain at a time when it was far from convinced of the need for war.

This interpretation, as Overy has convincingly shown, underestimates the extent of Germany's economic mobilisation (Overy, 1995). In the first two years of the war German military spending rose dramatically with a corresponding fall in consumer-goods production [**Doc. 41, p. 177**]. Output per head of all consumer goods declined by 22 per cent between 1938 and 1941. Paradoxically, however, despite the huge sums invested in the war economy, the actual production of weapons was disappointing. In 1940, for instance, Germany spent about US $6,000 million on armaments, while Britain spent only US $3,500 million, yet the latter managed to produce over 50 per cent more aircraft, 100 per cent more vehicles and nearly as many tanks as did Germany (Overy, 1995: 251). It is statistics such as these that have given rise to the economic *Blitzkrieg* myth. Far from being intentional, these low German production figures were the result of structural and economic factors. The war had broken out earlier than Hitler intended and much of the initial spending had gone into military infrastructure rather than weapons. The German armament effort was timed to reach its peak in 1941–42. Many of the smaller armament firms were also incompetent and reluctant to introduce modern mass-production techniques, while the armed forces insisted on quality rather than quantity of armaments, which inevitably slowed up production dramatically. Göring was also incapable of running the war economy at maximum efficiency and only told Hitler what he wanted to hear.

The German war economy was consequently in a state of deep crisis by the summer of 1941. The armed forces and Hitler were multiplying demands for complex new weapons at a time when conscription had removed another 6 million young males from the labour market, for which the increasing use of female, foreign and prisoner-of-war labour could not compensate. It was clear that the key to overcoming these problems was to rationalise production. On 3 December Hitler issued his *Führer* Command, 'Simplification and Increased Efficiency in Armaments Production', which laid the foundations for rationalising the war economy in 1942. By the time he was killed in an air crash in February 1942, Todt, the Armaments Minister, had already set up a series of 'Main Committees', each one of which was given responsibility for producing a particular class of weapon or equipment. Speer, who succeeded him, enjoyed the direct political support of Hitler and was able to solve technical and economic disputes with the armed forces by referring back to Hitler for key decisions. Speer also set up a liaison committee with Goebbels' Ministry of Propaganda, which was specifically devoted to 'armaments propaganda'. Speer's message was simply 'the best weapons bring victory' (Tooze, 2007: 555).

In January, in his *Führer* Command 'Armament 42', Hitler laid down yet another programme for an enormous increase in munitions and equipment. Over the next two years Speer was to achieve a 'production miracle' (Overy, 1995: 343). In April 1942 he successfully persuaded Hitler to create the Central Planning Board, which organised the allocation of raw materials to each sector of the economy. It was 'the true war cabinet of the German economy' (Tooze, 2007: 560). It was given additional clout by the regular attendance of Erhard Milch, who was in charge of aircraft production, Gauleiter Sauckel as special Plenipotentiary for Labour Mobilisation and Hermann Backe of the Food Ministry.

Industrialists were also encouraged to use new scientific management techniques to rationalise production, maximise their plant capacities and standardise designs. In the aircraft industry, for instance, Edward Milch decided to concentrate on the mass production of aircraft models which had already been tried and tested, and machine tools were set up to achieve a lengthy production run of the same models of aircraft. In 1943 Speer set up an armaments commission to coordinate weapon design and production so that production could be concentrated on a narrower range of artillery, tanks and vehicles. Rationalisation was further encouraged by the negotiation of fixed-price contracts with the industrialists, which forced firms to increase production if they were to make a profit.

Speer's efforts were rewarded by a steady increase in armaments production which, despite heavy Allied bombing, reached its peak in 1943–44 [**Doc. 18, p. 159**]. He did not achieve these successes through rationalisation alone. To enforce factory discipline he became ever more dependent on Himmler. In July 1943 he agreed to the SS overseeing plant security operations in the armaments factories. Increasingly (too) Speer relied on naked force to deal with recalcitrant or 'inefficient managers'. After the first wave of American bombing attacks in February 1944, Speer and Milch toured all the aircraft factories where they dispensed summary justice to those who were supposed to have failed in their duties. A few weeks later Milch informed a meeting of engineers that they had effectively *carte blanche* to 'knock down anybody who blocks your way' (Tooze, 2007: 628). Increasingly this injunction was carried out. For instance, in the construction of the huge underground plants in Thuringia for building the V2 rockets thousands of labourers from the concentration camps died.

FOOD SUPPLIES AND RATIONING

For most of the war the Nazi regime ensured that the German population was at least adequately fed and therefore not driven to desperation by hunger. It did not aim to maintain peacetime standards but rather to create a fair ration system and an '*Existenzminimum*', below which living standards would not be allowed to fall. Particular care was taken to ensure that the system was fair, even though in the first two years of the war the wealthy and party leaders were still able to buy luxuries in the free-market zone in Hamburg where goods were specially imported for foreign diplomats. Soldiers' families, in contrast to the First World War, were given special welfare payments, which were paid in kind with coupons for food and rent.

In April 1942, however, rations had to be cut as a result of poor grain harvests in Germany in 1940 and 1941. This delivered a potentially damaging blow to the morale of the civilian population, which galvanised Hitler into appointing Hermann Backe to replace Darré as Minister of Food and Agriculture. Backe, in close cooperation with Himmler, was determined to feed the Germans at the expense of the occupied territories. The *Wehrmacht* was to live off the land, while all surplus food was ruthlessly to be transported to the Reich. As Goebbels observed in his diary the decision had been taken that before Germans starved, 'it would be the turn of a number of other peoples' (Tooze, 2007: 544). The need to save by eliminating 'surplus' mouths was an added stimulant to the murder of the Jews in Poland.

By October 1942 the German food crisis was over and food rations for both Germans and foreigners working in the factories were substantially increased. Up to 1944 average consumers received rations which were between 7 and 15 per cent above the minimum calorific standard, although in the last year of the war these were increasingly cut.

Nevertheless, almost up to the end of the war food supplies and distribution were more effective than during the First World War.

SOLVING THE LABOUR CRISIS IN THE WAR INDUSTRIES

By 1939 females already made up 37.4 per cent of the total labour force. When the war broke out the government attempted to transfer much of the predominantly female workforce from the contracting consumer-goods sector to the war industries. It was assumed that short training courses would quickly familiarise the women with their new work, but the switch was far from harmonious and was bitterly resented. The longer hours meant that women had to neglect their families, and the fact that their wages were often lower compounded their sense of grievance. Consequently, as many as 236,000 married women workers took advantage of the government's relatively generous benefit system for soldiers' wives and left the labour market.

By the spring of 1940 the Reich Labour Ministry was again pushing for comprehensive female conscription, but the unpopularity of compulsion both at home and with married men on the front caused the party leadership to hold back. As an alternative, Polish labour was deployed, and then, after the defeat of France in June 1940, a million French POWs were drafted into German agriculture and industry. By the spring of 1941 labour shortages were again acute and the government tried with little success to persuade women to return to work by a mixture of patriotic appeals and financial bribes. Hitler, however, was not yet ready to sanction female conscription, until, as Bormann told Lammers in September 1941, 'a possible entry into the war by America' (Noakes and Pridham, IV, 1998: 321).

Potentially, the invasion of Russia in June 1941 gave the Nazi regime access to a vast pool of labour, but so certain was it of initial victory that there was at first little opposition to the policy of mass extermination of the Russian POWs through starvation [**Doc. 37, p. 174**]. Only with the military reverse before Moscow in December 1941 did industrialists, the Reich Labour Ministry and the armed forces begin to press for what was at first only a limited deployment of Russians in German industry. The proposal was seen as controversial by many Nazis, including Himmler, on both racial and security grounds, but once Speer was appointed to the Ministry for Armaments and War Production, the way was clear for the large-scale deployment of Russian POWs and civilians in Germany. Speer had the backing of industry, the armed services and, above all, of Hitler. Party reservations about Russian labour were overcome by the appointment of Fritz Sauckel to the post of Plenipotentiary for Labour Mobilisation. His office was a typical 'National Socialist hybrid of administration and party bureau' (Herbert, 1997: 181). Theoretically, Sauckel was responsible to Speer but in political terms he reported directly to Hitler. He was, as Ulrich Herbert has observed, 'a kind of link man between the technocratic and ideological aspects of National Socialism' (Herbert, 1997: 162). His task was both to bring foreigners into Germany on a massive scale and then to reconcile ways of getting the most out of them, which ideally involved treating then as well as possible, with the inevitable political and racial repression that would reassure Himmler and the Nazi faithful. Sauckel's recruitment commissions scoured occupied Russia and, through a mixture of promises of a better life in Germany and sheer terror, managed to recruit by November 1942 nearly 1.5 million Russians to work in the Reich.

By January 1943 the pressures on German manpower had intensified. On the eastern front German monthly losses amounted to 150,000 men, while over the same period of time only 60–65,000 reinforcements could be raised. Inevitably this led to fresh demands for calling up men in reserved occupations and replacing them with women and foreign workers. Under the slogan of total war, the war economy and the military demands took priority over ideology. On 27 January 1943 Hitler issued two decrees: all men between 16 and 65 who were not in the armed forces and all women between 17 and 45 had to register for war work. In practice, however, only about 900,000 women were called up as there were still a considerable number of exemptions for the self-employed, mothers with children, and so on [**Doc. 42, p. 178**]. Three days later the Reich Commissioners were given the power to close all non-essential trades and businesses and assign their workers to the war industries. This was a bitter blow to the small independent artisans who had formed Hitler's core support in 1933.

The employers of the large armament industries preferred efficient high-performing foreigners to low-performing women or men from small unmechanised workshops and plants, who were unused to modern mass-production techniques. Thus in 1943–44 efforts were redoubled to recruit foreign workers and a further 2.5 million were brought into the Reich. All in all, by the end of 1944 there were over 7 million foreign workers in Germany. To improve their production and morale, attempts were made to moderate Nazi racial policy. Goebbels launched a 'Europe against Bolshevism' campaign in which Germany was seen as the defender of European civilisation against the USSR (see page 101). Belatedly, within this context an attempt was made to win over the Russian POWs and workers. Goebbels, with Hitler's backing, even insisted that the Russians should no longer be singled out as 'beasts and barbarians', but be given equality of treatment with the western European workers (Noakes and Pridham, IV, 1998: 244).

In practice, though, this was unenforceable as the treatment of foreign prisoners was a matter for camp commanders, employers, managers and foremen. The western European workers, particularly the Flemish-speaking Belgians and the French, were treated almost as well as the Germans. They received the same wages and rations and were not guarded or supervised on the factory floor. The Italian prisoners of war and civilians who were conscripted for forced labour, once Italy had defected from the Axis side in September 1943 (see page 97), and the Russians and Poles were at the bottom of the pile, and usually had to live in conditions which were little better than slave labour. German society, with a workforce increasingly stratified by race, and with a large number of upper-middle-class families employing Ukrainian girls as maids, began to show, in Herbert's words, the characteristics of a 'quasi-colonial social order' (Herbert, 1997: 189).

Up to a point the huge influx of foreign labour 'made the German working class more or less passive accomplices in Nazi racial policy' (Burleigh and Wippermann, 1991: 295). More and more Germans were also drawn into the apparatus of surveillance and repression in the factories. There were certainly cases of horrendous brutality and 'reprisals' after air raids, but there were, too, examples of decency and humanity [**Doc. 46(b), p. 142**]. On the whole, however, the majority of German workers, immersed in their own problems, appear to have shown little interest in the fate of the foreign workers. As Herbert has written, 'the foreigners were simply there, as much part of wartime life as ration cards or air raid shelters. . . . Their own privileged position as Germans *vis-à-vis* these workers was likewise nothing exceptional, certainly no cause for misgiving' (Herbert, 1997: 396).

THE IMPACT OF WAR ON THE GERMAN PEOPLE, 1942–45

As the war intensified a large number of women not only had to play a major part in keeping industry and the transport infrastructure working, but also had to look after families and bolster the morale of their husbands or sons when, and indeed if, they returned from the front. Inevitably these multiple and often conflicting tasks were made more difficult by the disruption and chaos caused by the growing number of British and American air raids [**Doc. 43, p. 178**]. The war forced many married women to adopt more independent roles, which inevitably changed their lives and produced growing tension with their husbands when they returned hoping to find a domestic world unchanged in essentials since 1939. From June 1942 onwards girls in the Reich Labour Service were eligible to be called up to serve as auxiliaries in the armed forces, and in 1944 women replaced men in operating the searchlights attached to the anti-aircraft batteries. Some girls, too, were employed in the occupied areas. Loneliness, separation from families or husbands and, as the air raids intensified, the ever present threat of death also led to a greater sexual promiscuity.

The wives and daughters of small independent artisans and peasants were particularly severely hit by the war. The former had to cope if their husbands' businesses were shut down as part of Speer's rationalisation schemes and faced being drafted into war production (see page 117), while the latter had to run their farms without adequate labour. In the words of a military report from Nuremberg in 1942, 'a peasant wife whose husband is at the front . . . has not a single quiet minute from 4 in the morning until 9 at night' (Overy, 1995: 307). In the course of the war the peasantry became increasingly disillusioned with the regime and felt with some justification that for all the Nazi propaganda about blood and soil, their interests were in fact being sacrificed to the urban majority. As Jill Stephenson has pointed out, the 'problems which had dogged small-scale agriculture for decades were intensified in the abnormal circumstances of a second twentieth-century war' (Stephenson, 1997: 347). The peasantry were burdened with an oppressive system aimed at regulating and monitoring food production, while at the same time the government requisitioned their horses and called up the young men who worked the land. Later in the war they were burdened with evacuees who often did little to help. It is true that they were often allotted either a Polish or French POW, but this too brought problems in its wake, as the state laid down that there should be no fraternisation between foreign workers and Germans. When it did at times inevitably occur, the subsequent punishments meted out by the Nazi regime shocked the local community and alienated it still further.

In the western and southern rural areas the traditional family and community came under pressure, but they just about survived intact. In the cities the social impact of total war after 1942 was more radical. Those workers who were exempted from call-up had increasingly to work alongside new and inexperienced factory hands and had to adapt to the new mass-production work practices. Many factories were also forced to evacuate by the bombing. The fear of being sent to the eastern front and the dependence on employers for extra rations to some extent ensured that the discipline of the German workforce on the whole remained good despite the abolition of overtime payments and the extension of the working week to 60 hours in 1944. The large-scale influx of inexperienced workers and foreign labour also provided new opportunities for many of the original workforce as supervisors and foremen.

As the war progressed, German society increasingly became more atomised and resembled a 'kind of kicked-in anthill' (Aycoberry, 1999: 210). In 1940 possibly as many as two million children had been evacuated from the northern and western cities (see page 111). As the bombing campaign was stepped up in 1943–44 a further 9 million women, children and elderly men were evacuated or made their way independently to the countryside. Such a mass migration inevitably created acute problems in the countryside. The urban refugees, who were in receipt of adequate family allowances, frequently found country life tedious and made little effort to help their hosts. The **Regierungspräsident** of Upper Bavaria, for instance, reported in August 1943 that 'a majority of the local women are working, while the evacuees just try to make life for themselves as comfortable as possible' (Erker, 1988: 377).

A year later these evacuees were beginning to be joined by refugees from eastern Germany. In the autumn of 1944 the Red Army, filled with a desire

Regierungspräsident Literally, District President, who is in charge of a sub-division of a *Land* province – a *Regierungsbezirk*. These officials survived the Nazi take-over of power and were relied upon by the Ministry of the Interior in Berlin as a counter-balance to the *Gauleiter* and Reich Governors.

to revenge the terrible sufferings of the Russian people, reached East Prussia. A taste of what was to come was seen in the raping, mutilation and murdering of women and children in the small East Prussian village of Nemmersdorf. To escape this fate, large numbers of the German population in the eastern territories began to 'trek' westwards. From October 1944 to January 1945 four or five million civilians from East Prussia, the Warthegau, Danzig, Pomerania, Silesia and Eastern Brandenburg fled westwards. In 1969 the Federal Archives in Bonn calculated that at least 600,000 of these died and a further 2.2 million cases were 'unresolved' (Aycoberry, 1999: 231).

Once in the interior of the Reich, the surviving refugees found a society in disintegration where 50 per cent of the population were on the move. Many found temporary refuge in bombed-out ruins, but eventually the majority settled in rural areas such as Schleswig-Holstein or Bavaria. Immediately after the war a further 6.5 million Germans from the Sudetenland and the new western Polish territories were expelled from their homes. Ultimately these huge population transfers were to destroy the traditional structure and isolation of rural Germany for ever.

THE END OF THE HITLER REGIME

By the autumn of 1944 it was obvious to all but the most fanatical Nazis that the war was lost. Allied bombing had reduced oil supplies to a dangerously low level and disrupted transport facilities throughout the Reich, thereby dislocating the supply of coal, steel and other vital raw materials to the factories. The loss of the occupied territories and the increasing reluctance of the neutral states to sell raw materials to Germany also worsened the already chronic economic difficulties and shortages. Once the Russians occupied the industrial areas of Silesia in January and the British occupied the Ruhr in April 1945, the German war economy could no longer function.

In December 1944 Hitler gambled heavily on driving a wedge between the British and American forces in the west by striking unexpectedly through the Ardennes. When he failed, he retreated to his bunker in Berlin. He had become a physical wreck quite incapable of recognising political and military realities. His feelings for the German people, who had apparently not been worthy of him, turned to bitter, nihilistic scorn, and he planned to drag them into the abyss after him. He ordered Speer to prepare a scorched-earth policy which would leave Germany a desert for the invading Allies. Speer managed to circumvent Hitler's orders to destroy factories and power stations and, so he claimed, at one juncture considered gassing Hitler and his 'court' in the bunker, but in the final analysis he could not bring himself to betray his

Führer. There is much truth in Trevor-Roper's observation that 'Hitler still remained, in the universal chaos he had caused, the sole master whose orders were implicitly obeyed' (Trevor-Roper, 1947: 183).

Hitler and his mistress, Eva Braun, whom he had married only hours before, committed suicide in the bunker, which was already under Russian artillery fire, on 30 April 1945. He had nominated Admiral Dönitz as President of the Reich and Goebbels as Chancellor with Bormann as Party Minister. Both Göring and Himmler had been discredited because they had dared to take independent action in the mistaken belief that Hitler had either abdicated or died. Himmler had asked the Swedes to mediate with the western powers and his arrest was therefore ordered by Hitler, while Göring, acting on the assumption that Hitler was incapacitated in Berlin, had sent him a telegram on 23 April. In this he informed Hitler that unless he heard to the contrary before 10 o'clock that evening he would act according to the edict of 29 June 1941, which made him the *Führer*'s successor. Even at this late date the bitter rivalries within the Nazi oligarchy protected Hitler. Bormann immediately misconstrued the intention of the telegram, and Hitler stripped Göring of his offices and had him put under house arrest. A few days later Göring surrendered to the Americans.

Within hours of Hitler's death, Goebbels and Bormann, without consulting Dönitz, tried to negotiate a cease-fire with the Soviets, but the Russians insisted on unconditional surrender. Goebbels and his wife then committed suicide on 1 May after first killing their children, while Bormann attempted to escape, but only reached the *Invalidenstrasse* where he swallowed poison rather than risk falling into Soviet hands. In the early hours of 2 May the German army surrendered in Berlin.

POSTSCRIPT TO THE THIRD REICH: THE DÖNITZ GOVERNMENT

On hearing of Hitler's death, Dönitz, who was in Schleswig-Holstein, seized the initiative and broadcast to the Reich the news that Hitler had died in combat 'at his post in the Reich Chancellery, while fighting to the last breath against Bolshevism' (Kershaw, II, 2000: 832). Dönitz's immediate aim was to negotiate a separate armistice with the western powers, which would enable him to keep the fighting going long enough in the east to save as many German troops as possible from Soviet captivity. He hoped, too, to persuade the western powers to recognise him as the legal successor to Hitler. His cabinet was made up of a mixture of loyal Nazis such as Wilhelm Stuckart, Himmler's State Secretary in the Ministry of the Interior, and nationalists like

Hitler's Finance Minister, Krosigk, all of whom were determined to maintain an authoritarian state, purged of only the worst Nazi excesses. Initially Dönitz left Himmler in charge of security, but on 6 May he was dismissed and most of the SS officers were arrested by the *Wehrmacht*. Himmler then attempted to flee to Bavaria disguised as a corporal, but was arrested by British troops and committed suicide on 23 May.

Dönitz managed to delay capitulating to the Allies until 8 May, which enabled some 3 million German troops to avoid falling into Soviet hands. The Third Reich lingered on for two more weeks. Dönitz convinced the British and Americans that his administration, albeit under Allied supervision, was still needed to help with the mounting problems of hunger, disease, refugees and Communism. Increasingly, however, his position became untenable. He spoke openly of wanting to preserve 'the most beautiful and best that National Socialism has given us – the unity of the racial community' (Kitchen, 1995: 298). Neither did he dissolve the Nazi Party, and only reluctantly did he remove the symbols and flags of the Third Reich. Anti-Communism and hatred of the USSR still remained his fundamental ideology. He also became increasingly critical of the western Allies' de-Nazification policies and warned them that they were destroying those 'quiet, decent citizens' who stood between Germany and Communism (Kitchen, 1995: 300). On 23 May 1945 he and his cabinet were arrested and on 5 June the Allies became the sovereign rulers of occupied Germany.

11

The German opposition

In 1945, when the full horrors of the concentration camps and the 'Final Solution' became known, it was understandable for Allied observers to belittle the German opposition, especially since its members appeared, as Taylor caustically expressed it, to 'resolve to put their fine principles into action only when the Anglo-American armies had established themselves in Normandy and the Red Army was at the gates of Warsaw' (Taylor, 1961a: 262). However, over the ensuing decades it has become clearer that there was an extensive, though uncoordinated, opposition to Hitler and that it functioned in conditions of exceptional difficulty and danger. In 1939, according to Gestapo statistics, there were 27,367 German political prisoners, and between 1933 and 1939 a total of 112,432 German citizens had been sentenced for political offences (Prittie, 1964).

The German opposition existed in uniquely challenging conditions. Unlike the resistance movements in occupied Europe, it had to work among a population which by and large accepted Hitler with varying degrees of enthusiasm, but once war started many Germans who had reservations about Hitler regarded its activities as treasonable. Paradoxically, once the tide turned against Germany in 1942, the problems facing the opposition were intensified, because Nazi Germany had so alienated world opinion that the western powers at any rate were determined to demand unconditional surrender and to brush aside feelers from the German opposition groups. It also lacked any reliable base within Germany or, apart from the Communists whose umbilical cord tied them to Moscow, the firm support of a friendly power abroad. The Churches, the army, the unions, the Pope, the western powers and Stalin all initially attempted to bargain with Hitler, thereby making it doubly difficult for a root-and-branch opposition to flourish. Fear of the Gestapo and the police, who were often assisted by denunciations from the population, also inhibited dissent. In practice Hitler could only be overthrown by either a popular uprising – which, once organised labour movements had been broken, was hardly a viable proposition – a palace revolution engineered by one of his lieutenants, or a military coup. In fact only the third option was at all practical in the circumstances of the Third Reich.

RESISTANCE AND *RESISTENZ*

Only a small number of exceptionally brave people joined the active opposition. Many more who hated the Third Reich formed what Rothfels called the 'silent opposition' (Rothfels, 1970: 29), which defied Hitler unobtrusively by hiding Jews [**Doc. 46(a), p. 180**], listening to the BBC, reading banned literature or even coining anti-Nazi jokes. Some writers and intellectuals simply withdrew from public life and attempted to avoid contact with the regime (a process known as internal emigration), while others used learned articles or analyses of past tyrannies as vehicles for obliquely criticising the Nazi regime.

In the 1970s this concept of a more broadly based resistance was extended both by the publication of a large number of local studies of a predominantly working-class opposition by the left-wing publishing house Roderberg, and by the Bavaria project on 'Resistance and Persecution in Bavaria, 1933–1945'. These studies go beyond Rothfels's 'silent opposition' by defining resistance 'as every form of active or passive behaviour which allows recognition of the rejection of the National Socialist regime or a partial area of National Socialist ideology and was bound up with certain risks' (Kershaw, 1993: 158). Thus, as well as looking at the work of underground social democratic and Communist groups, it also analysed relatively minor acts of civil disobedience such as refusing to give the Heil Hitler salute, hanging out a church banner instead of the swastika flags, fraternising with foreign workers or peasants who bought from Jewish cattle-dealers. The Bavaria project was more interested in what Kershaw calls the 'functional' rather than 'intentional' dimension to opposition. It did not concentrate so much on the motives and intentions of the participants but rather on how grass-roots opposition in fact 'block[ed] or partially restrict[ed] Nazism's societal penetration' (Kershaw, 1993: 159).

Resistenz Medical term meaning immunity or resistance to a disease. Hence the failure of Nazi ideology to penetrate certain sections of the German population can also be characterized by the term *Resistenz*.

This approach gave rise to the controversial concept of **Resistenz**, which is a medical term but in this context implied immunity to Nazi ideology.

To what extent these minor examples of often accidental and superficial dissent, which usually were not inspired by principled opposition to the regime, can really be seen as part of the German resistance to Hitler is debatable. The Swiss historian Walter Hofer, for instance, complained that it 'leads to a levelling down of fundamental resistance against the system on the one hand and actions criticizing more or less superficial manifestations on the other' (Kershaw, 1993: 160). The concept of *Resistenz* does, however, show the limits to Nazi penetration of society and how individuals and particular groups tried to maintain an element of independence from the encroachments of the Nazi state.

OPPOSITION FROM THE CHURCHES

As Roland Freislar, the notorious President of the Nazi People's Court, observed during the trial of Count Helmuth von Moltke (see page 131), Christianity and Nazism had only one thing in common: 'we claim the whole man' (Conway, 1968: 289). The German Protestant and Roman Catholic Churches should therefore have been in the vanguard of the opposition to Hitler, and indeed. Nazi attacks on the Christian Churches generated considerable hostility from German Christians and the clergy, but in practice this opposition was tempered by partial support for some of Hitler's policies, particularly his foreign policy, anti-Bolshevism and in some circles anti-Semitism as well. Thus the Catholic Church, for instance, greeted the annexation of the Sudetenland with a 'festive peal of bells', while both evangelical and Catholic Churches, with few exceptions, remained silent in the aftermath of the *Reichskristallnacht* outrages (see page 77).

Thanks largely to Martin Niemöller and the several thousand priests who formed the breakaway Confessing Church (see page 28), the Protestant Churches defeated attempts to absorb them into a new, uniform Nazi **Reichskirche** under Bishop Müller, but this major victory by no means implied a political opposition to Hitler. Like the army, the new Confessing Church was intent primarily on preserving its independence rather than becoming 'the spearhead of political opposition to the Nazis' (Conway, 1968: 84). The Pope, too, had sought to preserve the Roman Catholic Church by coming to terms with Hitler in the Concordat of July 1933, which had the effect of blunting the opposition of Roman Catholic priests in Germany towards the Nazis and of reconciling their flocks to the new regime. As with the Protestant Churches, only in certain limited spheres did the Roman Catholics confront the Nazis. A stubborn battle was, for example, fought to prevent the absorption of Catholic youth groups into the Hitler Youth (see page 59).

If churchmen appeared to be unpatriotic or undermining national unity, they enjoyed little support from either their colleagues or congregations. For instance, on 30 September 1938 leading members of the Confessing Church planned to hold in their churches a service of intercession [or prayer] as they assumed that by then war would have broken out over the Sudetenland (see page 87). In the rubric of the service war was specifically described as a

Reichskirche The German National Church was an attempt to unite the various churches into which German Protestantism was divided, and was set up on 27 May 1933. The government refused to accept von Bodelschwingh as the new Reich Bishop and engineered the election of Ludwig Müller, a convinced Nazi. As this led to bitter dissension and the formation of the Confessing Church, Hitler withdrew his support for Müller.

punishment, and the forgiveness of God was sought for both the sins of the Germans and their nation. In fact the service was cancelled when the news of the Munich Conference was announced, but plans for the intercession found their way into Himmler's hands and were published. The majority of Protestants regarded them as little less than treason and rapidly distanced themselves from the Confessing Church. Not surprisingly, '[u]nder a barrage of accusations and vilification the Confessing Church members grew more and more confused between their political and their theological loyalties. Their resolution weakened and their morale sank to its lowest ebb' (Conway, 1968: 223). When war broke out a year later both the Catholic and Protestant Churches remained silent.

On one level, however, the war strengthened the role of the Churches within the community. Inevitably, attendance at church services increased as the 'imminence of mortality . . . became more immediate' (Stephenson, 1997: 352), and at the grass roots this strengthened the '*Resistenz*' of a growing number of Germans to party ideology. In Württemberg, for instance, even some Hitler Youth leaders were reported attending church services, and Christian funeral services were often held for loyal Nazis who had fallen at the front. When they enjoyed public support, the Churches could criticise the regime openly. In August 1941, for instance, Bishop Galen of Münster publicly attacked the euthanasia programme and forced Hitler to stop the large-scale gassing of mentally ill patients precisely because he spoke for a wide cross-section of the German people. This was at the very least a considerable victory for Christianity, even though euthanasia was in fact continued more secretly with other methods (see pages 70–71). It was, however, a protest over a single issue. It was not a root-and-branch attack on the regime. Galen was very careful to stress his loyalty to Germany and support for the war 'against the 'external enemy' and 'the enemy in our midst' (Burleigh, 2000: 724).

There was no blanket condemnation of the murder of the Jews from the Catholic Church. In 1937 the Pope had issued the famous encyclical 'With Burning Concern', which condemned Hitler's violations of the Concordat and his racial policy, but tragically this remained an exception to the general policy of tolerating the regime. Criticism by the Catholic bishops of Hitler's anti-Semitic policies was cautious and hesitant. In the winter of 1941, for example, they complained only about the fate of 'non-Aryan' Catholics or of Jews married to Catholics. The Confessing Church was similarly cautious, although belatedly in October 1943 it did address a pastoral letter to all its congregations in which it trenchantly stated that 'terms like "eradication", "liquidation" or "unfit to live" are not known in the law of God' (Conway, 1968: 266) [**Doc. 45, p. 179**].

The Churches as institutions were inevitably constrained by public opinion and the political situation. Active opposition was, however, pursued by some brave individuals. A considerable number of Protestant priests did openly criticise Hitler, as is testified by the death of nearly 400 in Buchenwald. Dietrich Bonhoeffer, the Protestant pastor and theologian, categorically described Hitler as the Anti-Christ to be rooted out, and became a major figure in the German opposition until he was arrested in 1943. Similarly, among the Catholics there were men of exceptional bravery. In November 1938, for instance, Father Lichtenberg, the Catholic Provost of Berlin, led his congregation in prayer for the persecuted Jews the day after *Reichskristallnacht*. He was duly arrested and died in a concentration camp in 1943. The Jesuit Father Alfred Delp was a member of the Kreisau Circle before he, too, was arrested and executed.

OPPOSITION ON THE LEFT

Initially, Hitler's most implacable opponents were found on the Left, but the destruction of the political parties and the trade unions deprived them of their power bases and forced them to operate from underground or abroad. The SPD established its party headquarters first in Prague and then in Paris, and up to 1939 managed to smuggle illegal literature across the frontiers. SPD and trade-union cells were from time to time established in factories and large cities but were so quickly broken up by the Gestapo that the party executive in Prague decided in 1937 to concentrate on merely maintaining communications with its supporters in the Reich so that after the collapse of the Hitler regime there would at least exist a nucleus for the revival of the party. As it was painfully clear that neither the SPD nor the unions could effectively oppose Hitler, several prominent SPD politicians in the underground, such as Wilhelm Leuschner, Julius Leber and Carlo Mierendorff, began to look to the army as the only workable opposition against Hitler and, consequently, contacted the conservative opposition groups and the disaffected generals.

The history of the Communist contribution to the German opposition was distorted by the Cold War. The East Germans exaggerated its importance, while the West Germans initially minimised or ignored it. The Communists were more skilled than the SPD in adapting their organisations to underground activities, and despite repeated Gestapo raids and heavy losses, Communist cells were never completely eliminated. The orthodox German Communists accepted without debate the party line as laid down in Moscow, where the German Central Committee in exile functioned. Initially the Communists concentrated on building up their membership in preparation for the proletarian revolution, but by 1935, in obedience to Stalin's instructions, they had belatedly begun to negotiate with the SPD for a united front against fascism, which after the years of mistrust and hostility between the two parties proved impossible to form. During the period of the Nazi–Soviet Pact, the Communist Party (KPD) was instructed to support Stalin's foreign policy but to oppose Hitler within Germany. In June 1941 Hitler's attack gave fresh impetus to the formation of Communist underground groups such as those set up by Bernhard Bästlein and Franz Jacob in Hamburg or Robert Uhrig and Anton Saefkow in Berlin, all of which acted from time to time independently of the Moscow party line. The most famous Communist group was the *Rote Kapelle* (Red Orchestra), which was run by a Polish Jew, Leopold Trepper, initially from Brussels and then from Paris. The German section was run by a *Luftwaffe* officer, Harro Schulze-Boysen, who worked in the Air Ministry and Arvid Harnack, a civil servant in the Ministry of Economics. It had cells both in industry and in several government ministries and supplied the Russians with much important information until it was uncovered by the Gestapo in 1942.

Left-wing opposition was not confined to members of the two big parties. There were numerous small, independent groups which, sickened by the divisions of the Left in the Weimar Republic, sought to bring about a realignment of left-wing forces in Germany. The *Roter Stosstrupp* (Red Assault Party), for example, called for a new party of the Left which would create a socialist society after the collapse of the Nazis, while another group, *Neu Beginnen* (New Start), aimed at reconciling the best elements in the KPD and SPD and at creating the basis for joint action against Hitler and cooperation in the reconstruction of society after the war. Gordon Craig has argued that the German resistance, 'despite its socialist and trade union component . . . never extended to the masses of the working class' (Craig, 1978: 667). It is undeniable that the Left failed to organise a mass movement, yet it is unfair to ignore the extent of anti-Nazi activity among the working classes. F.L. Carsten mentions 'the intense opposition working class activity in Berlin' after 1933 (Graml *et al.*, 1970: x), and it is hard to ignore the fact that in 1936, for example, more than 11,000 people were arrested for assisting the SPD underground movement.

THE CHALLENGE OF YOUTH CULTURE

With a few important exceptions youth subcultures and gangs in the Third Reich were not overtly political in their opposition. Nevertheless, in a society which National Socialism hoped to regulate down to the smallest detail, the natural desire for youth to rebel against the older generation or the 'establishment' was inevitably seen as a political challenge to the regime. In the late

1930s and early 1940s a series of youth groups sprang up in the large cities of the Reich. In many ways they were the precursors of the **Halbstarken** or 'Teddy Boys' of the 1950s.

In the western parts of the Reich at the end of the 1930s young working-class people between the ages of 14 and 18 began to get together to form the 'Edelweiss Pirate' groups, which were primarily a rebellion against regimentation in the workplace and in the Hitler Youth. They cultivated a deliberate scorn for the daily grind of work and at weekends would go off on hikes in the countryside or cycle rides to meet up with other like-minded groups. Their main act of opposition, as such, was to attack Hitler Youth patrols. Some, however, also distributed Communist stickers, leaflets or the flysheets which had been dropped by Allied planes during bombing raids.

In 1944 in Cologne-Ehrenfeld, a gang of 'Eidelweiss Pirates' linked up with an underground group which provided shelter for *Wehrmacht* deserters, escaped prisoners of war and foreign workers. Its members raided military depots and attacked the Nazis, and in one skirmish actually killed the head of the Cologne Gestapo before it was infiltrated and smashed by the Gestapo. In Leipzig, Dresden, Halle, Munich and Hamburg there were similar groups of working-class young people. Some of them, as in Leipzig, were influenced by the traditions of the KPD; others were less interested in politics.

Among the upper-middle-class youth the Swing Movement developed and formed dance clubs in most of the big cities [**Doc. 44, p. 179**]. On one level their activities were apolitical, but their enthusiasm for jazz, American dances like the 'jitterbug', adoption of American and British fashions, and open tolerance of Jews and half-Jews in their groups challenged Nazi social norms and led Himmler to threaten to put what he called their 'ringleaders' into concentration camps.

The most overtly politicised of the youth groups was the White Rose group in Munich, which was founded in 1942 by Hans and Sophie Scholl. It was initially a circle composed of a small group of students as well as the Swiss psychologist Professor Huber. Drawing on the teaching of Christianity and the legacy of **German idealism** which had developed at the end of the eighteenth century, they launched a brave but inevitably doomed campaign against the Nazi dictatorship. In the course of 1942–43 they distributed six typed, cyclostyled leaflets for the most part in Munich, which were intended to appeal to the conscience of the professional middle class. They also established contacts with other opposition groups in Berlin, Hamburg, Cologne and several other cities and made unsuccessful attempts to establish contact with the Kreisau Circle. In February 1943 they were arrested, tried and executed after they were reported by a porter at Munich University to the Gestapo for giving out subversive leaflets in the university courtyard.

Halbstarken Literally translated as half strong. The term was used in the 1950s to describe an adolescent subculture whose members were mostly male and working class and aggressive and provocative in public in the Federal Republic of Germany. The *Halbstarken* can be compared to the 'Teddy Boys' in Britain.

German idealism Philosophical movement originating in Germany in the late eighteenth and early nineteenth centuries. It developed from the work of Immanuel Kant, and became closely linked with romanticism and the revolutionary politics of the Enlightenment.

RESISTANCE BY THE MILITARY AND CONSERVATIVE ELITES

The potentially most effective resistance to Hitler was to be found in the national conservative opposition, which was composed of prominent individuals or 'notables' who worked within the system to destroy Nazism. The leading members were all important men in the traditional German establishment: Erwin Planck, for example, had been Papen's former State Secretary; Carl Goerdeler was Price Commissioner under both Papen and Hitler and Lord Mayor of Leipzig; Johannes Popitz was the Prussian Finance Minister; Ulrich von Hassell, the former German ambassador in Rome; and General Beck was Army Chief of Staff until 1938. Despite their isolation from the masses, these men had within their grasp the means of destroying Hitler, as they had close links with the army, and under certain circumstances, could win it over, although it would be necessary to wait until the Officer Corps was both disillusioned with Hitler and convinced that he was about to destroy Germany. Their first opportunity came in the summer of 1938, when the Officer Corps felt itself humiliated by Hitler's handling of the Blomberg–Fritsch affair and alarmed at his apparent intention to unleash a general European war for the sake of the Sudetenland (see page 87). With the assistance of Generals Beck, Witzleben, Hammerstein, Oster and Halder, a plan which was to be implemented once the western powers had declared war, was drawn up to have Hitler arrested, martial law declared and a constituent assembly summoned, but the Munich settlement ironically destroyed what has been judged to have been a 'most promising attempt to overthrow Hitler' (Hoffmann, 1977: 96).

There were also plans drawn up by members of the conservative opposition to overthrow the Nazi regime during the phoney war. In November 1939 it was agreed that the diplomat Erich Kordt would place a bomb in the Reich Chancellery at a time when Hitler was there, but the plan was abruptly aborted when Hitler cancelled the order for beginning the offensive in the west. Ironically, on 8 November, a lone assassin, Georg Elser, a carpenter, nearly managed to kill Hitler where the army had failed, when he succeeded in placing a bomb actually in a pillar in the *Bürgerbräu* beer cellar where Hitler was scheduled to speak. Hitler was only saved because bad weather conditions forced him to leave early to catch the train rather than a plane to Berlin. In the New Year the Beck–Goerdeler–Oster group worked together with Popitz and Hassell on a draft for a new constitution and the necessary emergency decrees for the period immediately after a successful coup. They also managed to establish contact with the British government via the British ambassador to the Vatican, but Hitler's victories first in Norway and then in France in May and June 1940 made the prospects for Hitler's removal very slim indeed. Yet, to their great credit, right through this period of spectacular victories the conservative resistance movement continued to give detailed thought to the shape of a post-Hitler world.

In 1941 the German opposition was strengthened by the formation of the Kreisau Circle which met at Kreisau, the Silesian estate of Count Helmuth James von Moltke. Its core was composed of the two groups that had formed around Moltke and his friend Peter Graf Yorck von Wartenburg. It represented a cross-section of the non-Communist opposition within Germany. There were social democrats like Mierendorff and Reichwein, two Jesuit priests, Delp and Rosch, Harald Poelchau and Eugen Gerestenmeier both of the Confessing Church, and several legal and administrative experts such as Hans Lukaschek, the former *Oberpräsident* of Upper Silesia, and Hans Peters, a jurist at Breslau University. It also had close links with Goerdeler and dissidents in both the Foreign Office and Officer Corps of the *Wehrmacht*. The Circle became the intellectual power house of the opposition. It set up small groups, which then presented their ideas at larger meetings which were disguised as country-house weekend parties. Although Moltke predominantly attracted the younger generation of resisters, he also had a profound impact on Goerdeler and on many of the Social Democrats as well. The Circle was smashed in January 1944 when Moltke was arrested by the Gestapo. He was executed 12 months later.

It has often been debated whether the conservative opposition was fundamentally reactionary or in reality the herald of the 1949 Bonn Republic. The foreign policy of the Goerdeler–Hassell group was strongly nationalistic and, at any rate up to 1942, based on what Graml calls 'seductive visions of a German Reich of medieval proportions', and Prussian and conservative in character (Graml *et al.*, 1970: 21). In April 1940 Hassell indirectly informed the British government that in any peace settlement Austria and the Sudetenland were to remain part of the Reich, while in the east the 1914 frontier with Poland would have to be restored. In January 1941, in a secret memorandum entitled 'The Goal', Goerdeler appeared to demand the return of Germany's colonies and proposed the setting up of a confederation of free European states under a benign German leadership. Under the influence of the Kreisau Circle, Goerdeler did begin to write about a future federal Europe but, understandably for a man of his generation, he never really abandoned his concept of Germany as an independent great power. The Kreisau Circle was more committed to a united European Federation. Although Moltke stipulated in 1943 that the Reich should remain 'the supreme leading power of the German nation', he also envisaged a European parliament and cabinet and an integrated economy (Noakes and Pridham, IV, 1998: 615).

In some ways the domestic policy of the conservative opposition was fundamentally illiberal and anti-democratic. Their ideas, as Kershaw has pointed out, 'were essentially oligarchic and authoritarian, resting heavily on

corporatist Used to
describe attempts to
defuse class hatred by
giving both the state,
capital and labour a role
in running industry.

corporatist and neo-Conservative notions advanced in the Weimar Republic, envisaging self-governing communities, limited electoral rights and the renewal of Christian values' (Kershaw, 1993: 154). Mommsen has characterised the constitutional draft devised by Goerdeler as 'exceed[ing] Papen's wildest dreams' and the proposals of Popitz and Hassell as 'predominantly fascist' (Graml *et al.*, 1970: 114). On the other hand, Moltke and the Kreisau Circle devised a Christian-socialist programme which Rothfels characterised as occupying a position between 'East and West' – that is, between Communism and capitalism (Rothfels, 1970: 115). Yet Moltke can also be regarded as a conservative who fundamentally mistrusted liberalism and democracy. He wanted, for example, to limit direct elections to the local and district levels and would have given heads of families an additional vote for each child under the age of 21. It is, however, wise to accept Bracher's warning of the futility of stamping the conservative German opposition with any label based on the few existing memoranda penned by individuals like Goerdeler or Moltke (Bracher, 1973). It is also important to remember that many of their surviving plans were primarily intended for the interim period following a coup against Hitler.

THE ROAD TO 20 JULY 1944

The tragic failure in 1943 of the White Rose group at Munich University and the risky but unsuccessful attempt by Popitz to divide the Nazis by persuading Himmler to depose Hitler in August 1943, emphasised afresh that the only effective way to bring down the regime was to assassinate Hitler, and it was the army that was best placed to bring this about. There were two main centres of opposition within the *Wehrmacht*: the Army Group Centre on the Russian front and the group of officers around General Olbricht in Berlin. The leading conspirator in Russia was Major-General Henning von Tresckow, who successfully managed to ensure that convinced anti-Nazis were appointed to key posts on the headquarters staff. In 1943 these groups managed to plan a series of assassination attempts against Hitler, but each one, as a result of 'a barely credible succession of trivial incidents' (Rothfels, 1970: 78), failed. First, on 13 March 1943 a bomb failed to explode on Hitler's aeroplane; two later attempts were also unsuccessful when Hitler defied the assassins' expectations by either not turning up for a meeting or remaining at an exhibition of captured Russian weapons for a much shorter time than expected. In January 1944 a further attempt to kill Hitler, while he was inspecting a display of new uniforms, was prevented by an air raid.

In early 1944 plans both to assassinate Hitler and stage a military *coup d'état* by mobilising the reserve army were given firmer shape by Colonel Claus Schenk Graf von Stauffenberg, who was working at the German Army Office in Berlin. Stauffenberg contacted activists on both the Right and the Left and became the key figure in planning 'Operation Valkyrie', the implementation of which would involve Hitler's assassination, the declaration of martial law, the setting up of a provisional government including Conservative, Centre, Social Democrat and non-party representatives, and immediate peace negotiations with the west. Stauffenberg's chance came when he was appointed Chief of Staff to General Fromm, the Commander-in-Chief of the Reserve Army, which enabled him to attend military briefings at Hitler's headquarters. After two unsuccessful attempts on 6 and 15 July his opportunity came on the 20th.

Although it is undeniable that the successful Allied landings in Normandy made action against Hitler even more urgent, Stauffenberg and his fellow conspirators were not simply fired by the desire to salvage what was left of Germany. They were also determined to prove to posterity that the German resistance dared, in Tresckow's words, to stake 'its life on risking the decisive throw' (Rothfels, 1970: 79) [**Doc. 47, p. 181**]. The tragic history of 20 July 1944 is well known. In a sense it can of course be said to have failed because 'Colonel Brandt kicked Stauffenberg's briefcase to the wrong side of the oak support of the conference table' (Prittie, 1964: 248), but it is also true that the bulk of the generals in Berlin dared not act decisively until they knew that Hitler was dead. If they had acted decisively on the afternoon of 20 July the *coup d'état* could still have succeeded. Not only did General Fromm refuse to implement Operation Valkyrie, but the plotters had left 'too many loose ends . . . dangling' (Kershaw, II, 2000: 677). They had failed to destroy the communications centre at the *Führer* headquarters, to devise plans for immediately seizing radio stations in Berlin, and to arrest party and SS leaders. Thus when it emerged that Hitler was still alive, the plot rapidly unravelled and the army both in Germany and France refused to cooperate. Its failure led to the virtual elimination of the opposition, as Hitler arrested more than 7,000 people, 5,000 of whom had been executed by April 1945.

Whatever the politics of the German resistance groups were, it is clear that its members were men of great personal bravery who opposed Hitler primarily for moral reasons. Their tragedy was, as Ritter has observed, that they received no backing 'from either within or without' (Ritter, 1958: 313). Those hundreds of thousands and perhaps millions of Germans who were secretly critical of the Third Reich behaved as the great majority of people of any nationality do in a dangerous and threatening situation, and earned Sophie Scholl's rebuke, delivered at her trial before the People's Court in

1943: 'What we have written and said is in the mind of all of you, but you lack the courage to say it aloud' (Bracher, 1973: 547).

WHY WAS THERE NO GERMAN REVOLUTION IN 1945?

Given that Germany was obviously losing the war by January 1945 and that disillusionment with the Nazi regime was rapidly growing, while food supplies were dwindling and transport, gas and electricity were in the throes of collapse, how is it that there was no German revolution, as in November 1918? Unlike 1918, the regime still exercised a decisive control over the home front. In the course of the war the apparatus of terror and repression had been greatly strengthened by Himmler, and right up to the end it was capable of ruthlessly destroying dissidents and opposition. It was no wonder then that the majority of the population followed the line of discretion rather than valour. One worker expressed this mood when he said: 'Rather than let them string me up I'll be glad to believe in victory' (Noakes and Pridham, IV, 1998: 638). It was also difficult for opposition to find a focus. There were no unions or socialist parties, as in 1918. Moreover, the cohesiveness of the workforce had been largely destroyed by the replacement of so many conscripted workers by women, foreign labourers and teenagers. Many of the older workers, who perhaps might have been able to provide leadership, were, by being made foremen or instructors, in fact integrated into the system and so less likely to rebel. Finally, there did not seem to be much option to fighting on. President Roosevelt, unlike his predecessor, Woodrow Wilson, in 1918, was intent on forcing the Germans into an unconditional surrender, while the brutal reputation and acts of the Red Army encouraged the population to hold out as long as possible did not make the prospects of a Soviet victory seem particularly pleasant. The bombing campaign also failed to break German morale. On the contrary, it made day-to-day survival a priority and took people's minds off political issues. A further factor inhibiting opposition to the regime was the fear of the 7 or 8 million foreign workers acting as a 'Trojan horse' within the Reich. The gangs of foreign workers which had cooperated with German criminals, *Wehrmacht* deserters and the 'Edelweiss Pirates' in Cologne and the Ruhr cities inevitably alarmed the majority of the German population and 'encouraged a solidarity with the existing order, or at least a concern not to undermine it' (Noakes and Pridham, IV, 1998: 639). Possibly this, too, was reinforced by both a feeling of guilt about Germany's treatment of the Jews, Russians and Poles and the fear of retribution from the Allies.

On the other hand, there was little enthusiasm for a people's war. The morale of the *Volkssturm* (see page 111). Units for the most part remained low, while attempts to set up semi-guerrilla organisations such as the *Freikorps Adolf Hitler*, which was supposed to be recruited from party officials, and the *Wehrwolf* groups, recruited from the Hitler Youth to conduct partisan war in occupied Germany, came to nothing. In October 1944 a secret report from the Stuttgart SD pointed out that '[i]n as restricted an area as Germany, in contrast to Russia, resistance by the population is out of the question. . . . It must not be forgotten that we are in the sixth year of the war and the population is weary' (Steinert, 1977: 281–82). When the Americans occupied Aachen on 13 October those inhabitants who had not been evacuated greeted them as liberators. Similarly, in Württemberg peasants ignored all party orders to resist as they were more interested in preserving their villages and farms than staging a pointless rearguard resistance.

Only in April, as the Allied troops advanced into Germany, was there a brief revival of the spirit of November 1918 and a sudden resurgence of political activity. Allied troops had released a significant number of SPD and KPD members from the concentration camps, who, together with local supporters, set up anti-fascist committees in the large cities. In Meissen, in central Germany, for instance, the anti-fascist committee was able to seize the *Rathaus* before Soviet troops entered the town. However, the occupying forces rapidly dissolved the committees and replaced them with martial law.

Part Three

ASSESSMENT

12

The Third Reich in retrospect

The history of the Third Reich has been extensively analysed but controversy about its every aspect shows no sign of abating. There is still no real consensus, for instance, about Hitler's role as *Führer*, Nazi foreign or economic policy, the structure of the Nazi state, the degree of popular support the regime enjoyed or the sequence of events that led to the Holocaust. The cataclysmic end of the Third Reich and the appalling suffering it caused have tended to ensure that German history between the years 1933 and 1945 has been studied as a uniquely horrendous event in world history. Auschwitz and the Holocaust have overshadowed not only the early years of the Third Reich, but the rest of modern German history. This feeling of horror has made it all the more difficult for historians to 'historicise' or normalise the Hitler regime and assess dispassionately the social and economic impact of the Hitler years on German history after 1945.

HITLER'S RISE TO POWER

Hitler's rise to power occurred in the context of the political, economic and social crisis of the early 1930s. The Nazi amalgam of *völkisch*, authoritarian and nationalist ideas provided a solution for both the middle classes and the elites. It could promise an element of 'restoration' but also of change and dynamism without destroying the actual structure of society in the way Bolshevism had in Russia. To the broad mass of its voters it offered the prospect of creating a 'national community' in which everyone would have his or her niche, provided of course they were 'Aryan'. Nazism was a charismatic and pseudo-religious movement which, as Peukert has pointed out, was 'the combined outcome of the experience of crisis, the yearning for security and the desire for aggression, all merged into a breathless dynamism that latched on to whatever was the next immediate event:

the next election campaign, the next mass demonstration, the next brawl' (Peukert, 1989: 42).

THE NAZI REGIME

As Chancellor, Hitler created a regime that was an uneasy alliance of the old elites and the National Socialist movement. With the passing of the Enabling Law and the destruction of organised labour the way was opened for replacing the pluralistic system of the Weimar Republic with the new 'national community'. National Socialism created a system of hegemony that preserved capitalism, but it created a dysfunctional regime based on the pre-1933 *Führer* party in which strong interest groups competed for power and influence under the overall umbrella of the charismatic *Führer*. The ultimate weakness of the regime was that it gradually undermined the tradition of stable, orderly government within Germany and replaced it with a chaos of competing agencies dependent on Hitler.

Kershaw argues that Hitler's style of charismatic leadership had an 'in-built tendency towards self-destruction' and that consequently his suicide on 30 April 1945 was 'not merely a welcome, but also a logical end to the Third Reich' (Kershaw, 1993: 336). How, then, did it manage to tap such reservoirs of strength in Germany and survive over five years of war against a growing coalition of formidable enemies? Here, perhaps, we need to bear in mind Martin Broszat's advice that we should not always study history backwards (Broszat, 1990). Those who initially supported Nazism could not foresee how the Third Reich would develop. The aims of both the elites and much of the German people overlapped with initial Nazi policy. Hitler's destruction of the Versailles Treaty and eventual provision of full employment were achievements which had universal backing. The German 'economic miracle' and the 'national community' helped appease the working classes, even if working hours increased and wages were controlled. Hitler's foreign-policy successes were exploited to the full by the *Führer* cult, and the frequent plebiscites were interpreted to show how he had the full support of the German people. The destruction of the trade unions, pressure groups and the political-parties, as well as the terror apparatus of the Gestapo and the SS made opposition on any large scale very difficult to achieve. Paradoxically despite the creation of the *Volksgemeinschaft*, German society was **atomised**.

atomised Literally reduced to individual atoms. In the political context the term means a society reduced to a total of isolated individuals lacking support from independent political parties or clubs.

By 1938 Hitler was in a position to begin to implement his ideas for fighting a racial war for *Lebensraum* in eastern Europe. Again, there was a bewildering overlap of aims between Hitler, the elites and the mass of the German people. There was general support for the destruction of Poland, although a deep reluctance to risk a general European war. However, the stunning victories over France and Britain in 1940 raised Hitler's popularity to unprecedented heights. Perhaps a different and more rational Hitler could probably, with patience, have weakened Britain in the Middle East and, through a naval and air war of attrition, brought about a negotiated peace that would have consolidated German hegemony on the continent, but a mere six months after the defeat of France he made the momentous decision to attack Russia. In retrospect, this does indeed seem to have been 'sheer lunacy' (Kershaw, II, 2000: 341), yet the decision did bring together neatly Hitler's strategic, military, economic and ideological aims. At a stroke, the defeat of Russia would force Britain to make peace, permanently make available Russian raw material resources and enable 'Jewish Bolshevism' once and for all to be eliminated. Instead, however, it provided the context in which, with the help of the western powers Hitler's armies would ultimately be defeated.

Within Germany the war was seen by the party faithful, to quote the words of the French revolutionary, Madame Roland, to be 'a great school of public virtue' in which the compromises of 1933 with the conservative elites could be finally swept away. Inside the old Reich pressure intensified on the Churches and the power of the party grew in inverse proportion to its decreasing popularity, although it was in the newly annexed and occupied territories that the full horrors of the Nazi racial, social and political revolution could develop, culminating in the death camps of Auschwitz, Belzec, Sobibor and Treblinka, and the murder of millions of Russians, Poles and foreign slave labourers. The increasing mobilisation of the German people for a total war and the doctrine of unconditional surrender announced at Casablanca by the western Allies gave the average sceptical, apolitical German little option but to support the regime and to hope that the *Führer* would again produce a 'miracle', as he had done in 1940.

Did the internal inefficiencies of the *Führer* system doom the Nazi state to ultimate failure? Would it ultimately have collapsed from internal 'dry rot', like the USSR in 1990–91? Such questions are, of course, hypothetical. The strengths of the regime were formidable, as we have seen, but the in-built momentum for war, change and racial revolution were permanently destabilising factors both within and without the Reich. As Rauschning observed in 1939, 'National Socialism cannot abandon this dynamic element: in doing so it would be abandoning itself' (Rauschning, 1939: 26).

HOW 'MODERN' WAS THE THIRD REICH?

Historians have to study the Third Reich in the round and attempt to put it within the context of its time as well as assessing its impact on the two successor German states. The present debate about the degree of modernisation in the Third Reich has led to the opening-up of fresh perspectives, which have made it easier to evaluate its legacy to the Federal Republic. Richard Overy, for instance, has shown how the foundations for the powerful West German car industry were laid in the Third Reich, while Michael Prinz and Rainer Zitelmann (1991) and many others have explored how the Labour Front first of all helped bring about 'the modernisation of leisure' (Roseman, 1997: 210) through the introduction of mass tourism for the working classes, and then, during the war, went on to produce elaborate plans for a post-war welfare state. Roseman even argues that the 'Nazi approach to labour relations in the factory . . . was less a return to feudal conditions than a National Socialist variant of the human relations approach being adopted in the USA' (Roseman, 1997: 211). In health care, too, there were elements that were distinctly 'modern' such as the new medical care and preventative measures made available for small children, mothers and indeed factory workers.

How can these new perceptions of the Nazi regime as a conscious modernising force be reconciled with its barbaric racial policies? Modernisation need not, of course, be synonymous with the development of pluralism and democracy. As Burleigh and Wippermann have shown, the novelty of the Nazi regime lay in its attempt to engineer 'an ideal future world, without "lesser races", without the sick, and without those whom they decreed had no place in the "national community"' (Burleigh and Wippermann, 1991: 306). Although in some areas economic and social policies were introduced which were in line with similar developments in Britain and the USA, racial engineering and *Lebensraum* were the core of Nazi policies. In Nazi Germany there was, as Peukert has argued, a juxtaposition of 'normality and modernity' with 'fascist barbarism', which raises profound questions about the 'pathologies and seismic fractures within modernity itself, and about the implicit destructive tendencies of industrial class society' (Peukert, 1989: 16).

THE LEGACY OF NAZI GERMANY

The immediate legacy of Hitler was a country of ruined cities, occupied and divided into four zones by the victorious powers. Its eastern territories were annexed by Poland and the USSR while wave after wave of refugees and expellees flooded into rump Germany. By provoking a world war with both the USA and the USSR Hitler was also, inadvertently, 'the architect of German disunity' up to 1990 (Gaddis, 1997: 115). He was indirectly the founding father of both the Marxist people's republic in the east and the liberal, capitalist state in the west.

It suited the politicians in both these states to argue that the surrender on 8 May 1945 marked 'Stunde Null' or zero hour, after which time began again. Yet inevitably there were some continuities in attitudes and personnel. The massive rearmament programmes of the Third Reich indirectly made possible the economic miracle of the 1950s. In 1945, for example, despite the bombing, German machine-tool holdings were over double those in Britain. The legacy of the Labour Front and Hitler Youth also contributed to better labour relations. Everhard Holtmann, in his study based on two small towns in the Ruhr, has shown how Hitler Youth veterans, for instance, brought into the SPD some of the more egalitarian ideas of National Socialism (James, 1991: 107). Initially the occupying powers attempted to pursue a thorough de-Nazification process, but with the onset of the Cold War in 1948 this was effectively dropped, and in the early years of the Federal Republic many of the dismissed former Nazi officials were allowed to return to work. The Cold War also enabled a virulent anti-Communism and hatred of the USSR to work as an integrating force for the new Federal Republic. In East Germany, the German Democratic Republic, a more radical purge of ex-Nazis took place. In 1949, backed by Soviet military power, a Communist dictatorship was created. In structure there were some similarities with the Third Reich, but essentially the model for the founding fathers was the totalitarianism of the USSR.

The legacy of the Third Reich also, of course affected the whole continent of Europe. Its defeat led not only to the division of Germany but also to the division of Europe into two hostile blocs. Mark Mazower has shown how the European Common Market which was established in 1958 in western Europe also revived some of the ideas, which a committee in the Reich Economics Ministry in 1940 after consulting widely with Belgian, Dutch and Swedish business leaders, had recommended. These involved the establishment of a 'European economic union' with a unified transport system, free movement of capital, a uniform tariff on imports from outside Europe and a rationalization of the European economy by 'finding areas of economic complementarity' (Mazower, 2008, 124).

Inevitably, then, despite the 'Stunde Null' myth, there was some continuity of development with Nazi Germany, especially in West Germany, but in reality the biggest legacy of the Hitler regime has been negative. It has provided a frightening example of how civilisation can crack and by its very example it has strengthened the exemplary determination of post-war Germans to avoid a repetition of such terrible events.

Part Four

DOCUMENTS

Document 1   THE NATURE OF FASCISM

Richard Lowenthal, under the name of Paul Serring, wrote an analysis of Hitler's seizure of power from a Marxist viewpoint, which was published in the journal of the exiled SPD, Zeitschrift für Sozialismus, *in September–October 1935. In this extract he is discussing the composition of the membership of the Nazi Party.*

. . . [T]his [fascist] party recruits itself from members of all classes, while within it certain groups are prevalent and form its nucleus, groups which have been called middle groups in a confusing terminology. The bourgeois is represented, but only the bourgeois which is in debt and needs support; the working class is represented, but only the workers who are chronically unemployed and unable to fight, living in distressed areas; the urban lower middle classes join, but only the ruined lower middle classes; the rentiers are included, but only the rentiers expropriated by inflation; officers and intellectuals lead, but only ex-officers and bankrupt intellectuals. These groups form the nucleus of the movement – it has the character of a true community of bankruptcy – and this allows the movement to expand beyond its nucleus into all social classes parallel with the crisis because it is socially interlinked with all of them.

Source: F.L. Carsten, 'Interpretations of Fascism', in W. Laqueur (ed.), *Fascism: A Reader's Guide*, Penguin (Harmondsworth, 1979), p. 462.

Document 2   HERMANN RAUSCHNING ON THE AIMS OF NAZISM, 1938

As a former Nazi and President of the Danzig Senate who fled to Switzerland in 1935, Rauschning sought in his perceptive book Germany's Revolution of Destruction *to inform the world of what he perceived to be the true nature of National Socialism.*

What then, are the aims of National Socialism which are being achieved one after another? Certainly not the various points of its programme: even if some of these are carried out, that is not the thing that matters. The aim of National Socialism is the complete revolutionizing of the technique of government, and complete dominance over the country by the leaders of the movement. The two things are inseparably connected: the revolution cannot be carried out without an elite ruling with absolute power, and this elite can maintain itself in power only through a process of continual intensification of revolutionary disintegration. National Socialism is an unquestionably genuine revolutionary movement in the sense of a final achievement on a vaster scale of 'the mass rising' dreamed of by Anarchists and Communists.

But modern revolutions do not take place through fighting across improvised barricades, but in disciplined acts of destruction. They follow irrational impulses, but they remain under rational guidance. . . .

Source: Hermann Rauschning, *Germany's Revolution of Destruction*, Heinemann (London, 1939), p. 20.

THE PARTY PROGRAMME   **Document 3**

The party programme of the German Workers' Party (which was about to change its name to the National Socialist German Workers' Party – NSDAP) was unveiled at a public meeting in the Hofbräuhaus *in Munich on 24 February 1920. It was drawn up by Hitler and Drexler, although Gottfried Feder probably influenced the formulation of Point 11. It was a mixture of anti-Semitism, anti-capitalism and intense nationalism.*

The Programme of the German Workers' Party is designed to be of limited duration. The leaders have no intention, once the aims announced in it have been achieved, of establishing fresh ones, merely in order to increase, artificially, the discontent of the masses and so ensure the continued existence of the Party.

1. We demand the union of all Germans in a Greater Germany on the basis of the right of national self-determination.

2. We demand equality of rights for the German people in its dealings with other nations, and the revocation of the Peace Treaties of Versailles and St-Germain.

3. We demand land and territory (colonies) to feed our people and to settle our surplus population.

4. Only members of the nation may be citizens of the state. Only those of German blood, whatever their creed, may be members of the nation. Accordingly, no Jew may be a member of the nation.

5. Non-citizens may live in Germany only as guests and must be subject to laws for aliens.

6. The right to vote on the state's government and legislation shall be enjoyed by the citizens of the state alone. We demand therefore that all official appointments, of whatever kind, whether in the Reich, in the states or in the smaller localities, shall be held by none but citizens. We oppose the corrupting parliamentary custom of filling posts merely in accordance with party considerations, and without reference to character or abilities.

7. We demand that the state shall make it its primary duty to provide a livelihood for its citizens. If it should prove impossible to feed the entire population, foreign nationals (non-citizens) must be deported from the Reich.

8. All non-German immigration must be prevented. We demand that all non-Germans who entered Germany after 2 August 1914 shall be required to leave the Reich forthwith.

9. All citizens shall have equal rights and duties.

10. It must be the first duty of every citizen to perform physical or mental work. The activities of the individual must not clash with the general interest, but must proceed within the framework of the community and be for the general good.

We demand therefore:

11. The abolition of incomes unearned by work.

The breaking of slavery of interest

12. In view of the enormous sacrifices of life and property demanded of a nation by any war, personal enrichment from war must be regarded as a crime against the nation. We demand therefore the ruthless confiscation of war profits.

13. We demand the nationalisation of all businesses which have been formed into corporations (trusts).

14. We demand profit-sharing in large industrial enterprises.

15. We demand the extensive development of insurance for old age.

16. We demand the creation and maintenance of a healthy middle class, the immediate communalising of department stores, and their lease at a cheap rate to small traders, and that the utmost consideration shall be shown to all small traders in the placing of state and municipal orders.

17. We demand land reform suitable to our national requirements, the passing of a law for the expropriation of land for communal purposes without compensation, the abolition of ground rent, and the prohibition of all speculation in land.

18. We demand the ruthless prosecution of those whose activities are injurious to the common interest. Common criminals, usurers, profiteers, etc., must be punished with death, whatever their creed or race.

19. We demand that Roman Law, which serves a materialistic world order, be replaced by a German common law.

20. The state must consider a thorough reconstruction of our national system of education (with the aim of opening up to every able and hard-working German the possibility of higher education and of thus obtaining advancement). The curricula of all educational establishments must be brought into line with the requirements of practical life. The aim of the school must be to give the pupil, beginning with the first sign of intelligence, a grasp of the notion of the state (through the study of civic affairs). We demand the education of gifted children of poor parents, whatever their class or occupation, at the expense of the state.

21. The state must ensure that the nation's health standards are raised by protecting mothers and infants, by prohibiting child labour, by promoting physical strength through legislation providing for compulsory gymnastics and sports, and by the extensive support of clubs engaged in the physical training of youth.

22. We demand the abolition of the mercenary [i.e. professional] army and the formation of a people's army.

23. We demand legal warfare on deliberate political mendacity and its dissemination in the press. To facilitate the creation of a German national press we demand:

(a) that all editors of, and contributors to newspapers appearing in the German language must be members of the nation;

(b) that no non-German newspapers may appear without express permission of the state. They must not be printed in the German language;

(c) that non-Germans shall be prohibited by law from participating financially in or influencing German newspapers, and that the penalty for contravening such a law shall be the suppression of any such newspaper, and the immediate deportation of the non-Germans involved. The publishing of papers which are not conducive to the national welfare must be forbidden. We demand the legal prosecution of all those tendencies in art and literature which corrupt our national life, and the suppression of cultural events which violate this demand.

24. We demand freedom for all religious denominations in the state, provided they do not threaten its existence nor offend the moral feelings of the German race.

The Party as such stands for positive Christianity, but does not commit itself to any particular denomination. It combats the Jewish-materialist spirit within and without us on the basis of the principle: the common interest before self-interest.

25. To put the whole of this programme into effect, we demand the creation of a strong central state power for the Reich; the unconditional authority of the political central Parliament over the entire Reich and its organisations; and the formation of Corporations based on estate and occupation for the purpose of carrying out the general legislation passed by the Reich in the various German states.

The leaders of the Party promise to work ruthlessly – if need be to sacrifice their lives – to translate this programme into action.

Source: J. Noakes and G. Pridham (eds), *Nazism, 1919–1945, Vol. I: The Rise to Power, 1919–1934* (2nd edn), Exeter University Press (Exeter, 1998), pp. 14–16.

Document 4   HITLER'S POWERS AS AN ORATOR

Hans Frank, who later became Governor-General of occupied Poland, recalled the first time he heard Hitler speak in January 1920 in Munich.

I was strongly impressed straight away. It was totally different from what was otherwise to be heard in meetings. His method was completely clear and simple. He took the overwhelmingly dominant topic of the day, the Versailles *Diktat*, and posed the question of all questions: What now German people? What's the true situation? What alone is now possible? He spoke for over two-and-a-half hours, often interrupted by frenetic torrents of applause – and one could have listened to him for much, much longer. Everything came from the heart, and he struck a chord with all of us. . . . He uttered what was in the consciousness of all those present and linked general experiences to clear understanding and the common wishes of those who were suffering and hoping for a programme. In the matter itself he was certainly not original . . . but he was the one called to act as spokesman of the people . . . he concealed nothing . . . of the horror, the distress, the despair facing Germany. But not only that. He showed a way, the only way left to ruined people in history, that of the grim new beginning from the most profound depths through courage, faith, readiness for action, hard work, and devotion to a great, shining, common goal . . . he placed before the Almighty in the most serious and solemn exhortation the salvation of the honour of the German soldier and worker as his life task. . . . When he finished, the applause would not die down. . . . From this evening onwards . . . I was convinced that if one man could do it, Hitler alone would be capable of mastering Germany's fate.

Source: Quoted in I. Kershaw, *Hitler, Hubris, Vol. I: 1889–1936*, Allen Lane (London, 1998), pp. 148–49.

Document 5   WORKING WITHIN THE CONSTITUTION

In September 1930 three young officers stationed in Ulm were accused of working illegally for the Nazi Party within the army. The three were put on trial before the Supreme Court at Leipzig. Hitler was called as a witness and in his statement he stressed how he aimed to achieve a 'legal' revolution by coming to power through constitutional means.

The National Socialist movement will try to achieve its aim with constitutional means in the state. The constitution prescribes my methods, not the aim. In this constitutional way we shall try to gain decisive majorities in the legislative bodies so that the moment we succeed we can give the state the form that corresponds to our ideas.

The chairman of the court summed up the statement to the effect that the setting up of the Third Reich was being worked for in a constitutional way.

Source: Noakes and Pridham (eds), *Nazism, 1919–1945, Vol. I: The Rise to Power, 1919–1934*, Exeter University Press (Exeter, 1998), p. 90.

HITLER AS SAVIOUR   **Document 6**

Speer describes why both he and his mother joined the Nazi Party in 1931. Speer, who was then a lecturer in architecture at the Berlin Institute of Technology, had just heard Hitler's speech to the students.

Here it seemed to me was hope. Here were new ideals, a new understanding, new tasks. . . . The perils of Communism which seemed inexorably on the way, could be checked, Hitler persuaded us, and instead of hopeless unemployment, Germany could move towards economic recovery. He had mentioned the Jewish problem only peripherally. But such remarks did not worry me, although I was not an anti-Semite; rather I had Jewish friends from my school days and university days, like virtually everyone else. . . . It must have been during these months that my mother saw an SA parade in the streets of Heidelberg. The sight of discipline in a time of chaos, the impression of energy in an atmosphere of universal hopelessness, seems to have won her over also.

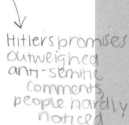

Hitler's promises outweighed anti-semitic comments, people hardly noticed

Source: A. Speer, *Inside the Third Reich*, Weidenfeld & Nicolson (London, 1970), pp. 16–18.

WHY THE CENTRE PARTY VOTED FOR THE ENABLING BILL   **Document 7**

Carl Bachem, who was the historian of the Centre Party, reflects on whether the Centre Party should have voted for the Enabling Bill.

If the Centre had voted against it, it would, given the current mood of the National Socialists, probably have been smashed at once just like the Social Democratic Party. All civil servants belonging to the Centre would probably have been dismissed. There would have been a great fracas in the *Reichstag*, and the Centrists would probably have been beaten up and thrown out. The parliamentary group would probably have made an heroic exit, but with no benefit to the Catholic cause or to the cause of the Centre Party. The links between the Centre and National Socialism would have been completely cut, all collaboration with the National Socialists and every possibility of influencing their policy would have been out of the question. Perhaps, then, it was right to make the attempt to come to an understanding and cooperate with the National Socialists, in order to be able to participate in a practical way in the reshaping of the future. . . .

In any case: as in 1919 we climbed calmly and deliberately into the Social Democrat boat, so in the same way, we were able to enter the boat of the National Socialists in 1933 and try to lend a hand with the steering. Between 1919 and 1933 this proved quite satisfactory: the Social Democrats, since they were not able to govern without the Centre, were unable to do anything particularly antireligious or dubiously socialistic. Will it be possible to exercise a similarly sobering influence on the National Socialists now?

Source: Noakes and Pridham (eds), *Nazism, 1919–1945, Vol. I: The Rise to Power, 1919–1934*, Exeter University Press (Exeter, 1998), pp. 157–58.

Document 8   GOEBBELS AND THE REICH MINISTRY OF POPULAR ENLIGHTENMENT AND PROPAGANDA

On 13 March, under pressure from Hitler, the cabinet agreed to set up a Reich Ministry of Popular Enlightenment and Propaganda. Its model was the Party Propaganda Directorate which Goebbels had set up in 1930. Its task was to spread 'enlightenment and propaganda within the population concerning the policy of the Reich Government and the national reconstruction of the German Fatherland' (Noakes and Pridham, II, 1984: 380). On 25 March Goebbels gave the following explanation to a meeting of radio officials and reporters.

The ministry has the task of achieving a mobilization of mind and spirit in Germany. It is therefore, in the sphere of the mind what the Defence Ministry is in the sphere of defence. Thus, this ministry will require money and will receive money because of a fact which everybody in the Government now recognizes, namely that the mobilization of the mind is as necessary as, perhaps even more necessary than, the mobilization of the nation. The proof is: in 1914 we had been mobilized in material terms as no other nation had – what we lacked was the mobilization of the mind . . . which provided the basis for material mobilization. We did not lose the war because our artillery gave out but because the weapons of our mind did not fire. . . .

Source: J. Noakes and G. Pridham (eds), *Nazism, 1919–1945, Vol. II: State, Economy and Society, 1933–1939*, Exeter University Press (Exeter, 1984), p. 382.

HITLER'S SPEECH TO THE *REICHSSTATTHALTER*, 6 JULY 1933 **Document 9**

Hitler was worried that interference by the party and the SA would threaten economic recovery and alienate the army, big business and the bureaucracy. At this early stage he did not wish to risk a show-down with the old elites which would delay rearmament and economic recovery. Therefore he spoke to the Reichsstatthalter *(Reich Governors) on 6 July.*

The revolution is not a permanent state of affairs, and it must not be allowed to develop into such a state. The stream of revolution released must be guided into the safe channel of evolution . . . we must therefore not dismiss a businessman if he is a good businessman, even if he is not yet a National Socialist; and especially not if the National Socialist who is to take his place knows nothing about business. In business ability must be the only authoritative standard. . . .

History will not judge us according to whether we have removed and imprisoned the largest number of economists, but according to whether we have succeeded in providing work. . . . The ideas of the programme do not oblige us to act like fools and upset everything, but to realize our trains of thought wisely and carefully. In the long run our political power will be all the more secure, the more we succeed in underpinning it economically. The *Reichsstatthalter* must therefore see to it that no organization or Party Offices assume the functions of government, dismiss individuals and make appointments to offices, to do which the Reich Government alone – and in regard to business the Reich Minister of Economics – is competent.

Source: N. Baynes, *Hitler's Speeches, 1922–39* (Vol. 1), Oxford University Press (Oxford, 1942), pp. 865–66.

HITLER'S PLANS FOR THE ARMY **Document 10**

On 28 February 1934 Hitler summoned the leaders of the SA and most of the senior Reichswehr *generals to a meeting. He promised to preserve the* Reichswehr *and rejected the alternative of creating a fascist militia on the Italian pattern. An account survives in the unpublished memoirs of Field Marshal von Weichs.*

. . . a militia, as Röhm suggested, would not be the least bit suitable for national defence. He sought to establish this by examples from military history. In the course of this he came to his own experience. The hastily and superficially trained division, to which he belonged in 1914 as a private, had come to grief at Langemarck with the most heavy losses. Therefore he was resolved to raise a people's army, built up on the *Reichswehr*, rigorously trained and equipped with the most modern weapons. He also rejected a

Fascist Militia on the Italian pattern. This new army would have to be ready for any defence purposes after five years, and after eight years suitable also for attacking. The SA must confine itself to internal tasks. . . .

Source: R.J. O'Neill, *The German Army and the Nazi Party*, Cassell (London, 1966), pp. 40–41.

Document 11   PAPEN WARNS HITLER ON 17 JUNE 1934

On 17 June Papen gave an address, which had been drafted by Edgar Jung, to the professors and students in the Auditorium Maximum of the University of Marburg. Papen warned Hitler with considerable clarity of the dangers of a 'second revolution' as threatened by Röhm.

Whoever toys with such ideas should not forget that a second wave of revolution might be followed by a third, and that he who threatens to employ the guillotine may be its first victim.

Nor is it clear where such a second wave is to lead. There is much talk of the coming socialization. Have we gone through the anti-Marxist revolution in order to carry out a Marxist programme? . . . Would the German people be better for it, except perhaps those who scent booty in a pillaging raid? . . . No people can afford to indulge in a permanent revolt from below if it would endure in History. At some time the movement must come to a stop and a solid structure arise. . . . Germany must not embark on an adventure without a known destination, nobody knowing where it will end. History has its own clock. It is not necessary continually to urge it on. . . . Great men are not created by propaganda, but grow until their deeds are acknowledged by History. Nor can Byzantium cheat these laws of Nature. Whoever speaks of Prussians should first of all think of quiet, selfless service, and of reward or recognition only at the very last, or best not at all.

Source: quoted in A. Bullock, *Hitler: A Study in Tyranny*, Penguin (Harmondsworth, 1962), p. 299.

Document 12   HITLER'S LIFESTYLE

As Hitler's architect, Speer had a unique chance to observe the Führer's inefficient work patterns.

When, I would often ask myself, did he really work? Little was left of the day; he rose late in the morning and conducted one or two official conferences;

but from the subsequent dinner on he more or less wasted his time until the early hours of the evening. His rare appointments in the late afternoon were imperilled by his passion for looking at building plans. The adjutants often asked me: 'please don't show any plans today'. Then the drawings I had brought with me would be left by the telephone switchboard at the entrance and I would reply evasively to Hitler's enquiries. Sometimes he would see through this game and would himself go to look in the anteroom or the cloakroom for my roll of plans.

In the eyes of the people Hitler was the Leader who watched over the nation day and night. This was hardly so. But Hitler's lax scheduling could be regarded as a lifestyle characteristic of the artistic temperament. According to my observations, he often allowed a problem to mature during the weeks when he seemed entirely taken up with trivial matters. Then after the 'sudden insight' came, he would spend a few days of intensive work giving final shape to his solution. . . . Once he had come to a decision, he relapsed again into his idleness.

Source: A. Speer, *Inside the Third Reich*, p. 131.

'WORKING TOWARDS THE *FÜHRER*'   **Document 13**

The State Secretary in the Prussian Agricultural Ministry, Werner Willikens, in a speech on 21 February 1934 to representatives from the agricultural ministries in the Länder, *gave his advice on how to interpret the will of the* Führer, *when no precise instructions were given by him.*

Everyone with opportunity to observe it knows that the *Führer* can only with great difficulty order from above everything that he intends to carry out sooner or later. On the contrary, until now everyone has best worked in his place in the new Germany, if, so to speak, he works towards the *Führer*. . . . Very often, and in many places, it has been the case that individuals, already in previous years, have waited for commands and orders. Unfortunately, that will probably also be so in the future. Rather, however, it is the duty of every single person to attempt, in the spirit of the *Führer*, to work towards him. Anyone making mistakes, will come to notice it soon enough. But the one who works correctly towards the *Führer* along his lines and towards his aim will in future as previously have the finest reward of one day suddenly attaining legal confirmation of his work.

Source: J. Noakes and G. Pridham (eds), *Nazism 1919–45, Vol. II: State, Economy and Society, 1933–39*, p. 13.

Document 14   A BRITISH VIEW OF HITLER

David Lloyd George, British Prime Minister 1916–22, paid Hitler a three-hour visit at the Berghof in September 1936. Later he wrote about him in the Daily Express.

The old trust him, the young idolize him. It is not the admiration accorded to a popular leader. It is the worship of a national hero who has saved the country from utter despondency and degradation . . . he is immune from criticism as a king in a monarchical country. He is something more. He is the George Washington of Germany – the man who won for his country independence from all oppressors. To those who have not actually seen and sensed the way Hitler reigns over the heart and mind of Germany, this description may appear extravagant. All the same it is the bare truth.

Source: *Daily Express*, 17 November 1936.

Document 15   THE NUMBER OF UNEMPLOYED (IN MILLIONS)

Year	January	July
1932	6.042	5.392
1933	6.014	4.464
1934	3.773	2.426
1935	2.974	1.754
1936	2.520	1.170
1937	1.853	0.563
1938	1.052	0.218
1939	0.302	0.038

Source: B. Gebhardt, *Handbuch der Deutschen Geschichte* (Vol. 4), edited by K.D. Erdmann, Union Verlag (Stuttgart, 1959), p. 352.

Document 16   THE FOUR YEAR PLAN

Hitler's memorandum was aimed at silencing economic objections, but it was also a clear statement of his basic philosophy and foreign and economic policy intentions.

... Since the outbreak of the French Revolution, the world has been moving with ever-increasing speed towards a new conflict, the most extreme solution of which is Bolshevism; and the essence and goal of Bolshevism is [sic] the elimination of those strata of mankind which have hitherto provided the leadership and their replacement by world-wide Jewry.

No nation will be able to avoid or abstain from this historical conflict. Since Marxism, through its victory in Russia, has established one of the greatest empires as a forward base for its future operations, this question has become a menacing one. Against a democratic world which is ideologically split stands a unified aggressive will based on an authoritarian ideology.

The military resources of this aggressive will are meantime increasing rapidly from year to year. One only has to compare the Red Army as it actually exists today with the assumption of military men 10 or 15 years ago to realize the menacing extent of this development. Only consider the results of a further development over 10, 15 or 20 years and think what conditions will be like then.

Germany

Germany will, as always, have to be regarded as the focus of the Western world against the attacks of Bolshevism. I do not regard this as an agreeable mission but rather as a handicap and burden for our national life, regrettably resulting from our disadvantageous position in Europe. We cannot, however, escape this destiny. ...

At the moment there are only two countries in Europe which can be regarded as standing firm against Bolshevism – Germany and Italy. The other nations are either corrupted by their democratic way of life, infected by Marxism and therefore likely to collapse in the foreseeable future or ruled by authoritarian governments, whose sole strength lies in their military resources; this means, however, that being obliged to protect their leadership against their own peoples by the armed hand of the Executive, they are unable to use this armed hand for the protection of their countries against external enemies. None of these countries would ever be capable of waging war against Soviet Russia with any prospects of success. In fact, apart from Germany and Italy, only Japan can be considered as a power standing firm in the face of world peril. ...

Germany's economic situation

Just as the political movement among our people knows only one goal, the preservation of our existence, that is to say, the securing of all the spiritual and other prerequisites of our existence for the self-assertion of our nation, so neither has the economy any other goal than this. The nation does not live for the economy, for economic leaders or for economic or financial theories; on the contrary, it is finance and the economy, economic leaders and theories, which all owe unqualified service in this struggle for self-assertion. . . .

. . . It is not sufficient merely to establish from time to time raw material or foreign exchange balances or to talk about the preparation of a war economy in time of peace; on the contrary, it is essential to ensure all the food supplies required in peacetime and, above all, those means for the conduct of a war which can be secured by human energy and activity. I therefore draw up the following programme for a final provision of our vital needs:

I. Parallel with the military and political rearmament and mobilization of our nation must go its economic rearmament and mobilization, and this must be effected in the same tempo, with the same determination, and if need be with the same ruthlessness as well. In future the interests of individual gentlemen can no longer play any part in these matters. There is only one interest, the interest of the nation: only one view, the bringing of Germany to the point of political and economic self-sufficiency.

II. For this purpose, foreign exchange must be saved in all those areas where our needs can be satisfied by German production, in order that it may be used for those requirements, which can under no circumstances be fulfilled except by import.

III. Accordingly, fuel production must be now stepped up with the utmost speed and brought to final completion within eighteen months. . . .

IV. The mass production of synthetic rubber must also be organized and achieved with the same urgency.

V. The question of cost of producing these raw materials is also quite irrelevant. . . . There has been time enough in four years to find out what we cannot do. Now we have to carry out what we can do.

I thus set the following tasks:

I. The German armed forces must be operational within four years.

II. The German economy must be fit for war within four years.

Source: Noakes and Pridham (eds), Nazism, 1919–1945, Vol. II: State, Economy and Society, 1933–1939, Exeter University Press (Exeter, 1984), pp. 281–87.

Document 17   ACHIEVEMENTS OF THE FOUR YEAR PLAN, 1936–42

The main failure of the Four Year Plan was to meet the target for synthetic fuel. Much of the necessary plant to meet the demands for the plan was only in full production by the early 1940s. In 1939 Germany still needed to import one-third of its raw material needs from abroad.

		(in thousands of tons)		
Commodity	1936 output	1938 output	1942 output	Plan target
Mineral oil	1,790	2,340	6,260	13,830
Aluminium	98	166	260	273
Buna rubber	0.7	5	96	120
Nitrogen	770	914	930	1040
Explosives	18	45	300	223
Powder	20	26	150	217
Steel	19,216	22,656	20,480	24,000
Iron ore	2,255	3,360	4,137	5,549
Brown coal	161,382	194,985	145,918	240,500
Hard coal	158,400	186,186	166,059	213,000

Source: D. Petzina, *Autarkiepolitik im Dritten Reich. Der national-sozialistische Vierjahresplan*, Deutsche Verlags-Anstalt (Stuttgart, 1968), p. 182.

GROSS NATIONAL PRODUCT AND MILITARY EXPENDITURE IN GERMANY, THE USA AND BRITAIN, 1933–45

Document 18

Year	Germany (billions RM)			USA (billions $)			Britain (billions £)		
	GNP	Military expend.	(%)	GNP	Military expend.	(%)	National income	Military expend.	(%)
1933	59	1.9	3	56	0.5	1	3.7	0.1	3
1934	67	4.1	6	65	0.7	1	3.9	0.1	3
1935	74	6.0	8	73	0.9	1	4.1	0.1	2
1936	83	10.9	13	83	0.9	1	4.4	0.2	5
1937	93	11.7	13	91	1.0	1	4.6	0.3	7
1938	105	17.2	17	85	1.0	1	4.8	0.4	8
1939	130	30.0	23	91	1.3	1	5.0	1.1	22
1940	141	53.0	38	101	2.2	2	6.0	3.2	53
1941	152	71.0	47	126	13.8	11	6.8	4.1	60
1942	165	91.0	55	159	49.6	31	7.5	4.8	64
1943	184	112.0	61	193	80.4	42	8.0	5.0	63
1944				211	88.6	42	8.2	5.1	62
1945				214	75.9	36	8.3	4.4	53

Source: B. Carroll, *Design for Total War: Arms and Economics in the Third Reich*, Mouton (The Hague, 1968), p. 184.

Document 19   A NAZI HISTORY SYLLABUS

A model course for contemporary German history as recommended by the National Socialist Educator (the official pedagogical paper in the Third Reich) for senior secondary children.

Weeks	Subject	Relations to the Jews	Reading material
1–4	Pre-war Germany, the Class-War, Profits, Strikes.	The Jew at large!	Hauptmann's *The Weavers*.
5–8	From Agrarian to Industrial State. Colonies.	The peasant in the claws of the Jew!	Descriptions of the colonies from Hermann Löns.
9–12	Conspiracy against Germany, encirclement, barrage around Germany.	The Jew reigns! War plots.	Beumelburg: *Barrage . . . Life of Hindenburg, Wartime Letters*.
13–16	German struggle – German want. Blockade! Starvation!	The Jew becomes prosperous! Profit from German want.	Manke: *Espionage at the Front*. War Reports.
17–20	The Stab in the Back. Collapse.	Jews as leaders of the November insurrection.	Pierre des Granges: *On Secret Service in Enemy Country*. Bruno Brehm: *That Was the End*.
21–24	Gemany's Golgotha. Erzberger's Crimes! Versailles.	Jews enter Germany from the East. Judah's triumph.	Volkmann: *Revolution over Germany*. Feder: *The Jews*. The *Stürmer* newspaper.
25–28	Adolf Hitler. National Socialism.	Judah's Foe!	*Mein Kampf*. Dietrich Eckart.
29–32	The bleeding frontiers. Enslavement of Germany.	The Jew profits by Germany's misfortunes.	Beumelburg: *Germany in Chains*. Wehner: *Pilgrimage to Paris*.
	The Volunteer Corps. Schlageter.	Loans (Dawes, Young).	Schlageter – a German hero.
33–36	National Socialism at grips with crime and the underworld.	Jewish instigators of murder. The Jewish press.	Horst Wessel.
37–40	Germany's Youth at the Helm! The Victory of Faith.	The last fight against Judah.	Herbert Norkus. Reich Party: The Congress.

Source: quoted in R.A. Brady, *The Spirit and Structure of German Fascism*, Gollancz (London, 1937), p. 112.

THE LEAGUE OF GERMAN GIRLS

Document 20

Christa Wolf, who later became one of East Germany's best-known authors, described in her autobiography the impact that the League of German Girls made on her as a child, and how her membership caused friction with her socialist mother. Joining was an act of rebellion against her family.

. . . What a pleasure it was to enjoy the joviality of the leader, a merry young woman by the name of Marianne, called Micky. Just call me Micky, I look like Micky [sic] Mouse anyway. Another kind of pleasure was to crowd around the leader, together with all the others, at the end of the evening, forgetting one's own shyness, to grasp her hand, to enjoy the extraordinary familiarity. And on the ride home, to become familiar with a new word by repeating it to herself: 'comradeship'. It meant the promise of a loftier life, far removed from the small area of the store, filled with cans of fish, bags of sugar, loaves of bread, sausages hanging from the ceiling . . . far removed also from the white figure in the store smock who was standing outside waiting for Nelly: her mother had probably been waiting for a long time. Why had she been this late? . . . Not a word about 'comradeship'. She wiped her feet [Not a word to her mother]. Nor could she admit to her mother that Micky sang and played and marched with them . . . there was something her mother couldn't give her, something she didn't want to miss. . . .

Source: quoted in C. Koonz, *Mothers in the Fatherland: Women, the Family and Nazi Politics*, Jonathan Cape (London, 1987), p. 193.

WOMEN'S PLACE IN THE NAZI STATE

Document 21

In his address to the National Socialist Women's Section on 8 September 1934, Hitler summed up the Nazi view of the woman's position in society.

If one says that man's world is the State, his struggle, his readiness to devote his powers to the service of the community, one might be tempted to say that the world of woman is a smaller world. For her world is her husband, her family, her children and her house. But where would the greater world be if there were no one to care for the small world? . . . Providence has entrusted to women the cares of that world which is peculiarly her own. . . .

Every child that a woman brings into the world is a battle, a battle waged for the existence of her people. . . .

Source: Baynes, *Hitler's Speeches* (Vol. 1), Oxford University Press (Oxford, 1942), pp. 528–29.

Document 22   POPULATION STATISTICS

Year	No. of marriages	Live births
1932	516,793	933,126
1933	638,573	971,174
1934	740,165	1,198,350
1935	651,435	1,263,976
1936	609,631	1,277,052
1937	618,971	1,275,212

Source: C.W. Guillebaud, *The Economic Recovery of Germany from 1933 to the Incorporation of Austria in March, 1938* (London, 1939), p. 275.

Document 23   THE EGALITARIAN STATE

In a speech made in Berlin on 1 May 1937 Hitler claims to have broken with the old class system.

We in Germany have really broken with a world of prejudices. I leave myself out of account. I, too, am a child of the people; I do not trace my line from any castle: I come from the workshop. Neither was I a general: I was simply a soldier, as were millions of others. It is something wonderful that amongst us an unknown from the army of the millions of German people – of workers and of soldiers – could rise to be head of the Reich and of the nation. By my side stand Germans from all walks of life who today are amongst the leaders of the nation: men who once were workers on the land are now governing German states in the name of the Reich. . . . It is true that men who came from the bourgeoisie and former aristocrats have their place in this

Movement. But to us it matters nothing whence they come if only they can work to the profit of our people. That is the decisive test. We have not broken down classes in order to set new ones in their place: we have broken down classes to make way for the German people as a whole.

Source: Baynes, *Hitler's Speeches* (Vol. 1), Oxford University Press (Oxford, 1942), pp. 620–21.

'DO-IT-YOURSELF' WAGE BARGAINING **Document 24**

The abolition of the unions and the increasing shortage of skilled workers enabled individual employees to make unofficial wage agreements with their employers. Detlev Peukert argues that this led to an '[e]very man for himself mentality' which persisted even after 1945. The following report by the SOPADE, the German Social Democratic Party in Exile, in 1935 emphasises this new individualism of the workers, which began in the Depression of 1930–33.

The National Socialists are well aware that the sense of solidarity is the source of the working class's strength, and as a result the aim of all their measures, whether directed for or against the workers, is to stifle the sense of that solidarity. . . . The damage they have done to the workers, as far as wages, taxes and welfare insurance are concerned, has always been so designed as to avoid affecting large groups in equal measure. General damage might possibly provoke counter-moves. It is debatable how successful this policy of the National Socialists has been, not least because the destruction of the sense of solidarity began earlier during the economic crisis. The crisis induced the worker to place a low value on negotiated wage agreements – the most precious achievement of collective action – and to seek work at any price. The National Socialists have now reduced the worker to the point that he often goes to the boss on his own to try to avert a deterioration in wages, especially over piece rates, and gets a concession out of the boss on the condition that he tells his workmates nothing about it. One often has the impression, particularly with young workers that the idea no longer even occurs to them that their demands might carry more weight if backed by collective action – even if only on the smallest scale.

Source: D.A. Peukert, *Inside Nazi Germany: Conformity, Opposition and Racism in Everyday Life*, Penguin (Harmondsworth, 1989), p. 114.

Document 25   LABOUR RELATIONS AND THE GESTAPO

Employers were often ready to make concessions, especially, as we have seen above, on an individual basis, in order to retain their workforce and to complete their orders on time. However, in the background there was always the threat of the Gestapo as the following SOPADE *report of January 1939 on a factory in Silesia shows.*

The company D reduced the piece work rates in the lathe shop, the paint shop, and for the boiler makers without having previously informed the workforce. This produced a storm of protest and work came to a halt as groups of workers met to discuss the issue. The works manager charged furiously through the plant ordering people to resume work. When this had no effect, he shouted to the workers: 'Go and see the Trustee, he ordered the reduction'. He vanished and phoned the Gestapo which came at once. There were informers among those involved in discussions who denounced to the Gestapo those stirring up opposition. Twenty-two workers were arrested and taken to the Brown House in Görlitz. The other workers were threatened with immediate dismissal and transfer to forced labour in the event of repetition. In the meantime 8 out of 22 have been released. They did not, however, return to the factory but had to go to fortification works in the West.

Source: Noakes and Pridham (eds), *Nazism, 1919–1945, Vol. II: State, Economy and Society, 1933–1939*, Exeter University Press (Exeter, 1984), pp. 368–69.

Document 26   THE IMPACT OF THE 'BEAUTY OF LABOUR' AND 'STRENGTH THROUGH JOY' SCHEMES

Underground SPD sources gave mixed reports about the reception of the 'Beauty of Labour' and 'Strength through Joy' schemes. The latter appeared to be genuinely popular, while the former were viewed with cynicism.

Berlin, February 1936
Under the rubric 'Beauty of Labour' some large firms have laid out sports fields and built swimming baths, etc. in their grounds for the use of their employees. But the workers are compelled to build these facilities in their spare time without pay. There is great indignation about this and many are of the opinion: 'It is simply intended to look good. The bosses are certainly not thinking of their workers and of their well being.'

Central Germany, April 1939

While Beauty of Labour makes no impression whatsoever – the splendours are normally built near to the entrance so that visitors can see them – Strength through Joy is not without its impact. However, workers' wages are only barely sufficient for essentials and nobody can afford a trip to Madeira, 150 RM per person – 300 with the wife. Even the shorter trips produce so many additional expenses that they often double the cost. But some people like them nonetheless. Anybody who has never made a trip in his life and sees the sea for the first time is much impressed. The effect is:

'The Nazis have done some good things after all'. The enthusiasm is, however, greater on the first trip. On the second, many are put off by the crowds. . . .

Source: Noakes and Pridham (eds), *Nazism, 1919–1945, Vol. II: State, Economy and Society, 1933–1939*, Exeter University Press (Exeter, 1984), p. 352.

DEVELOPMENT OF WAGES AND COST OF LIVING INDEX, 1929–40 **Document 27(A)**

The Nazi regime was able to keep down wages with considerable success. Profits, on the other hand, rose by 36.5 per cent between 1935 and 1939.

	Real earnings (1925/29 = 100)	Money wages (1913/14 = 100)	Cost of living index (1913/14 = 100)
1929	107	177	154.0
1932	91	144	120.6
1933	87	140	118.0
1934	88	140	121.1
1935	91	140	123.0
1936	93	140	124.5
1937	96	140	125.1
1938	101	141	125.6
1939	n.a.	141	126.2
1940	n.a.	141	130.1

Source: adapted from R. Overy, *War and Economy in the Third Reich*, Clarendon Press (Oxford, 1995), p. 216.

Document 27(B)   AVERAGE GROSS HOURLY EARNINGS IN SELECTED INDUSTRIES, 1935–38

	1935	1936	1937	1938
	(In Reichspfennig)			
Building and construction	72.4	72.1	72.3	75.4
Chemicals	82.0	82.0	84.6	85.3
Iron and steel	–	86.3	94.5	96.1
Casting/founding	–	–	88.2	96.3
Metal working	83.6	85.7	88.9	91.1
Clothing	53.8	54.5	55.7	59.6
Textiles	55.0	54.6	55.8	59.1

Source: Peukert, *Inside Nazi Germany*, pp. 114–15.

Document 28   HITLER ON THE RACIAL STATE

In Mein Kampf *Hitler clearly described his intention of creating the racial state where eugenics would strengthen the race and the 'physically and mentally unhealthy and unworthy' would be sterilised.*

The Folkish (*völkisch*) state must . . . set race in the centre of all life. It must take care to keep it pure. It must declare the child to be the most precious treasure of the people. It must see to it that only the healthy beget the children; but there is only one disgrace: despite one's own sickness and deficiencies, to bring children into the world, and one's highest honour: to renounce doing so. And conversely, it must be considered reprehensible to withhold healthy children from the nation. Here the state must act as a guardian of a millennial future in the face of which the wishes and the selfishness of the individual must appear as nothing and submit. It must put the most modern medical means in the service of this knowledge. It must declare unfit for propagation all who are in any way visibly sick or who have inherited a disease and can therefore pass it on, and put this into actual practice. Conversely, it must take care that the fertility of the healthy woman is not limited by the financial irresponsibility of a state regime which turns the blessing of children into a curse for the parents. It must put an end to that lazy, nay criminal, indifference, with which the social premises for a fecund family are treated today, and must instead feel itself to be the higher guardian of this most precious blessing of a people. Its concern belongs more to the child than to the adult.

Those who are physically and mentally unhealthy and unworthy must not perpetuate their suffering in the body of their children. In this the folkish state must perform the most gigantic educational task. And some day this will seem to be a greater deed than the most victorious wars of our present bourgeois era. By education it must teach the individual that it is no disgrace but only a misfortune deserving of pity, to be sick and weakly, but that it is a crime and hence at the same time a disgrace to dishonour one's misfortune by one's own egotism in burdening innocent creatures with it. . . .

A prevention of the faculty and opportunity to procreate on the part of the physically degenerate and mentally sick, over a period of 600 years would not only free humanity from an immeasurable misfortune, but would lead to a recovery which today seems scarcely conceivable. If the fertility of the healthiest bearers of the nationality is thus consciously and systematically promoted, the result will be a race which at least will have eliminated the germs of our physical and hence spiritual decay.

Source: A. Hitler, *Mein Kampf*, with an introduction by D.C. Watt, Hutchinson (London, 1974), pp. 367–68.

HIMMLER'S CIRCULAR ON THE 'GYPSY NUISANCE'   **Document 29**

Himmler's control of the Reich Criminal Police ensured that he could dictate the agenda of the Reich Central Office for the 'fight against the Gypsy Nuisance', as this came under the jurisdiction of the former organisation. On 8 December 1938 he issued a circular of which the following is an extract.

Treatment of the Gypsy question is part of the National Socialist task of regeneration. A solution can only be achieved if the philosophical perspectives of National Socialism are observed. Although the principle that the German nation respects the national identity of alien peoples is also assumed in the fight against the Gypsy Nuisance, nonetheless the aim of measures taken by the state to defend the homogeneity of the German nation must be the physical separation of Gypsydom from the German nation, the prevention of miscegenation, and finally the regulation of the way of life of pure and part Gypsies. The necessary legal foundation can only be created through a Gypsy law, which prevents further intermingling of blood, and which regulates all the most pressing questions which go together with the existence of Gypsies in the living space of the German nation.

Source: quoted in M. Burleigh and W. Wippermann, *The Racial State: Germany 1933–1945*, Cambridge University Press (Cambridge, 1991), p. 121.

Document 30   HITLER AND THE JEWS

To Hitler 'the Jew' was 'the mightiest counterpart to the Aryan' (Mein Kampf, 1974: 272). The former's ultimate aim was global economic and political domination. In Chapter 11 of Mein Kampf *he sketched out in a lurid and hate-inspired section how the Jews had first settled in Germany and then gradually penetrated the social, political and economic systems. With the advent of liberalism and then democracy Hitler argued that the Jew had become the 'spokesman of a new era' (1974: 285).*

In the organised mass of Marxism [the Jew] has found the weapon which lets him dispense with democracy and in its stead allows him to subjugate and govern the peoples with a dictatorial and brutal fist.

He worked systematically for revolutionisation [sic] in a twofold sense: economic and political. Around peoples who offer too violent a resistance to attack from within he weaves a net of enemies, thanks to his international influence, incites them to war, and finally, if necessary, plants the flag of revolution on the very battlefields.

In economics he undermines the states until the social enterprises, which have become unprofitable, are taken from the state and subjected to his financial control.

In the political field he refuses the state the means for its self-preservation, destroys the foundations of all national self-maintenance and defence, destroys faith in the leadership, scoffs at its history and past, and drags everything that is truly great into the gutter.

Culturally he contaminates art, literature, the theatre, makes a mockery of natural feeling, overthrows all concepts of beauty and sublimity, of the noble and the good, and instead drags men down into the sphere of his own base nature.

. . . Now begins the great last revolution. In gaining political power the Jew casts off the few cloaks that he still wears. The democratic people's Jew becomes the blood Jew and tyrant over peoples. In a few years he tries to exterminate the national intelligentsia and by robbing the peoples of their natural leadership makes them ripe for the slave's lot of permanent subjugation.

The most frightful example of this kind is offered by Russia where he killed or starved about 30 million people with positively fanatical savagery, in part amid inhuman tortures, in order to give a gang of Jewish journalists and stock exchange bandits domination over a great people.

Source: A. Hitler, *Mein Kampf*, with an Introduction by D.C. Watt, Hutchinson (London, 1974), pp. 295–96.

HITLER THREATENS THE JEWS WITH ANNIHILATION **Document 31**

In a speech delivered to the Reichstag on 30 January 1939 Hitler specifically warned the Jews of their fate should war break out.

Today I will once more be a prophet: If the international Jewish financiers in and outside Europe should succeed in plunging the nations into a world war, then the result will not be bolshevization of the earth and thus the victory of Jewry, but the annihilation of the Jewish race in Europe!

Source: Baynes, *Hitler's Speeches* (Vol. 1), Oxford University Press (Oxford, 1942), p. 741.

HITLER'S THINKING ON FOREIGN POLICY IN *MEIN KAMPF* **Document 32**

(a) Hitler is quite specific about Germany's need for Lebensraum *or settlements in Russia.*

And so we National Socialists consciously draw a line beneath the foreign-policy tendency of our pre-war period. We take up where we broke off 600 years ago. We stop the endless German movement to the south and west, and turn our gaze towards the land in the east. At long last we break off the colonial and commercial policy of the pre-war period and shift to the soil policy of the future.

If we speak of soil in Europe, we can primarily have in mind only Russia and her vassal border states. . . .

Our task, the mission of the National Socialist movement, is to bring our own people to such a political insight that they will not see their goal for the future in the breath-taking sensation of a new Alexander's,[1] but in the industrious work of the German plough, to which the sword need only give soil.

[1]Reference to Alexander the Great's conquests.

Source: Hitler, *Mein Kampf*, with an Introduction by D.C. Watt, Hutchinson (London, 1974), pp. 598–99.

(b) Hitler also advocated alliances with Britain and Italy against France.

Anyone who undertakes an examination of the present alliance possibilities for Germany from the above standpoint must arrive at the conclusion that the last practicable tie remains with England. . . . We must not close our eyes to the fact that a necessary interest on the part of England in the annihilation of Germany no longer exists today; that, on the contrary, England's policy from year to year must be directed more and more to an obstruction of France's unlimited drive for hegemony. . . . And Italy, too, cannot and will not desire a further reinforcement of the French position of superior power in Europe. . . .

Source: Hitler, *Mein Kampf*, pp. 564–66.

(c) In criticising Wilhelmine foreign policy for pursuing too many goals at once, Hitler outlines an alternative programme, which Hillgruber (1974) and Hildebrand (1973) argue he covertly adopted in the 1930s.

The correct road would even then have been the third: a strengthening of our continental power by gaining new soil in Europe, and precisely this seemed to place a completion by later acquisitions of colonial territory within the realm of the naturally possible. This policy, to be sure, could only have been carried out in alliance with England or with so abnormal an emphasis on the military implements of power that for forty or fifty years cultural tasks would have been forced into the background.

Source: A. Hitler, *Mein Kampf*, p. 558.

Document 33   THE HOSSBACH MEMORANDUM

On 5 November 1937 Hitler called a meeting of his most important ministers and service chiefs. An account of the meeting was compiled some five days later by Hitler's adjutant, Colonel Hossbach, which in 1946 was accepted by the Nuremberg Tribunal as a 'blueprint' of Hitler's intentions to wage war.

. . . [Hitler's] exposition to follow was the fruit of thorough deliberation and the experience of his four-and-a-half years of power . . . and [he] asked, in the interest of a long-term German policy, that his exposition be regarded, in the event of death, as his last will and testament.

The *Führer* then continued:

The aim of German policy was to make secure and to preserve the racial community and to enlarge it. It was therefore a question of space. . . .

The question for Germany was: Where could she achieve the greatest gain at the lowest cost? German policy had to reckon with two hate-inspired antagonists, Britain and France, to whom a German colossus in the centre of Europe was a thorn in the flesh, and both countries were opposed to any further strengthening of Germany's position either in Europe or overseas. . . .

Germany's problem could only be solved by the use of force, and this was never without attendant risk. The Silesian campaigns of Frederick the Great, Bismarck's wars against Austria and France, had involved unheard-of risks, and the swiftness of Prussian action in 1870 had kept Austria from entering the war. If the resort to force, with its attendant risks, is accepted as the basis of the following exposition, then there remains still to be answered the questions 'When?' and 'How?' In this matter there were three contingencies to be dealt with:

Contingency 1: Period 1943–45

After this date only a change for the worse, from our point of view, could be expected.

The equipment of the Army, Navy and *Luftwaffe*, as well as the formation of the officer corps, was nearly completed. Equipment and armament were modern; in further delay there lay the danger of their obsolescence. . . . Our relative strength would decrease in relation to the rearmament, which would by then have been carried out by the rest of the world. If we did not act by 1943–45 any year could, owing to a lack of reserves, produce the food crisis, to cope with which the necessary foreign exchange was not available, and this must be regarded as a 'waning point of the regime'. Besides, the world was expecting our attack and was increasing its counter-measures from year to year. It was while the rest of the world was still fencing itself off that we were obliged to take the offensive. Nobody knew today what the situation would be in the years 1943–45. One thing was certain, that we could wait no longer. . . . If the *Führer* was still living, it was his unalterable determination to solve Germany's problem of space by 1943–45 at the latest. . . .

Contingency 2

If internal strife in France should develop into such a domestic crisis as to absorb the French army completely and render it incapable of use for war against Germany, then the time for action against the Czechs would have come.

Contingency 3

If France should be so embroiled in war with another State that she could not 'proceed' against Germany.

For the improvement of our politico-military position our first objective, in the event of our being embroiled in war, must be to overthrow Czechoslovakia and Austria simultaneously in order to remove the threat to our flank in any possible operation against the West. . . .

The *Führer* saw contingency 3 coming definitely nearer; it might emerge from the present tensions in the Mediterranean, and he was resolved to take advantage of it whenever it happened, even as early as 1938.

In the light of past experience, the *Führer* saw no early end to the hostilities in Spain. . . .

Source: *Documents on German Foreign Policy, 1918–1945*, Series D, Vol. I (1937–41), HMSO (London, 1950), pp. 29–38.

Document 34   HITLER SURVEYS THE INTERNATIONAL SITUATION, 22 AUGUST 1939

On 22 August 1939, the day before the signature of the Nazi–Soviet Pact, Hitler summoned his military commanders to the Berghof, his mountain retreat near Berchtesgaden, and gave them a survey of the current situation. No official minutes were issued, but notes were taken unofficially by Admiral Canaris, the head of the Counter-Intelligence Service, of which the following is an extract.

It was clear to me that a conflict with Poland had to come sooner or later. I had already made this decision in the Spring, but I thought that I would first turn against the West in a few years, and only after that against the East. But the sequence of things cannot be fixed. Nor should one close one's eyes to the threatening situations. I wanted first of all to establish a tolerable relationship with Poland in order first to fight against the West. But this plan, which appealed to me, could not be executed, as fundamental points had changed. It became clear to me that, in the event of a conflict with the West, Poland would attack us. Poland is striving for access to the sea. The further development appeared after the occupation of the Memel territory and it became clear to me in certain circumstances a conflict with Poland might come at an inopportune moment.

. . . The relationship with Poland has become unbearable. My Polish policy hitherto was contrary to the views of the people. My proposals to Poland [Danzig and the Corridor] were frustrated by England's intervention. Poland changed her tone towards us. A permanent state of tension is intolerable. The power of initiative cannot be allowed to pass to others. The present moment is more favourable than in two or three years' time. An attempt on my life or Mussolini's could change the situation to our disadvantage. One cannot for ever face one another with rifles cocked. One compromise solution suggested to us was that we should change our convictions and make gestures. They talked to us again in the language of Versailles. There was a danger of losing prestige. Now the probability is still great that the West will not intervene. We must take the risk with ruthless determination. The politician must take a risk just as much as the general. We are faced with harsh alternatives of striking or certain annihilation sooner or later.

Source: J. Noakes and G. Pridham (eds), *Nazism, 1919–1945, Vol. III: Foreign Policy, War and Racial Extermination*, Exeter University Press (Exeter, 1988), pp. 739 and 741.

HITLER GIVES THE ORDER TO PREPARE FOR AN ATTACK ON THE USSR   **Document 35**

Hitler saw the defeat of Russia as the key to defeating Britain and to keeping America out of the war. General Halder, the Chief of Staff, recorded Hitler's assessment of the military and diplomatic situation at a military conference on 31 July 1940.

Führer:

(a) Stresses his scepticism regarding technical feasibility [of an invasion of Britain]; however satisfied with results produced by Navy.

(b) Emphasizes weather factor.

(c) Discusses enemy resources for counteraction. Our small Navy is only 15 per cent of enemy's. . . . In any decision we must bear in mind that if we take risks, the prize too is high.

(d) In the event that invasion does not take place, our action must be directed to eliminate all factors that let England hope for a change in the situation. To all intents and purposes the war is won. . . . Submarine and air warfare may bring about a final decision, but this may be one or two years off. Britain's hope lies in Russia and the United States. If Russia drops out of the picture, America too is lost for Britain, because elimination of Russia would tremendously increase Japan's power in the Far East.

Russia is the Far Eastern sword of Britain and the United States pointed at Japan. . . . Japan has her programme which she wants to carry through before the end of the war. . . .

With Russia smashed, Britain's last hope would be shattered. Germany will then be master of Europe and the Balkans. Decision: Russia's destruction must therefore be made part of this struggle. Spring 1941. The sooner Russia is crushed, the better. Attack achieves its purpose only if the Russian state can be shattered to its roots with one blow. . . . Holding part of the country alone will not do. Standing still for the following winter would be perilous. So it is better to wait a little longer but with resolute determination to eliminate Russia. . . .

Source: Noakes and Pridham (eds), *Nazism, 1919–1945, Vol. III: Foreign Policy, War and Racial Extermination*, Exeter University Press (Exeter, 1988), p. 790.

Document 36   THE *EINSATZGRUPPEN*

The Einsatzgruppen, *or mobile task forces, moved into the USSR behind the front-line German troops on 23 June 1941. Heydrich issued the following orders to their commanders.*

All of the following are to be executed:
   Officials of the Comintern . . . top and medium-level officials and radical lower-level officials of the Party, Central Committee, and district and sub-district committees.
   The people's Commissars.
   Jews in Party and state employment, and other radical elements (saboteurs, propagandists, snipers, assassins, inciters, etc.).

Source: M. Burleigh, *The Third Reich*, Macmillan (London, 2000), p. 602.

Document 37   GERMAN TREATMENT OF RUSSIAN PRISONERS OF WAR

The ordinary Russian soldier was also treated abominably by the Germans during the winter of 1941–42. Between June 1941 and February 1942 more than 2 million died of starvation and maltreatment. However, belatedly, the economic pressures of total war forced Hitler to tolerate their employment in the German war industries. The following eye-witness report gives an account of treatment of Russian troops at the Prisoners' Camp at Blizin, near Skarzysko, Poland.

The camp consists of four huts, situated in the fields near the village, so that everything that happens there can be observed by the neighbours. Trainloads of prisoners which arrived here had taken over a fortnight to reach the new camp and were without food or water. Each wagon when opened contained scores of dead bodies. The sick who could not move were thrown out. They were ordered to sit down on the ground near the camp and were shot by the S.S. men before the eyes of the rest. The camp contains about 2,500 prisoners. The average daily death rate is about 50. The dead bodies are thrown out on to the fields and sprinkled with lime, often lying some days after that unburied. . . . The prisoners received ¼ kg of bread made of horse-chestnut flour and potatoskins, and soup made of rotten cabbage. . . .

Source: *German Crimes in Poland*, i–ii (Warsaw, 1946), pp. 268–69.

RESETTLEMENT POLICIES IN POLAND **Document 38**

Goebbels comments on the adverse economic and political effects of Himmler's resettlement policies in the Lublin area in 1943. Ernst Zoerner was an old guard Nazi who had been appointed Mayor of Dresden in 1933.

Zoerner has resigned as Governor of Lublin. He called on me to give the reasons for his resignation. He had succeeded on the whole in squeezing an unusual amount of food out of the Lublin district. Understandably so, for this district is the most fertile in the entire General Government. Suddenly, however, he received orders for resettlement that had a very bad effect upon morale. Some 50,000 Poles were to be evacuated to begin with. Our police were able to grab only 25,000; the other 25,000 joined the partisans. It isn't hard to imagine what consequences that had for the whole area. Now he was to evacuate about 190,000 more Poles. This he refused to do, and in my opinion he was right. His district will now be governed from Warsaw by Governor Dr Fischer. Although Dr Frank, the Governor General, agreed with Zoerner's views, he hasn't sufficient authority to put his foot down on the encroachments of the police and the S.S. It makes you want to tear out your hair when you encounter such appalling political ineptitude. At home we are waging total war with all its consequences and are subordinating all philosophical and ideological aims to the supreme aim of final victory: in the occupied areas, however, things are done as though we were living in profound peace. . . .

Source: J. Goebbels, *The Goebbels Diaries*, Hamish Hamilton (London, 1948), pp. 313–14.

Document 39   HITLER'S RACIAL PRIORITIES

In February 1941 both Göring and the Reich Ministry of Labour were pressing for the employment of eastern European Jews in the German war industries, but this was vetoed by Hitler. On 22 April 1941 an official of the Reich Ministry for Armaments and Munitions issued this statement.

Following a directive from the *Führer* . . . there should be no attempt to transfer Jews from the east to the Reich for use as labour.

It is thus no longer possible to contemplate using Jews as replacements for labour which has been withdrawn, particularly from the building sector and from textile plants.

Source: Noakes and Pridham (eds), *Nazism, 1919–1945, Vol. III: Foreign Policy, War and Racial Extermination*, Exeter University Press (Exeter, 1988), p. 1084.

──────◀◉▶──────

Document 40   THE WANNSEE CONFERENCE

Heydrich had been given responsibility by Göring in November 1941 to make the necessary preparations 'for a complete solution of the Jewish question in Europe'. The meeting was originally called for 9 December 1941, but had to be cancelled after the Japanese attack on Pearl Harbor. On 20 January 1942 key officials met secretly to discuss the matter in a lakeside villa in the Berlin suburb of Wannsee. The following is an extract from the minutes prepared by Eichmann.

In pursuance of the final solution, the Jews will be conscripted for labour in the east under appropriate supervision. Large labour gangs will be formed from those fit for work, with the sexes separated, which will be sent to those areas for road construction and undoubtedly a large number of them will drop out through natural wastage. The remainder who survive – and they will certainly be those who have the greatest powers of endurance – will have to be dealt with accordingly. For if released, they would, as a natural selection of the fittest, form a germ cell from which the Jewish race could regenerate itself. (That is the lesson of history.)

In the process of carrying out the final solution, Europe will be combed through and through from west to east . . . The evacuated Jews will be initially brought in stages to so-called transit ghettos in order to be transported there further east. . . .

Source: Noakes and Pridham (eds), *Nazism, 1919–1945, Vol. III: Foreign Policy, War and Racial Extermination*, Exeter University Press (Exeter, 1988), p. 1131.

──────◀◉▶──────

COMPARISON BETWEEN THE BRITISH AND GERMAN WAR EFFORTS **Document 41**

	1939	1940	1941	1942	1943	1944
Index of consumer expenditure						
(per capita: 1938 = 100)						
Germany	95.0	88.4	81.9	75.3	75.3	70.0
Britain	97.2	89.7	87.1	86.6	85.5	88.2
Industrial workforce working on war orders						
Germany	21.9	50.2	54.5	56.1	61.0	–
Britain	18.6	–	50.9	–	–	–
Proportion of women in the native workforce						
Germany	37.3	41.4	42.6	46.0	48.8	51.0
Britain	26.4	29.8	33.2	34.8	36.4	36.2
War expenditure as a percentage of national income						
Germany	32.2	48.8	56.0	65.6	71.3	–
Britain	15.0	43.0	52.0	52.0	55.0	54.0

Source: Overy, *War and Economy in the Third Reich*, p. 312.

THE INEFFICIENCIES OF LABOUR CONSCRIPTION **Document 42**

On 27 January 1943 Hitler permitted Fritz Sauckel, Plenipotentiary-General for Mobilisation, to issue a decree by which all women between the ages of 17 and 45 had to register for work, but the effectiveness of this decree was undermined by both the reluctance of many women, who had hitherto escaped war work, to register and the fact that employers found foreign labour much more effective. The following is an extract from an SD (Security Service) report of 4 February 1943.

The reports note that, in particular, those national comrades who have been employed in important war work had expected tough regulations. However, after the publication of the details of the decree they were astonished that so many exemptions had been given. The disapproval of this manifested itself in some cases in quite drastic remarks such as 'rubber decree', etc. . . . .

Already women and girls from every social class have been contacting numerous labour offices to try to prove that they are not available for labour mobilisation. . . . It was already evident that some of these women were trying to claim they were suffering some illness or other with a doctor's certificate in order to evade recruitment. . . .

Source: Noakes and Pridham (eds), *Nazism, 1919–1945*, Vol. IV: *The German Home Front in World War II*, Exeter University Press (Exeter, 1998), p. 333.

Document 43   THE STRAINS OF WAR ON THE FAMILY

By the autumn of 1943 bombing, evacuation and the heavy fighting in Russia were all taking their toll on family life as the following extracts from an SD report of 18 November 1943 show.

. . . Many women are also concerned that the stability of their marriages and the mutual understanding of their partners is [sic] beginning to suffer from the lengthy war. The separation which, with short breaks, has now been going on for years, the transformation in their circumstances through total war and in addition, the heavy demands which are nowadays made on every individual are changing people and filling their lives. When on leave, the front-line soldier often no longer shows any understanding for his family's domestic circumstances, which are governed by the war, and remains indifferent to the many daily cares of the home front. This often produces an increasing *distance between the married couple*. Thus wives often point out that having looked forward to being together again during their husband's leave, the occasion is spoilt by frequent rows caused by mutual tensions. That even happens in marriages which were previously models of harmony. . . .

The *splitting up of families* without the possibility of making visits with all the accompanying problems is in the long run felt to be an intolerable burden both by men but in particular by women. . . . Above all, the married men say that their family is the only compensation they have for their heavy work load. One shouldn't take away from them the only thing that makes life worth living. But the wives are no less subjected to a heavy mental burden because they want to live in their own homes, to look after them and to care for their husbands and children. . . .

. . . The majority of the evacuated women and children are accommodated in small villages and rural parishes under the most primitive conditions. They have to cook in the same kitchens with their hosts, which often give cause for conflict, since people look into each other's pots and get jealous if the other family has something better to eat. In a number of cases there can be no question of family life since sometimes not all children can be accommodated with their mother in the same house, and further, more often the only living room that is available has to be shared with the host family. . . .

Source: Noakes and Pridham (eds), *Nazism, 1919–1945, Vol. IV: The German Home Front in World War II*, Exeter University Press (Exeter, 1998), pp. 360–62.

THE SWING MOVEMENT   **Document 44**

The Swing Movement developed among upper-middle-class teenagers who rebelled against völkisch *music and the banality of popular musical hits. Instead, they preferred swing and jazz. Initially live concerts of this music did take place legally, but Hitler Youth officials rapidly had them closed down. The following is an extract from one internal Hitler Youth report on a swing festival in Hamburg in February 1940.*

. . . [T]he jazz music was all English and American. Only swing dancing and jitterbugging took place. At the entrance to the hall stood a notice on which the words 'swing prohibited' had been altered to 'swing requested'. The participants accompanied the dances and songs, without exception, by singing English words. Indeed, throughout the evening they attempted only to speak English; at some tables even French.

The dancers were an appalling sight. None of the couples danced normally; there was only swing of the worst sort. Sometimes two boys danced with one girl; sometimes several couples formed a circle, linking arms and jumping, slapping hands, even rubbing the backs of their heads together; and then bent double, with the top half of the body hanging loosely down, long hair flopping into the face, they dragged themselves round practically on their knees. When the band played the rumba, the dancers went into wild ecstasy. They leapt around and joined in the chorus in broken English. The band played wilder and wilder items; none of the players was sitting down any longer, they all 'jitterbugged' on the stage like wild creatures. Several boys could be observed dancing together, always with two cigarettes in the mouth, one in each corner. . . .

Source: quoted in Peukert, *Inside Nazi Germany*, Penguin (Harmondsworth, 1989), pp. 186–87.

THE CONFESSING CHURCH EMPHASISES THE FIFTH COMMANDMENT, 1943   **Document 45**

The Confessing Church did eventually condemn the Nazi policy of ethnic cleansing in 1943, when its Prussian Synod addressed a pastoral letter to all its congregations in which the obligations of the Fifth Commandment were specifically spelt out.

The state is not entrusted with the powers to take away life, except in the case of criminals or war time enemies . . . terms like 'eradication', 'liquidation', or 'unfit to live' are not known in the law of God. The murdering of men solely because they are members of a foreign race, or because they are old, or mentally ill, or the relatives of a criminal, cannot be considered as carrying out the authority entrusted to the state by God.

Source: quoted in J.S. Conway, *The Nazi Persecution of the Churches, 1933–1945*, Weidenfeld and Nicolson (London, 1968), pp. 266–7.

Document 46   INDIVIDUAL ACTS OF OPPOSITION

(a) Many Germans defied the Nazi regime by hiding Jews. In Berlin, for example, some 5,000 survived thanks to such efforts. Below is an extract from the account of a German-Jewish woman.

I was constantly sent for by the Gestapo. In 1942 these interrogation sessions became even more threatening and I therefore went underground. In the middle of May 1942 I went to Silesia and stayed in several places without officially registering myself. I lived in Breslau, Gleiwitz, Hindenburg, in the countryside and in Spahlitz (in the district of Oels). It was here that I remained hidden for months at the house of a German lawyer. . . . (Later after I was arrested this brave man had another Jewish woman hidden in his house.) . . .

Source: Wiener Library, *Eye Witness Accounts*, PIIc, no. 153.

(b) Most Germans in the war were preoccupied with their own worries and tended to ignore the problems of foreign workers. The incident described below was, as Peukert has stressed, 'exceptional'.

Memorandum from Franz Otto Colliery to Duisburg Gestapo, 13 October, 1943
We wish to inform you of an incident which occurred underground here on 9.10 in Franz Otto Colliery, Duisburg Neuenkamp.

At the end of a shift the foreman . . . who is in charge of coal extraction from the faces of one district of the pit, ordered one of the Russian prisoners of war employed there to stay on longer and help extract a wedge of coal that had remained in the rock.

Since the Russian refused, despite repeated requests to comply with this instruction, [the foreman] forcibly attempted to compel him to perform this task.

In the course of the altercation the apprentice face-worker Lapschiess, Max . . . turned on the foreman and defended the POW in a manner such as to encourage the latter to strike the foreman on the head with his lamp. [The foreman] received a gaping wound on his face which has required stitches, and he has since been on sick leave. He is a diligent man and a member of the colliery Political Action Squad.

We should be grateful if you could make it clear to Lapschiess, who has already been in a concentration camp (1935–39), that his interference with instructions issued to the Russian prisoners of war constitutes a disturbance in the colliery's operation and that he may under no circumstances take the part of a POW.

This morning Lapschiess declared in impudent fashion to my face that he would continue to intervene if Russian prisoners of war were assaulted. . . .

Source: quoted in Peukert, *Inside Nazi Germany*, Penguin (Harmondsworth, 1989), p. 142.

GENERAL VON TRESCKOW ON THE SIGNIFICANCE OF THE OPPOSITION   **Document 47**

After the war Fabian von Schlabrendorff, then a young officer, recalled his conversation with Tresckow on the Russian front on 21 July after news of the failure of Operation Valkyrie had just been received. Shortly after this Tresckow committed suicide. Tresckow observed:

. . . The whole world will vilify us now. But I am still firmly convinced that we did the right thing. I consider Hitler to be the arch enemy not only of Germany but of the world. When in a few hours, I appear before the judgment seat of God, in order to give an account of what I have done and left undone, I believe I can with good conscience justify what I did in the fight against Hitler. If God promised Abraham that he would not destroy Sodom if only 10 righteous men could be found there, then I hope for our sakes God will not destroy Germany. None of us can complain about our own deaths. Everyone who joined our circle put on the robe of Nessus to die for his convictions.

Source: Noakes and Pridham (eds), *Nazism, 1919–1945, Vol. IV: The German Home Front in World War II*, Exeter University Press (Exeter, 1998), p. 618.

Document 48   CONTRASTING ATTITUDES TOWARDS HITLER IN MARCH 1945

(a) Speer was desperately trying to persuade the Gauleiter to defy Hitler's orders to destroy German industrial plants before Allied troops arrived. To his surprise, as he wrote later, he still found reserves of optimism and confidence that Hitler would save Germany.

I drove to the Ruhr area once more. Saving its industry was the crucial question for the post-war era. In Westphalia a flat tyre forced us to stop. Unrecognized in the twilight I stood in a farm-yard talking to farmers. To my surprise, the faith in Hitler which had been hammered into their minds all these last years was still strong. Hitler could never lose the war, they declared. 'The Führer is still holding something in reserve that he'll play at the last moment. Then the turning point will come. It's only a trap, his letting the enemy come so far into our country.' Even among members of the government I still encountered this naïve faith in deliberately withheld secret weapons that at the last moment would annihilate an enemy recklessly advancing into the country. Funk [the Economics Minister], for example, asked me: 'We still have a special weapon, don't we? A weapon that will change everything?'

Source: Speer, *Inside the Third Reich*, Weidenfeld and Nicolson (London, 1967), p. 446.

(b) On the other hand a local policeman reported the following at a ceremony on 11 March at the war memorial in Mark Schellenberg, a small town near Hitler's residence at the Berghof in Bavaria.

When the leader of a *Wehrmacht* unit at the end of his speech for the remembrance called for a 'Sieg Heil' for the *Führer*, it was returned neither by the *Wehrmacht* present, nor by the *Volkssturm* nor by the spectators of the civilian population who had turned up. This silence of the masses . . . had a depressing effect, and probably reflects better than anything the attitudes of the population.

Source: quoted in I. Kershaw, *Hitler, Vol. I: 1936–1945, Nemesis*, Penguin (Harmondsworth, 2000), p. 766.

Guide to further reading

The following books are all in English. For readers who wish for access to German sources, J. Hiden, *Republican and Fascist Germany* (Longman, London, 1996) contains an excellent biographical essay.

The most comprehensive collection of sources in English on Nazism is the four volumes on *Nazism, 1919–45*, edited by J. Noakes and G. Pridham (Exeter University Press, Exeter, 1983–2000). The documents cover most aspects of Nazism and the Third Reich and are accompanied by an illuminating commentary. Other useful document collections are *Documents on German Foreign Policy, 1918–1945*, Series C (1933–37), Series D (1937–45) (HM Stationery Office, London, 1957–66) and The Trial of the Major War Criminals before the International Military Tribunal (at Nuremberg), *Proceedings*, vols I–XXIII; *Documents in Evidence*, vols XXIV–XLII (HM Stationery Office, London, 1947–49). For understanding Hitler and his ideology *Mein Kampf*, ed. D. Watt (Hutchinson, London, 1977) is an indispensable source, especially volume 2. This can be supplemented by *Hitler's Secret Book*, ed. T. Taylor (Grove Press, New York, 1961) and *Hitler's Table Talk*, with an introductory essay 'The Mind of Adolf Hitler' by H.R. Trevor-Roper (Weidenfeld & Nicolson, London, 1953). For English readers a useful collection of Hitler's speeches is still N. Baynes, ed., *Hitler's Speeches, 1922–39*, 2 vols (Oxford University Press, Oxford, 1942) but it needs to be supplemented by Max Domerus, ed., *Hitler: Speeches and Proclamations, 1932–45*, 3 vols (I.B. Tauris, London, 1990–97).

For general accounts, which put the Third Reich into the context of German history, G.A. Craig, *Germany, 1866–1945* (Oxford University Press, Oxford, 1978), H.A. Holborn, *History of Modern Germany, 1840–1945* (Eyre & Spottiswoode, London, 1969) and P.G. Pulzer, *Germany 1870–1945: Politics, State Formation and War* (Oxford University Press, Oxford, 1997) provide useful overall surveys, while V. Berghahn, *Modern Germany*, 2nd edn (Cambridge University Press, Cambridge, 1987) and David G. Williamson, *Germany since 1815: A Nation Forged and Renewed* (Palgrave Macmillan,

Basingstoke, 2005) also cover post-war Germany and the Nazi legacy.
T. Kirk, *The Longman Companion to Nazi Germany* (Longman, London, 1995)
is a useful reference book.

For an understanding of the intellectual roots of Nazism, G.L. Mosse, *The
Crisis of German Ideology: Intellectual Origins of the Third Reich* (Weidenfeld
& Nicolson, 1964) and F. Stern, *The Politics of Cultural Despair: A Study in
the Rise of the Germanic Ideology* (University of California Press, Berkeley, CA,
1974) are key texts. Attempts to define what Nazism was have led to an
intense debate, which shows no sign of stopping. The best introduction
to the complexity of these debates is to be found in I. Kershaw, *The Nazi
Dictatorship: Problems and Perspectives*, 4th edn (Arnold, London, 2000),
W. Laqueur, ed., *Fascism: A Reader's Guide* (Penguin, London, 1976),
K. Hildebrand, *The Third Reich* (especially Part Two: 'Basic Problems and
Trends of Research') (Routledge, London, 1984) and R. Evans, *In Hitler's
Shadow: West German Historians and the Attempt to Escape from the Nazi Past*
(I.B. Tauris, London, 1989). The most thought-provoking contemporary
study on the nature of Nazism is H. Rauschning, *Germany's Revolution of
Destruction* (Heinemann, London, 1939).

There are a large number of books on the origins of Nazism and Hitler's
rise to power. As representative of those historians who see strong continuities with Imperial Germany, H.-U. Wehler, *The German Empire, 1871–1918*
(Berg, Leamington Spa/Dover, NH, 1984) and V. Berghahn, *Germany and the
Approach of War in 1914* (Macmillan, London, 1973) are required reading,
but their arguments are questioned by D. Blackbourn, *History of Germany,
1780–1918: The Long Nineteenth Century* (Fontana, London, 1997). Good
general studies which place Hitler's rise to power in the context of the
Weimar Republic are A.J. Nicholls, *Weimar and the Rise of Hitler* (Macmillan,
London, 1968), H. Mommsen, *The Rise and Fall of Weimar Democracy*
(University of North Carolina Press, Chapel Hill, NC, 1996), H. Heiber, *The
Weimar Republic* (Blackwell, Oxford, 1993) and E.J. Feuchtwanger, *From
Weimar to Hitler, 1918–33* (Macmillan, London, 1993). There are a series
of penetrating and informative essays in I. Kershaw, ed., *Weimar: Why Did
German Democracy Fail?* (Weidenfeld & Nicolson, London, 1990). There are
several local studies of Nazism, which enable the historian to analyse its
growth at local level: J. Noakes, *The Nazi Party in Lower Saxony, 1921–33*
(Oxford University Press, Oxford, 1971), G. Pridham, *Hitler's Rise to Power:
The Nazi Party in Bavaria, 1921–33* (Hart-Davis, London, 1973), J. Grill, *The
Nazi Movement in Baden, 1920–1945* (University of North Carolina Press,
Chapel Hill, NC, 1983) and C.-C.W. Szejnmann *Nazism in Central Germany:
The Brownshirts in 'Red' Saxony* (Berghahn Books, New York, 1999). Thomas
Childers, *The Nazi Voter* (University of North Carolina Press, Chapel Hill,
NC, 1983) analyses the composition of the Nazi vote by class and occupation.

M. Broszat, *Hitler and the Collapse of Weimar Germany* (Berg, Leamington Spa, 1987) provides a concise account of the final years of the Republic. H.A. Turner Jr., *German Big Business and the Rise of Hitler* (Oxford University Press, New York/Oxford, 1985) is essential reading for the relations of the NSDAP with big business. D. Orlow, *The History of the Nazi Party, Vol. I: 1919–1933* (David & Charles, Newton Abbot, 1971) provides a detailed study of the Nazi Party until the seizure of power.

The most recent and comprehensive study of the Third Reich is contained in the three volumes by R.J. Evans: *The Coming of the Third Reich*, *The Third Reich in Power* and *The Third Reich at War* (Allen Lane, London, 2003–9). Other useful overviews are: K. Bracher, *The German Dictatorship: The Origins, Structure and Consequences of National Socialism* (Penguin, Harmondsworth, 1973), N. Frei, *National Socialist Rule in Germany: The Führer State, 1933–45* (Blackwell, Oxford, 1993), M. Burleigh, *The Third Reich: A New History* (Macmillan, London, 2000), M. Kitchen, *The Third Reich. Charisma and Community* (Pearson, Harlow, 2008) and T. Kirk, *Nazi Germany* (Palgrave Macmillan, 2007). There are a large number of Hitler biographies. A. Bullock, *Hitler: A Study in Tyranny* (Penguin, Harmondsworth, 1962) is still well worth reading especially for the years 1933–34, and J.C. Fest, *Hitler* (Penguin, Harmondsworth, 1977) is well written and has much information. However, beyond doubt the best and most detailed biography is I. Kershaw, *Hitler, Vol. I: 1889–1936, Hubris* (1998); *Vol. II: 1936–1945, Nemesis* (2000) (Allen Lane, London). It has become indispensable to any study of the Third Reich. A brief but perceptive biography is N. Stone, *Hitler* (Hodder & Stoughton, London, 1980).

There is an enormous bibliography on every aspect of the Third Reich. For the administration of the Third Reich, M. Broszat, *The Hitler State: The Foundation and Development of the Internal Structure of the Third Reich* (Longman, London, 1981) is a difficult but important book. A short but informative study on the civil service is J. Caplan, 'Bureaucracy, Politics and the National Socialist State', in P.D. Stachura, ed., *The Shaping of the Nazi State* (Croom Helm, London, 1978).

D. Orlow, *The History of the Nazi Party, Vol. II, 1933–1945* (David & Charles, Newton Abbot, 1973) is a comprehensive study of the development and role of the party (including the SS) from 1933 to 1945. The development of the SS state is studied in greater depth in H. Krausnick, H. Buchheim, M. Broszat and H.-A. Jacobsen, *Anatomy of the SS State* (Collins, London, 1968) and R.L. Koehl, *The Black Corps: The Structure and Power Struggles of the Nazi SS* (University of Wisconsin Press, Madison, WI, 1983), while the best study of how the Gestapo worked and the degree of support it received from the German population is R. Gellately, *The Gestapo and German Society* (Oxford University Press, Oxford, 1990). Gellately further explores the question of consent in *Backing Hitler: Consent and Coercion in Nazi Germany* (Oxford University Press, Oxford, 2001). Jane Caplan, 'Political Detention and the Origin of the Concentration Camps', in N. Gregor, ed., *Nazism, War and Genocide. New Perspectives on the Third Reich* (University of Exeter Press, Exeter, 2005) sheds some interesting light on the early years of the concentration camps.

An old but still informative study of Hitler's role in the government of the Nazi state is E.N. Peterson, *The Limits of Hitler's Power* (Princeton University Press, Princeton, NJ, 1969). K.D. Bracher, 'The Role of Hitler: Perspectives of Interpretation' and H. Mommsen, 'National Socialism: Continuity and Change', which are both in W. Laqueur, ed., *Fascism: A Reader's Guide* (Penguin, Harmondsworth, 1979) are short introductions to the same subject. For the importance of Hitler as an integrative figure in the Third Reich see I. Kershaw, *The Hitler Myth: Image and Reality in the Third Reich* (Oxford University Press, Oxford, 1987).

For a study of the economy, R.J. Overy, *War and Economy in the Third Reich* (Clarendon Press, Oxford, 1995) and A. Tooze, *The Wages of Destruction The Making and Breaking of the Nazi War Economy* (Allen Lane, London, 2006) are key works. A.S. Milward, who puts the 'guns and butter' argument in *The German Economy at War* (Athlone Press, London, 1965), is still worth reading, as is T. Mason, who argues in 'Labour in the Third Reich, 1933–39', *Past and Present*, Vol. XXXIII (1966), pp. 112–41 and in *Social Policy in the Third Reich: The Working Class and the Community* (Berg, Oxford, 1993) that Hitler went to war to escape economic restraints. A. Schweitzer, *Big Business in the Third Reich* (Eyre & Spottiswoode, London, 1964) is still a very useful survey. The relations between particular industries and the Nazi state have been studied by J.R. Gillingham, *Ruhr Coal, Hitler and Europe. Industries and Politics in the Third Reich* (Methuen, London, 1985) and by P. Bellon, *Mercedes in Peace and War: German Automobile Workers, 1903–45* (Columbia University Press, New York, 1990). The best analysis of Nazi agricultural policy is J. Farquharson, *The Plough and the Swastika: The NSDAP and Agriculture in Germany, 1928–1945* (Sage, London, 1976). U. Herbert, *Hitler's Foreign Workers* (Cambridge University Press, Cambridge, 1997) is an excellent study of the role of foreign workers in the wartime economy and their treatment by the Germans.

Two books with the same title, P. Aycoberry, *The Social History of the Third Reich* (The New Press, New York, 1999) and R.A. Grünberger, *Social History of the Third Reich* (Penguin, Harmondsworth, 1974), provide overviews of German society during the Third Reich, while D. Schoenbaum's indispensable classic *Hitler's Social Revolution* (Weidenfeld & Nicolson, 1967) only covers the years 1933–39. There are some good essays on different aspects of life in Nazi Germany in R. Bessel, ed., *Life in the Third Reich* (Oxford

University Press, Oxford, 1987). In this collection, Ulrich Frei, 'Good Times, Bad Times: Memories of the Third Reich', based on oral history, is particularly interesting, as is D. Geary, 'Working Class Identities in the Third Reich' in N. Gregor, ed., Nazism, *War and Genocide. New Perspectives on the Third Reich* (University of Exeter Press, Exeter, 2005). There is a growing literature on women in the Third Reich. T. Mason's two articles 'Women in Germany, 1925–1940', *History Workshop*, vol. 1 (Spring 1976), pp. 74–113 and vol. 2 (Autumn 1976), pp. 5–32 are concise and stimulating. J.S. Stephenson's two books *Women in German Society* (Croom Helm, London, 1975) and *The Nazi Organization of Women* (Barnes and Noble, New York/ London, 1981), as well as C. Koonz, *Mothers in the Fatherland: Women, the Family and Nazi Politics* (Jonathan Cape, London, 1987), are more detailed studies. D.A. Peukert, *Inside Nazi Germany: Conformity, Opposition and Racism in Everyday Life* (Penguin, Harmondsworth, 1989) is an important study of everyday life in Nazi Germany in which there is much on youth and the workers. His essay 'Youth in the Third Reich', in R. Bessel, ed., *Life in the Third Reich* (Oxford University Press, Oxford, 1987) is a good introduction to the subject. The best essay in English on the whole complex question of how 'modern' National Socialism was is M. Roseman, 'Socialism and Modernisation', in R. Bessel, ed., *Fascist Italy and Nazi Germany: Comparisons and Contrasts* (Cambridge University Press, Cambridge, 1997). For the Churches during the Third Reich, J.S. Conway, *The Nazi Persecution of the Churches, 1933–45* (Weidenfeld & Nicolson, London, 1968) and E.C. Helmreich, *The German Churches under Hitler* (Wayne State University Press, Detroit, MI, 1979) provide comprehensive accounts. For German society during the war, M. Kitchen, *Nazi Germany at War* (Longman, London, 1995) and T. Charman, *The German Home Front 1939–1945* (Barrie and Jenkins, London, 1989) provide good overall accounts, and M. Roseman's essay, 'World War II and Social Change in Germany', in C. Emsley, A. Marwick and W. Simpson, eds, *War, Peace and Social Change in Twentieth-century Europe* (Open University Press, Milton Keynes, 1989) is brief but illuminating.

For Hitler's racial and eugenic policies, M. Burleigh and W. Wippermann, *The Racial State: Germany 1933–45* (Cambridge University Press, Cambridge, 1991) is the best overall analysis. There is an enormous amount of literature on Nazi anti-Semitism and the Holocaust. D. Bankier, 'Hitler and the Policy-making Process on the Jewish Question', *Holocaust and Genocide Studies*, vol. III, no. 1 (1988), pp. 1–20 and M.R. Marrus, 'The History of the Holocaust: A Survey of Recent Literature', *Journal of Modern History*, vol. 59, no. 1 (1987), pp. 114–60 provide a good guide through the intentionalist/ structuralist maze. S. Friedländer, *Nazi Germany and the Jews: The Years of Persecution 1933–1939* (HarperCollins, New York, 1997) and *The Years of Extermination: Nazi Germany and the Jews, 1939–1945* (HarperCollins, New

York, 2007) provide a comprehensive analysis of the whole period. S. Friedländer, *Nazi Germany and the Jews, 1933–45* (Phoenix, London, 2009) is an abridged version. L.S. Dawidowicz, *The War against the Jews, 1933–45* (10th anniversary edition, Penguin, Harmondsworth, 1986) provides a trenchant example of the intentionalist case. K.A. Schleunes, *The Twisted Road to Auschwitz. Nazi Policy towards German Jews* (Deutsch, London, 1972) and H. Graml, *Antisemitism in the Third Reich* (Blackwell, Oxford, 1992) are excellent analyses of the complex events that led to the Holocaust. H. Mommsen, 'The Realization of the Unthinkable: The "Final Solution" of the Jewish Question in the Third Reich' and L. Kettenacker, 'Hitler's Final Solution and Its Rationalization', both in G. Hirschfeld, ed., *The Politics of Genocide* (Allen & Unwin, London, 1986) and M. Broszat, 'Hitler and the Genesis of the "Final Solution"', in H.W. Koch, ed., *Aspects of the Third Reich* (Macmillan, London, 1985) are all articles by leading structuralist historians. D. Yisraeli, 'The Third Reich and the Transfer Agreement', *Journal of Contemporary History*, vol. 6, no. 2 (1971), pp. 129–48 sheds some interesting light on Nazi policy and Jewish emigration in the 1930s. D.J. Goldhagen, *Hitler's Willing Executioners: Ordinary Germans and the Holocaust* (Abacus, New York, 1997) is a controversial analysis of German attitudes towards the persecution of the Jews.

The most comprehensive study of German foreign policy in English up to 1939 is G.L. Weinberg, *The Foreign Policy of Hitler's Germany, Vol. I: Diplomatic Revolution in Europe, 1933–36* (1970); *Vol. II: Starting World War II, 1937–39* (1980) (University of Chicago Press, Chicago, IL). A succinct and informative book is J. Wright, *Germany and the Origins of the Second World War* (Palgrave Macmillan, Basingstoke, 2007). N. Rich, *Hitler's War Aims, Vol. I, Ideology, the Nazi State and the Course of Expansion* (1973); *Vol. II: The Establishment of the New Order* (1974) (Deutsch, London) cover the period right up to the occupation of continental Europe. D.C. Watt, *How War Came* (Heinemann, London, 1989) is a massively detailed study of the immediate events leading up to war in September 1939. W.M. Carr, *Arms, Autarky and Aggression*, 2nd edn (Edward Arnold, London, 1979) is a much briefer analysis of the years 1933–39, while K. Hildebrand, *The Foreign Policy of the Third Reich* (Batsford, London, 1973) is a succinct study of Nazi foreign policy up to 1945 from an intentionalist point of view. A.J.P. Taylor, *The Origins of the Second World War* (Hamish Hamilton, London, 1961) is a classic that remains essential reading. E.M. Robertson, ed., *The Origins of the Second World War: Historical Interpretations* (Macmillan, London, 1971) contains some important essays, particularly A. Bullock, 'Hitler and the Origins of the Second World War' and T. Mason, 'Some Origins of the Second World War'. For Hitler's decision to attack Russia, G.L. Weinberg, *Germany and the Soviet Union, 1939–41* (Brill, Leyden, 1954) is still an interesting analysis, while R. Cecil, *Hitler's Decision to Invade Russia* (Davis-Poynter, London, 1975) is concise and well argued. E.M. Robertson, 'Hitler Turns from the West to Russia, May–December 1940', in R. Boyce and E.M. Robertson, eds, *Paths to War* (Macmillan, London, 1989) is also well worth reading. M. Mazower, *Hitler's Empire* (Penguin, London, 2008) is a comprehensive and indispensable analysis of Nazi policy in occupied Europe. G. Wright, *The Ordeal of Total War, 1939–45* (Harper & Row, New York, 1968) and N. Rich, *Hitler's War Aims, Vol. II: The Establishment of the New Order* (Deutsch, London, 1974) also give excellent overviews of German policy in occupied Europe. The best book in English on German policy in Russia is still A. Dallin, *German Rule in Russia, 1941–45* (Macmillan, London, 1957, reprinted Octagon, New York, 1990). J.T. Gross, *Polish Society under German Occupation* (Princeton University Press, Princeton, NJ, 1979) gives a good account of the German occupation in Poland, while Vichy France is covered by P. Burrin, *Living with Defeat: France under German Occupation, 1940–44* (Arnold, London, 1996).

Much of the literature on German resistance to Hitler is still concentrated on the Church and the conservative elites. E. Bethge, *Bonhoeffer, Exile and Martyr* (Collins, London, 1975) and G. Ritter, *The German Resistance: Carl Goerdeler's Struggle against Tyranny* (Allen & Unwin, London, 1958) are biographies of two prominent figures in the resistance movement. T. Prittie, *Germans against Hitler* (Hutchinson, London, 1964), E. Zeller, *The Flame of Freedom: The Struggle against Hitler* (Oswald Wolff, London, 1967), H. Rothfels, *The German Opposition to Hitler* (Oswald Wolff, London, 1973), P. Hoffmann, *The History of the German Resistance to Hitler*, 3rd edn (MacDonald and Janes, Montreal, 1996) and M. Balfour, *Withstanding Hitler in Germany, 1933–45* (Routledge London, 1988) all give accounts of the various resistance groups in Germany. H. Graml, H. Mommsen, H.-J. Reich and E. Wolf, *The German Resistance to Hitler*, rev. edn (Harvard University Press, Cambridge, MA, 1970) is an important collection of articles, which also assesses the ideas of the opposition. A more recent collection of essays on the resistance is D.C. Clay, ed., *Contending with Hitler: Varieties of German Resistance in the Third Reich* (Harvard University Press, Cambridge, MA, 1991). I. Kershaw, *Popular Opinion and Popular Dissent in the Third Reich: Bavaria, 1933–45* (Oxford University Press, Oxford, 1983) and D.A. Peukert, *Inside Nazi Germany: Conformity, Opposition and Racism in Everyday Life* (Penguin, Harmondsworth, 1989) explore the theme of *Resistenz*. Peukert is also very good on youth rebellion.

For the legacy of the Third Reich, H. James, 'The Preview of the Federal Republic', *Journal of Modern History*, vol. 63 (March 1991), pp. 99–115 is an excellent introductory article. There is also a discussion of the Nazi legacy to both German states in D.G. Williamson, *Germany from Defeat to Partition* (Pearson Education, Harlow, 2001).

References

Abelshauser, W. and Faust, A., 'Wirtschafts-und Sozialpolitik. Eine Nationalsozialerevolution?', in *Nationalsozialismus im Unterricht, Studieneinheit 4*, Deutsches Institut für Fernstudien an der Universität von Tübingen, Tübingen, 1983.

Aycoberry, P., *The Social History of the Third Reich*, New Press, New York, 1999.

Bankier, D., 'Hitler and the Policy-making Process on the Jewish Question', *Holocaust and Genocide Studies*, vol. III, no. 1 (1988), pp. 2–6.

Baynes, N., ed., *Hitler's Speeches, 1922–39* (2 vols), Oxford University Press, Oxford, 1942.

Berger, S., 'The German Tradition of Historiography, 1800–1995', in M. Fulbrook, ed., *German History since 1900*, Arnold, London, 1997.

Berghahn, V., *Germany and the Approach of War in 1914*, Macmillan, London, 1973.

Bessel, R., ed., *Life in the Third Reich*, Oxford University Press, Oxford, 1987.

Blackbourn, D., *Germany, 1780–1918: The Long Nineteenth Century*, Fontana, London, 1997.

Bracher, K., *The German Dictatorship: The Origins, Structure and Consequences of National Socialism*, Penguin, Harmondsworth, 1973.

Brady, R.A., *The Spirit and Structure of German Fascism*, with a foreword by H.J. Laski, Gollancz, London, 1937.

Broszat, M., *The Hitler State: The Foundation and Development of the Internal Structure of the Third Reich*, Longman, London, 1981.

Broszat, M., 'Hitler and the Genesis of the "Final Solution"', in H.W. Koch, ed., *Aspects of the Third Reich*, Macmillan, Basingstoke, 1985.

Broszat, M., 'A Plea for the Historicisation of National Socialism', in P. Baldwin, ed., *Reworking the Past: Hitler, the Holocaust and the Historians' Debate*, Beacon Press, Boston, MA, 1990.

Buchheim, H. *et al.*, *Anatomy of the SS State*, Collins, London, 1968.

Bullock, A., *Hitler. A Study in Tyranny*, Penguin, Harmondsworth, 1962.

Bullock, A., 'Hitler and the Origins of the Second World War', in E.M. Robertson, ed., *The Origins of the Second World War*, Macmillan, London, 1971.

Bullock, *Hitler and Stalin*, Fontana, London, 1998

Burleigh, M., *The Third Reich: A New History*, Macmillan, London, 2000.

Burleigh, M. and Wippermann, W., *The Racial State: Germany 1933–45*, Cambridge University Press, Cambridge, 1991.

Butler, R., *The Roots of National Socialism, 1783–1933*, Faber & Faber, London, 1941.

Carr, W.M., *Arms, Autarky and Aggression*, Edward Arnold, London, 1972.

Carr, W.M., 'National Socialism: Foreign Policy and *Wehrmacht*', in W. Laqueur, ed., *Fascism: A Reader's Guide*, Penguin, Harmondsworth, 1979.

Cecil, R., *Hitler's Decision to Invade Russia*, Davis-Poynter, London, 1975.

Conway, J.S., *The Nazi Persecution of the Churches, 1933–45*, Weidenfeld & Nicolson, London, 1968.

Craig, G.A., *Germany, 1866–1945*, Oxford University Press, Oxford, 1978.

Dahrendorf, F., *Society and Democracy in Germany*, Weidenfeld & Nicolson, London, 1967.

Dallin, A., *German Rule in Russia, 1941–45*, Macmillan, London, 1957.

Dawidowicz, L.S., *The War against the Jews, 1933–45* (10th anniversary edn), Penguin, Harmondsworth, 1986.

Erker, P., 'Landbevölkerung und Flüchtlingszustrom', in M. Broszat, K.-D. Henke, and H. Wolle, eds, *Von Stalingrad zur Währungsreform: Zur Sozialgeschichte des Umbruchs in Deutschland*, Oldenbourg Verlag, Munich, 1988.

Evans, R.J., *The Third Reich in Power*, Penguin, London, 2006.

Evans, R.J., *The Third Reich at War*, Penguin, London, 2009.

Falter, J.W., 'Die Wähler der NSDAP 1928–1933: Sozialstruktur und parteipolitische Herkunft', in M. Michalka, ed., *Die nationalsozialistische Machtergreifung*, Schöningh, Paderborn/Munich, 1984, pp. 47–59.

Farquharson, J.E., *The Plough and the Swastika. The NSDAP and Agriculture in Germany, 1928–45*, Sage, London/Beverly Hills, CA, 1976.

Fest, J.C., *Hitler*, Penguin, Harmondsworth, 1977.

Fest, J., *The Face of the Third Reich*, Penguin, Harmondsworth, 1979.

Fox, J., 'Holocaust as History', *Modern History Review*, vol. III, no. 2 (1991), pp. 2–6.

Frei, N., *National Socialist Rule in Germany: The Führer State, 1933–45*, Blackwell, Oxford, 1993.

Friedländer, S., *Nazi Germany and the Jews*, Phoenix, London, 2009.

Friedrich, C.J. and Brzezinski, Z.K., *Totalitarian Dictatorship and Autocracy*, Harvard University Press, Cambridge, MA, 1956.

Gaddis, J.L., *We Know Now: Rethinking Cold War History*, Oxford University Press, Oxford, 1997.

Gellately, R., *Backing Hitler*, Oxford University Press, Oxford, 2001.

Graml, H., *Antisemitism in the Third Reich*, Blackwell, Oxford, 1992.

Graml, H., Mommsen, H., Reich, H.-J., and Wolf, E., *The German Resistance to Hitler*, Batsford, London, 1970.

Grünberger, R., *A Social History of the Third Reich*, Penguin, Harmondsworth, 1974.

Helmreich, E.C., *The German Churches under Hitler*, Wayne State University Press, Detroit, MI, 1979.

Herbert, U., *Hitler's Foreign Workers*, Cambridge University Press, Cambridge, 1997.

Hiden, J.W., *Republican and Fascist Germany: Themes and Variations in the History of Weimar and the Third Reich, 1918–1945*, Longman, London, 1996.

Hildebrand, K., *The Foreign Policy of the Third Reich*, Batsford, London, 1973.

Hildebrand, K., 'Hitlers Ort in der Geschichte des preussisch-deutschen Nationalstaates', *Historische Zeitschrift*, vol. 217 (1974), pp. 584–632.

Hildebrand, K., *The Third Reich* (trans. P.S. Falla), Routledge, London, 1991.

Hillgruber, A., *Hitlers Strategie, Politik und Kriegsführung, 1940–1941*, Bernard & Graefe, Frankfurt am Main, 1965.

Hillgruber, A., 'England's Place in Hitler's Plans for World Dominion', *Journal of Contemporary History*, vol. 9, no. 1 (January 1974), pp. 5–22.

Hitler, Adolf, *Mein Kampf*, ed. D. Watt, Hutchinson, London, 1974.

Hoffmann, P., *The History of the German Resistance to Hitler*, MacDonald and Janes, London, 1977.

Irving, D., *Hitler's War*, Viking, London, 1977.

Jackel, E., *Hitler in History*, Hanover/London, 1984.

James, H., 'The Preview of the Federal Republic', *Journal of Modern History*, vol. 63 (March 1991), pp. 99–115.

Kershaw, I., *Popular Opinion and Dissent in the Third Reich*, Oxford University Press, Oxford, 1984.

Kershaw, I., *The Hitler Myth*, Oxford University Press, Oxford, 1987.

Kershaw, I., *The Nazi Dictatorship: Problems and Perspectives* (3rd edn), Arnold, London, 1993 (4th edn, 2000)

Kershaw, I., *Hitler, Vol. I: 1889–1936, Hubris* (1998); *Vol. II: 1936–1945, Nemesis* (2000), Allen Lane, London.

Kettenacker, L., 'Hitler's Final Solution and Its Rationalization', in G. Hirschfeld, ed., *The Politics of Genocide*, Allen and Unwin, London, 1986.

Kitchen, M., *Nazi Germany at War*, Longman, London, 1995.

Kirk, T., *Nazi Germany*, Palgrave Macmillan, Basingstoke, 2007.

Klein, B.H., *Germany's Economic Preparations for War*, Harvard University Press, Cambridge, MA, 1959.

Koonz, C., *Mothers in the Fatherland: Women, the Family and Nazi Politics*, Jonathan Cape, London, 1987.

Marrus, M.R., 'The History of the Holocaust: A Survey of Recent Literature', *Journal of Modern History*, vol. 59, no. 1 (1987), pp. 114–160.

Mason, T., 'Labour in the Third Reich, 1933–39', *Past and Present*, vol. XXXIII (1966), pp. 112–41.

Mason, T., 'Some Origins of the Second World War', in E.M. Robertson, ed., *The Origins of the Second World War*, Macmillan, London, 1971.

Mason, T., 'Women in Germany, 1925–1940 (Family, Welfare and Work. Part I)', *History Workshop*, vol. I (Spring 1976), pp. 74–113.

Mason, T., 'Intention and Explanation: A Current Controversy about the Interpretation of National Socialism', in G. Hirschfeld and L. Kettenacker, eds, *The Führer State: Myths and Realties. Studies on the Structure and Politics of the Third Reich*, Kletta Cotta/German Historical Institute, Stuttgart/London, 1981.

Matzerath, H. and Volkman, H., 'Modernisierungstheorie und National-sozialismus', in J. Kocka, ed., *Theorien in der Praxis des Historikers*, Vandenhoeck and Ruprecht, Göttingen, 1977.

Mazower, M., *Hitler's Empire*, Allen Lane, London, 2008.

Michalka, W., ed., *Die nationalsozialistische Machtergreifung*, Schöningh, Paderborn/Munich, 1984.

Milward, A.S., *The German Economy at War*, Athlone Press, London, 1965.

Mommsen, H., 'National Socialism: Continuity and Change', in W. Laqueur, ed., *Fascism: A Reader's Guide*, Penguin, Harmondsworth, 1979.

Mommsen, H., 'The Realization of the Unthinkable: The "Final Solution" of the Jewish Question in the Third Reich', in G. Hirschfeld, ed., *The Politics of Genocide*, Allen and Unwin, London, 1986.

Neumann, F., *Behemoth: The Structure and Practice of National Socialism*, Cass, London, 1967 (1st edn, 1942).

Noakes, J. and Pridham, G., eds, *Nazism, 1919–1945, Vol. I: The Rise to Power, 1919–1934* (1983; 2nd edn, 1998); *Vol. II: State, Economy and Society, 1933–1939* (1984, reprinted 1991; 2nd edn, 2000); *Vol. III: Foreign Policy, War and Racial Extermination* (1988); *Vol. IV: The German Home Front in World War II* (1998), Exeter University Press, Exeter.

Nolte, E., *Three Faces of Fascism: Action Française, Italian Fascism, National Socialism*, Mentor, New York, 1969.

Nolte, E., 'Between Myth and Revisionism? The Third Reich in the Perspective of the 1980s', in H.W. Koch, ed., *Aspects of the Third Reich*, Macmillan, Basingstoke, 1985.

Orlow, D., *The History of the Nazi Party, Vol. I: 1919–1933* (1971); *Vol. II: 1933–1945* (1973), David & Charles, Newton Abbot.

Overy, R.J., *War and Economy in the Third Reich*, Clarendon Press, Oxford, 1995.

Overy, R.J., *The Dictators: Hitler's Germany, Stalin's Russia*, Allen Lane, London, 2004.

Peterson, E.N., *The Limits of Hitler's Power*, Princeton University Press, Princeton, NJ, 1969.

Peukert, D.A., *Inside Nazi Germany. Conformity, Opposition and Racism in Everyday Life*, Penguin, Harmondsworth, 1989.

Prinz, M. and Zitelmann, R., eds, *Nationalsozialismus und Modernisierung*, Wissenschaftliche Buchgesellschaft, Darmstadt, 1991.

Prittie, T., *Germans against Hitler*, Hutchinson, London, 1964.

Rabinbach, A.G., 'The Aesthetics of Production in the Third Reich', *Journal of Contemporary History*, vol. 11, no. 4 (October 1976), pp. 43–74.

Rauschning, H., *Germany's Revolution of Destruction*, Heinemann, London, 1939.

Rich, N., *Hitler's War Aims* (2 vols), Deutsch, London, 1973–74.

Ritter, G., *The German Resistance: Carl Goerdeler's Struggle against Tyranny*, Allen and Unwin, London, 1958.

Roseman, M., 'National Socialism and Modernisation', in R. Bessel, ed., *Fascist Italy and Nazi Germany: Comparisons and Contrasts*, Cambridge University Press, Cambridge, 1997.

Rothfels, H., *The German Opposition to Hitler*, Oswald Wolff, London, 1970.

Schleunes, K.A., *The Twisted Road to Auschwitz: Nazi Policy towards German Jews*, Deutsch, London, 1972.

Schoenbaum, D., *Hitler's Social Revolution*, Weidenfeld & Nicolson, London, 1967; paperback, Norton, New York, 1980.

Schweitzer, A., *Big Business in the Third Reich*, Eyre & Spottiswoode, London, 1964.

Speer, A., *Inside the Third Reich*, Weidenfeld & Nicolson, London, 1970.

Steinert, M., *Hitler's War and the Germans: Public Mood and Attitude during the Second World War*, Ohio University Press, Athens, 1977.

Stephenson, J.S., *Women in Nazi Society*, Croom Helm, London, 1975.

Stephenson, J.S., 'Nazism, Modern War and Rural Society in Württemberg, 1939–45', *Journal of Contemporary History*, vol. 32, no. 3 (1997), pp. 339–56.

Stern, J., *Hitler, the Führer and the People*, Fontana, London, 1975.

Taylor, A.J.P., *The Course of German History*, Methuen, London, 1961a.

Taylor, A.J.P., *The Origins of the Second World War*, Hamish Hamilton, London, 1961b.

Taylor, T., ed., *Hitler's Secret Book*, Grove Press, New York, 1961.

Thorne, C., *The Approach of War*, Macmillan, London, 1967.

Tooze, A., *The Wages of Destruction*, Penguin, London, 2007.

Trevor-Roper, H., *The Last Days of Hitler*, Macmillan, London, 1947.

Trevor-Roper, H., ed., 'The Mind of Adolf Hitler', in *Hitler's Table Talk*, Weidenfeld & Nicolson, London, 1953.

Turner, H.A., 'Fascism and Modernization', in H.A Turner, ed., *Reappraisals of Fascism*, New Viewpoints, New York, 1975.

Vansittart, R., *Black Record: Germans Past and Present*, Hamish Hamilton, London, 1941

Vermeil, E., *Germany's Three Reichs: Their History and Culture*, E.W. Dickes, London, 1945.

Wehler, H.-U., *The German Empire, 1871–1918*, Berg, Leamington Spa/Dover, NH, 1985.

Wheeler-Bennett, J.W., *The Nemesis of Power: The German Army in Politics, 1918–45*, Macmillan, London, 1961.

Weinberg, G.L., *Germany and the Soviet Union, 1939–41*, Brill, Leyden, 1954.

Weinberg, G.L., *The Foreign Policy of Hitler's Germany, Vol. I: Diplomatic Revolution in Europe, 1933–36* (1970); *Vol. II: Starting World War II, 1937–39* (1980), University of Chicago Press, Chicago, IL.

Williamson, D., *Poland Betrayed: The Nazi-Soviet Invasions of 1939*, Pen and Sword, Barnsley, 2009.

Wright, G., *The Ordeal of Total War, 1939–45*, New York, Harper & Row, 1968.

Wright, J., *Germany and the Origins of the Second World War*, Palgrave Macmillan, Basingstoke, 2007.

Index